HUNTER BOYS

Other books by Richard Pike

HUNTER BOYS

TRUE TALES FROM PILOTS OF THE HAWKER HUNTER

RICHARD PIKE

GRUB STREET • LONDON

Published by
Grub Street
4 Rainham Close
London
SW11 6SS

A CIP record for this title is available from the British Library

ISBN-13: 978-1-909808-03-4

Designed by Sarah Driver
Edited by Sophie Campbell

Printed and bound by Berforts Information Press Ltd

Grub Street Publishing only uses
FSC (Forest Stewardship Council) paper for its books.

CONTENTS

For Sue with such marvellous memories of our time in Croyde

INTRODUCTION AND ACKNOWLEDGEMENTS

Submissions for this book have been sent to me in various forms, sometimes coming from unusual and unexpected sources as the book progressed. Chapters, therefore, have been written and edited by me although I've used the first person singular throughout and sought each person's approval before finalising the script.

My sincere thanks to the owner of The Aviation Bookshop, Mr Simon Watson, who, during a visit to India, was made aware of the diary notes which form the basis of Chapter 11. While the original diarist, H K Singh, could not be traced, his colleagues encouraged use of the notes which I have condensed in the chapter.

Also particular thanks to aviation artist Chris Stone who painted the picture on the front cover especially for this book, and Ray Deacon for kind use of his extensive collection of Hunter photos.

Richard Pike, 2014

CHAPTER 1

BUILDING BRIDGES

ALAN POLLOCK MADE HIS PRESENCE KNOWN

Change was not just in the wind but blasting through my world at a speed high on the Beaufort scale. I was an operational Hawker Hunter pilot on a ground tour because the commander-in-chief of Royal Air Force Germany needed an *aide-de-camp* – a job for which I'd been duly selected, against his received advice, eventually from a cast of one. Determined to scrounge myself as much flying as possible, I became quite good at arranging *ad hoc* flights in various aircraft types (nine different types, in fact, at four different airfields). It was in September 1959 when I decided to ring a squadron friend of mine, a Hunter pilot at RAF Gütersloh, to gain his co-operation. "I'm on my way," I said obliquely.

"You are?"

"My boss is away and I've been able to borrow an aircraft – a Chipmunk."

"You have?"

"It'll be almost nine pm by the time I land at Gütersloh," I went on. "Could you kindly pick me up from station flight, please?"

"Mmmm... no problem."

"Thanks," I said. "Thanks a lot...see you there and you'll know when I've arrived – I'll just fly over the officers' mess." As if in a swift and unpremeditated gesture by my friend, I heard a click and the phone went dead.

Quite quickly after this I managed to drive down to RAF Wildenrath and get airborne that night, soon to be lulled by the soothing sound of the de Havilland Chipmunk's Gipsy Major engine which hummed happily as I headed eastwards from Wildenrath *en route* to Gütersloh. The weather conditions were ideal with a clear, cloudless sky illuminated by the brilliance of a full moon. Below, like a giant jigsaw map, moonlit fragments of the German landscape moved steadily as the Chipmunk made progress. It can be a lonely place, the sky, and the ghostly motion of car headlights stood out like lost benighted creatures travelling through

*26(AC) Squadron singleton F. Mk6 'M' XE546 in landing configuration
on the final approach at Gütersloh.*

dark transparent space as if stray souls struggled to discover where they were, what
they were, where they ought to be. Trimmed out and with a torch to hand, it was
easy to check my aviation map regularly to ensure that, in my own case, I knew
exactly where I was.

If I suffered a sense of isolation this was eased when, within one hour, the
distinctive lights of Royal Air Force Gütersloh came into view. The visibility was
still excellent and it struck me that the most expeditious way to alert my friend
was to perform a couple of aerobatic manoeuvres in the vicinity of the officers'
mess. I chose a suitable section of airfield perimeter track not far from the mess
as the ground reference point. I advanced the throttle to select full power on the
Gypsy Major Mk 8 engine as I commenced a dive to pick up the 130 knots airspeed
needed for a loop followed by another loop. This is the life, I reckoned, as the trusty
Chipmunk hurtled unhesitatingly round the sky in a magnificent moonlight sonata.
Regretfully, however, I was unaware that below, in addition to alerting my friend,
a senior officer had by chance happened to step outside the officers' mess into the
crisp night air at the very precise and very inverted moment of loop number one.

Summonsed the next morning to the senior officer's presence, his voice was
edged with melancholy and he looked cross when he announced: "As you well
know, Pollock, night aerobatics are prohibited... strictly prohibited. Consider
yourself grounded!"

"But I'm already on a ground tour, sir," I said plaintively.

"You are?"

"Yes, most certainly!"

"In that case you're grounded on a ground tour... which must be something of a record," he scowled.

My state of grounding did not last long. Within just one hour of my twenty-four-hour period of formal grounding, one of the Hawker Hunter squadrons based at Gütersloh – 26 (Army Co-operation) Squadron – was short of a pilot. I was needed urgently. So it was, on that September day in 1959, that I flew a Mark 6 Hunter of 26 Squadron despite my state of double grounding.

*

It was some months later, in the spring of 1960, that I flew five sorties in one day for 26 Squadron. For the last of these flights, which was at night, I had a sense of satisfaction as I flew a navigational exercise at high altitude above the north German plain. My Hawker Hunter, XJ690, pointed towards the black, freezing vault of the night sky studded with stars so brilliant that they looked unreal. The red glow of my Hunter's flight instrument lights induced a familiar feeling of cosiness within the cockpit. Occasionally, a ground controller's voice would interrupt my reverie and I could picture the individuals who, as they sat at their radar consoles, chatted convivially and sipped at steaming cups of coffee while simultaneously monitoring radio calls and watching aircraft 'blips' on radar screens.

It was on the last leg of my pre-planned navigational route when I heard the distress call. Another Hunter was in trouble and the pilot had transmitted a 'PAN' urgency message. I followed events as I listened on the aircraft radio and tried to work out the implications for my own recovery and landing at Gütersloh. By now my remaining fuel state was not too bad provided that I flew at endurance airspeed to eke out reserves. During this process, however, another Hunter promptly declared an emergency. Again, I monitored the aircraft radio to determine what was going on and to assess whether I should divert to an alternative airfield. Within minutes, though, my attention was drawn to the abrupt appearance of a pair of red lights situated low down in the cockpit. These lights were adjacent to, and to the right of, the engine oil pressure gauge, and their steady red glow revealed bad news. Within moments I knew that my aircraft had suffered a 'turret drive' failure with consequent loss of both of the Hunter's electrical generators and failure of the aircraft's hydraulic system. With nine minutes of battery reserves left before I'd lose all aircraft electrics, diversion to another airfield was no longer an option; it was a case of 'Gütersloh or bust'.

Carefully, I carried out the stipulated procedures, reverting straightaway to manual (non-hydraulically assisted) flight control and off-loading non-essential electrical items, but I decided to delay my declaration of an emergency. I realised that the controllers at Gütersloh were already stretched without the addition of my difficulties. Announcement of the news, though, could not be postponed indefinitely and when, eventually, I felt that the moment was right, I attempted to suppress an almost apologetic tone as I broadcast: "*PAN – PAN – PAN… total electrical and hydraulic failure…*"

At this instant I could imagine the approach controller's head drop dolefully, the very picture of woe, but to his credit he remained calm when, after a perceptible pause, he acknowledged my call. Meanwhile, as the dramas ahead of me began to unfold, it became evident that the runway was blocked by a Hawker Hunter ensnared in the crash barrier at the eastern end of the landing run, and that the second Hunter now blocked the opposite end of the runway. By this juncture in a state of minor shock and awe, I could barely believe my luck – or more to the point, my lack of luck – at having to attempt to land on a runway with both ends blocked and which technically, therefore, was 'state black' and thus unavailable. Another recourse – to eject – was distinctly unappealing, so I remained cool-headed while I worked out a plan of action.

I had checked that the surface wind was light and from a westerly direction. I set myself up, therefore, for an approach into wind with the aim of flying at a height of four to six feet above the Hunter and the crash barrier which, as it was night, I'd never even see. This, I estimated, should offer *just* sufficient runway length to allow me to stop before a collision with the Hunter stuck at the other end of the runway. Without the benefit of hydraulic power, my flight controls were heavy to operate and I had to be wary of the Hunter's tendency to 'Dutch roll' (a possible out-of-phase yaw-rolling motion) when flown at lower airspeed without hydraulics and exacerbated by crosswinds and turbulence. During the last stages of my approach to landing I planned to shut-down the engine so that, with just enough decaying airspeed, I could glide in above the Hunter still in the crash barrier. I had to land as judiciously as possible before I applied the single-shot emergency braking provided by the back-up wheel-brake accumulator. Fine judgement would be the key to success. The situation was unique and the antithesis of carefully planned, regular procedures. If things didn't work out on my first attempt, there'd be no second chance.

When I reached the downwind leg of the airfield circuit, the runway lighting helped me to make out some of the general scene. I was aware that, faced with this one-off opportunity, my flying experience would be put to the test in no uncertain terms. I reached for the undercarriage and flap emergency operating mechanisms and felt promptly reassured when, after operation, the back-up high pressure air bottle accumulators obligingly lowered the Hunter's wheels; I had indications of 'three greens' and full flaps down. With my eyes largely glued towards the touch-down point beyond the enmeshed Hunter, I felt strangely relieved at not being able to see what I was trying to avoid! My flight instruments, height and airspeed accuracy, fine judgement and some luck would prove critical to a successful outcome.

Now, as I turned XJ690 onto finals, I decided to maintain an airspeed of fifteen knots faster than normal until the crucial instant of stop-cocking the engine. At what I reckoned to be a range of forty or so yards from the major obstacles, I brought back my throttle through the gate to close down the engine. XJ690 was now a glider. My downward vision could hardly spot the netted Hunter flash below me while I focused on my planned touch-down point ahead.

Holding the Hunter steady in its downward float to round out, I soon felt the normal, gentle Hawker 'kiss' as the aircraft's splendidly wide undercarriage touched *terra firma*. In one long, steady action and with my stick moving hard back, I progressively squeezed the brake lever to gain maximum benefit before the accumulator ran out. The runway lights rushed past in a blur which gradually became slower and slower.

Still with some flare-path and runway ahead of me I came to a halt. With a sense of deliverance, and not entirely nonchalantly, I applied the parking brake. I de-clutched and slid back my hood manually, inserted the ejection seat's lower safety pin, released my seat straps and stood up to insert the ejection seat's top safety pin. With a slight shiver in the cold air, I looked around me.

Ahead I could hear, and soon see, an approaching Land Rover with tow bar. I looked back at the Hunter still ensnared in the crash barrier and now in the probe of several headlights, then turned to gaze at the other Hunter, by this stage virtually cleared from the end of the runway some 200 yards beyond my nosewheel.

I glanced up at the night sky. Events had worked out for me; I'd been fortunate, amazingly so, and I knew it. I could not have known, of course, that the impact on my mind would be such that, even well over fifty years later, that chain of events would remain as fresh in my memory as if they had occurred just yesterday.

A Bridge Too Far
It was eight years less a day after this particular episode that a very heavy cold, prescribed drugs, and a tip-off from my Red Arrow friends about the official cancellation of the RAF fiftieth anniversary flypast and our own 1(F) Squadron's substitute flypasts (and leaflet drops) would form a chain of events to ensure that my service with the Royal Air Force came to an abrupt end. I suppose you might call it my nemesis and it was something for which I was entirely unprepared – as unprepared, indeed, as the circumstances which had led up to such a drastic conclusion. In any case, after landing my Hunter Mk 9 at RAF West Raynham in Norfolk on that portentous day in early April 1968, there were some things that I wanted to do urgently. I knew only too well that it was just a matter of time before the thunder of the gods descended on my head with a vengeance.

I felt the need, firstly, to destroy the quarter-million scale aviation map which

I'd used to navigate myself northwards after take-off from RAF Tangmere in Sussex. Apart from anything else, from a professional point of view I felt a little ashamed of this map with its scribbled markings and overall tatty appearance. As casually as possible, therefore, I walked into the operations section at West Raynham and asked to borrow some matches. Everyone there seemed quite relaxed; evidently the news had yet to reach them. I borrowed the matches, sneaked outside and as discreetly as possible set fire to the map.

Next, I wanted to telephone my wife and both sets of parents. Having thanked the operations personnel, I nonchalantly bade them farewell before, when clear of the block, I hastened to the mechanical transport section. Once there, I chatted-up the switchboard girl who agreed that I could put through a private call. My call included a relayed message for my wife, mother-in-law and parents. I told them what had happened and why. I said that I would be under close arrest for at least a couple of days and that on no account should they say anything to the press. The telephone operator somewhat apologetically said then that there would be a small delay as she'd just had two 'lightning' priority calls – something quite outside her long experience. "The balloon's possibly gone up," I said drily without offering her too much revelation.

At that juncture I left the telephone operator to her calls and began to head towards our squadron set-up at 1(F) Squadron. I walked quite slowly now and, as I did so, perhaps it was inevitable that recent events should course through my mind. I was aged thirty-two and at a stage in my service career when I had gained a fair amount of experience as a fighter pilot and flying instructor. I was by no means alone in the strong views I held about the treatment of the Royal Air Force by politicians, in particular about the cavalier way in which successive governments, including that of the current Labour government led by Mr Harold Wilson, seemed to regard the service. The country had seen a shift away from manned aircraft to the use of guided missiles, a policy instituted in 1957 by Defence Minister Duncan Sandys. Sacked in 1966 from Mr Edward Heath's shadow cabinet, Sandys would see his policies reversed but by then it was too late: orders at home and overseas had been lost, research had been cut back, good companies had gone out of business.

Under a Labour administration, devaluation had followed, and decimation of the British aircraft industry with the cancellation of the TSR2, P1154 and AW681 projects. It appeared to me that national morale was rock bottom, as exemplified by the abortive 'Wilson coup' plot in the spring of 1968. Despite later governmental dissimulation, the anniversary flypast originally planned to mark fifty years since the foundation of the Royal Air Force had been cancelled.

It had seemed at that point that a few unofficial initiatives would be appropriate. As senior flight commander on 1(F) Squadron, I organised on Monday 1st April 1968 some celebratory leaflet raids against a few other Royal Air Force stations. The reactions were illuminating. Two RAF stations, Chivenor and Valley, telephoned their congratulations, however Coltishall and Wattisham complained of dangerous flying, bad example, untidy debris (admittedly Wattisham was due for an inspection by their air officer commanding the next day) and poor airmanship. This attitude, frankly, made me see red – although I could understand that a Hunter dropping fiftieth anniversary leaflets with accuracy and style could appear dangerous to some commanders of the Lightning boys. For the next few days I quietly fumed. Then, on Thursday 4th April 1968, four of our 1 Squadron Hunter Mk 9s were scheduled to take part in an event at RAF Tangmere, a famous fighter airbase in Sussex and 1(F) Squadron's spiritual home. I felt this was appropriate for the RAF's oldest squadron (motto: *in omnibus princeps* – first in all things) whose four detached Hunters would land at Tangmere after their flypast over the station's Freedom of Chichester parade.

When, on that Thursday, our four pilots (callsign: 'Princeps Red') took off from West Raynham, the formation of Hunter Mk 9s overflew Brighton as part of the town's air display. Our Hunters then headed due west to overfly exactly on time, to the very second, indeed, Tangmere's formal parade at Chichester. This demonstrated, I believed, the RAF's high standard of professionalism which politicians seemed so readily to disregard. We'd been told to expect some press interest after landing so all four pilots, as we taxied in, exchanged our 'bone dome' flying helmets for traditional straw boaters (the press, though, were not there).

At a party in the Tangmere officers' mess that evening, the combination of lack of sleep, ongoing exasperation, and drugs for a heavy cold all stimulated my inclination to express strong views about the state of the service in general and, in particular, the lack of celebratory effort in this year of such special significance for which even our VIPs appeared unaware. The following morning, I awoke early after just two-and-a-half hours of sleep. Images, irritations, events started to rush through my mind; I found it impossible to go back to sleep. The more I thought about things, the more I seemed to become incensed. How dare those ignorant, negligent politicians treat our fine service in such a way? It was outrageous, intolerable.

It must have been during these early morning mental machinations that the idea first entered my head. If, I reasoned to myself, 'officialdom' had proved so inadequate, then why not perform some kind of individual demonstration? Furthermore, my line of logic continued, I felt well placed right now for the task in hand. Our Hunters were due to return to West Raynham today, a flight that would take us not far from the environs of London. With the RAF's fiftieth anniversary week drawing to a close, surely a celebration 'flagwave' across Westminster would not go amiss? Moreover, I reckoned that a key and intriguing consideration was that, unlike a ground-level protester accessible to the forces of the law, as a fighter pilot I'd face no such constraint. Alone in the skies I'd be untouchable until the point of return to *terra firma*. Any subsequent court martial to express a patriotic point of view would be definitely worthwhile.

So it was that, early in the morning of Friday, 5th April 1968, the germ of the celebratory 'flagwave' idea was conceived, an idea which, for years to come, would have far reaching repercussions.

I needed now to make my clandestine plans. One positive aspect was that the weather conditions were ideal for low flying and my route over London would have to be flown at low altitude; by flying at very low level I knew that I'd be less likely to encounter other air traffic. To minimise noise and nuisance to Londoners, I decided that I should reduce my airspeed and lower the Hunter's flaps when flying over built-up areas. Making best use of my fifteen years of flying experience, I was aware that I'd have to break the odd regulation here and there, nonetheless I intended to conduct the flight in as careful and professional manner as possible. On my quarter-million scale map (later to be ignominiously burnt) I scribbled rough timing marks for various airspeeds; 420 knots initially, 360 knots as I approached London, a quiet 180 knots over built-up London until I reached the River Thames. At that point I would increase to 300 knots and later to 420 knots after an exit stage right via the eastern suburbs. Having marked headings to steer and fuel figures to note, I folded the map down my highlighted route.

One problem was my lack of a detailed target map of central London. Without trying to attract attention I stowed my quarter-million scale map in a flying suit pocket and set off in search of something suitable. In what was by then an airmen's crew room (but used by 601 Squadron in the Battle of Britain and featured in famous photographs taken in July 1940 by Charles Brown of *The Daily Mirror*) a kindly chief technician let me peruse his Automobile Association book. Ignoring some perplexed looks, I scrutinised a small, symbolic map of central London and felt suddenly so uneasy that I nearly aborted the whole plan. I realised that this part of my scheme would have to be played, as they say, a bit by ear.

Now I needed to consider another hurdle; that of parting company with my colleagues after our formation take-off from Tangmere. This would have to be done with guile, in a manner that did not arouse suspicion. In the event, though, the solution was far easier than I'd anticipated. When the formation took off from Tangmere in two pairs and a singleton (the latter machine flown by the squadron commanding officer who had joined us), the CO's aircraft broke away starboard from the rest of the formation after take-off so as to perform farewell manoeuvres over the airfield. As number four in the second pair and holding an echelon port position, it was easy for me to slip away unobserved when the formation wheeled to the right. I eased back my throttle, reversed my bank gently away from the other three so as to stay down at low level and point my Hunter XF442 (H-for Hotel) towards London. After a delay of two minutes or so, I used the 'speechless' system to relay to my leader that I'd suffered radio failure and that I'd lost visual contact with the rest of the formation. With the radio issue now resolved, I could continue in relative peace and quiet. I was on my own; the scene was set; London here I come!

En route to London I knew that I'd pass close to Dunsfold airfield, a World War 2 site whose lease had been acquired by the Hawker Company in 1950 specifically for development of the Hawker Hunter (in preference to Beaulieu airfield on the advice, so he told me one time, of test pilot Neville Duke). I'd be in the vicinity, in other words, of the home of the Hawker Hunter, including XF442, and I knew that it would be regarded as remiss to do anything other than streak at high speed and low altitude across the aerodrome. Having checked that the area was clear, that was precisely what I did.

With Dunsfold's anniversary flyby accomplished, I had just a couple of minutes before my planned 'initial point', the great water reservoirs some three miles south east of Heathrow Airport. Ahead of these as I banked to the right. At this low level I was safely clear of Heathrow's airliners, which was confirmed when I could spot a distant Boeing 707 pursue its stately path down the glide slope towards the airport's westerly runway. By complete coincidence, I was now flying near enough to be heard by Hawker's design and assembly teams at Kingston and Ham as I cut the corner across the green expanse of Richmond Park to continue along the silvery-brown ribbon of the River Thames as it snaked due east. Captivated, I flew above the striking, functional symmetries of Hammersmith Bridge, Putney Bridge and a whole series of further bridges before I reached Lambeth Bridge.

The weather conditions remained ideal; the angle and brilliance of the sun, the cloudless sky, the lack of wind all helped to magnify my sense of the surreal. As I peered ahead, suddenly I detected my target: the classic sight of the Houses of Parliament and Big Ben emerging on my left. Certainly sensing the enormity of what I was doing, I felt a curious relief and satisfaction that I had now reached my main target area. As the spectacular and familiar silhouette loomed, I climbed slightly and banked to circle the historic seat of British government. In order to maintain a good tight orbit, I opened my throttle to full power thereby increasing the Rolls-Royce Avon's noise level which up to now I'd been so careful to keep as low as possible. However, I decided that this was perhaps what was really needed to wake up our members of parliament and to remind other august, chair-bound figures snoozing at their ministerial desks that the country still had a fighting air force, one small unit of which was celebrating a noble anniversary despite the dead hand of government policy, the sickening cutbacks of previous years and the rock bottom national morale.

Three times I circled the Houses of Parliament. Twelve times Big Ben's big bell struck noon. Like Jonathan Swift's Gulliver, I surveyed in dazed fascination the Lilliputian scene below; Swift's opinion of the state of European government seemed ironically apposite. My views were at once privileged and remarkable. I kept well clear of Buckingham Palace but the 387-feet bulk of the Vickers Millbank tower block, constructed five years previously, interfered annoyingly with the uniform radius of my turning circle. I felt cross that, with no suitable self-briefing and from my Whitehall-angled sight-lines, I was unable to pick out the prime minister's residence at number 10, Downing Street. I recall wondering idly how many regulations I was breaking at this exclusive and delicious moment. Then, quite abruptly, I started to feel rather tired. Perhaps, despite a conscious state of denial, my subconscious understood well enough that this could be my last flight as a member of the Royal Air Force.

Later, I heard that my message to Westminster had been received all right. A debate in the House of Commons had been interrupted and a cross-party group of four members of parliament had tabled a motion of support for my action. The motion, however, had been ruled out-of-order and deleted, so I was told, from the official Hansard record.

After my third and last orbit I levelled out over the River Thames, dipped my Hunter's wings in salute as I flew past the Royal Air Force memorial and the statue of Viscount Trenchard (for whom my father, John Pollock, had once worked in 1934 when they were both at Scotland Yard), then I continued in an easterly direction to follow the line of the Thames. Later, I was told by Group Captain Duncan Smith DSO DFC, whom I knew, that he was actually in the office of Chief of the Air Staff Sir John Grandy GCB KBE DSO (and whose ADC I had also been for his first ten days as commander of Second Allied Tactical Air Force), when they were both drawn to the window at around midday by the sound of a jet aircraft nearby. Duncan Smith spotted me straightaway but then had to correct Sir John's sightline: "No, sir, not up there. He's below – down there!"

Now above Hungerford Bridge, I noted Cleopatra's Needle to my left and the Royal Festival Hall on the right before I passed over Waterloo Bridge. Ahead and some distance to the left rose the striking structure of the Post Office Tower and as I approached Blackfriars Bridge the dome of St Paul's Cathedral stood upright and defiant, just as in the Blitz against Nazi bombs, but currently with a latticework of scaffolding which disguised its famous silhouette. For minutes I had felt almost intoxicated by the views and by the surrounding sense of history. Beyond Blackfriars Bridge lay Southwark Bridge and London Bridge, the latter shortly to be sold to an American citizen and rebuilt in Arizona, USA (he would later deny rumours that his intention was to buy Tower Bridge but that, regretfully, he had muddled up the names).

Suddenly, with London Bridge now below me, I realised that I had to make an intriguing decision. Until that moment I had given no thought to the matter of tackling the iconic Tower Bridge, not even giving thought to the fact that it would

Mike Rondot's impression of the dramatic moment, as featured in Flypast.

be there. As with the previous bridges, I reckoned that it would be a straightforward case of flying above this famous landmark. However, I was instantly struck with the idea of flying not above but between the spans. My brain cells began to race; I had just three seconds in which to decide, though it seemed much longer. Flying low gained me an extra split second of study time and helped me to line up for a straight run at the bridge. From the perspective of any trained fighter ground-attack pilot, this was an interesting penetration problem. Down at ultra-low level in my Hunter, in the Upper Pool of London, I was well below a serried rank of tall mechanical cranes that stood like puzzled spectators along the right-hand riverbank.

Ahead at Tower Bridge I noticed road traffic on the bascule section, including a red double-decker London bus which lumbered slowly from north to south. Now with just a short distance to run, I realised that it would be easy enough to fly under the bridge's upper walkway. My thoughts began to churn...*keep her steady... that gap looks like it's well wide enough for my wingspan of nearly 34 feet...no problem at all...no problem at all?...I must stay as high as possible over that double-decker bus; I wonder if the passengers have noticed me yet...I'll aim to fly as near as I can to the upper walkway...easily the safest plan...I'll have to watch out, though – the Hunter's height is around thirteen feet...I'll make it like a reverse skip-bombing run with the cues above rather than below...My God!...now the bridge's steel girders look incredibly close...the girders appear to explode above, below and all around my cockpit...I've surely over-cooked it...the top of my fin, thirty-four feet back from my head, will strike the upper walkway...*

For that microsecond, logged by the bridge-master, Mr Tapper, as at two minutes past noon, I remained convinced that my Hunter's fin must strike the bridge's upper walkway. My heart missed a couple of beats but the Hunter, still in one piece, flew on. The flight controls felt normal; my fin was apparently intact. Now I was aware of an acute physical reaction as my heart began to fire up again.

Soon, while I continued to follow the River Thames due east, I swept past Wapping, round the big 'S' bends through Limehouse Reach and on past a Royal Naval frigate moored at Greenwich. After Barking Reach I turned north east over Hornchurch Marshes before I commenced a slow climb and headed for Clacton-on-Sea. With nothing to hide any more, I decided to resume my use of the aircraft radio. I adopted a special anniversary callsign – Romeo Alfa Foxtrot 1 – a nice touch, I reckoned, even though the significance appeared to be lost on the controllers I contacted. With due clearance from air traffic control I flew low across RAF Wattisham whose station commander (an ex-English Electric Canberra man) had lambasted our station commander at West Raynham calling on him to put a stop to Monday's leaflet raids. From Wattisham I headed for Lakenheath and with permission flew low over our sister squadron of the USAF (492 Tactical Fighter Squadron equipped with F-100 Super Sabres) before I set course for RAF Marham, home of 55 Squadron's and 57 Squadron's Handley Page Victor air-to-air refuelling fleet. By this stage, not exactly flush with fuel, my low pass over a rather less co-operative RAF Marham was intended to cover former Fighter Command and Bomber Command bases currently in the process of amalgamation to form the new Strike Command.

So it was that with thoughts of *sic transit gloria* (glory fades) spinning through my mind I set off on the brief final leg of my unauthorised flight of fancy. I conducted a somewhat hasty and inadequate inverted run across my squadron's hangars at RAF West Raynham before I broke downwind, airbrake in, lowered my undercarriage and flap, and turned finals for landing. On touchdown, I streamed my Hunter's brake parachute which billowed out contentedly behind and below XF 442's perfectly intact fin.

As I taxied-in after the landing, I speculated on the nature of my reception committee. I'd experienced these once or twice in the past so I was not altogether unfamiliar with the *modus operandi*. On this occasion, however, all seemed normal: just the usual cheery airman to guide me onto the Hunter's wheel-chocks. Amazed and pleased that evidently I had a few more moments of grace, I decided to destroy my quarter-million scale aviation map before I made those urgent private telephone calls from the nearby mechanical transport section. I then walked to my squadron buildings and climbed the stairs that led

How newspapers in April, 1968 reacted to Pollock's flying escapade.

up to the offices where I presented myself to the squadron commanding officer, the wing commander flying and the station commander. To my considerable surprise, all three were apparently quite unruffled. No doubt well acquainted with fast moving events, they appeared to take the situation in their stride and my squadron CO seemed strangely relieved that Whitehall wasn't littered with 1(F) Squadron's anniversary leaflets. At length, it was left to me to suggest my own arrest, a suggestion that was duly taken up.

After this, the wing commander in charge of administration, a splendid officer, escorted me to the officers' mess where I was examined by the station medical officer. The good doctor declared that in his opinion I was sane but that I'd be required to await the arrival of a Royal Air Force psychiatrist. This man eventually turned up at 8.30 that evening and after an hour's examination he, too, declared me officially sane but tired and with a heavy cold. A day-and-a-half ensued while my fate was decided and in this period, naturally enough, I grew restless especially as no-one appeared keen on my proposal that I should be released from close arrest to open arrest.

Still in high spirits and feeling frustrated, I became mischievous, seized my officer guard and locked him up. Following this event I was transferred home and then to the RAF Hospital at Nocton Hall in Lincolnshire. However, as a former regular climber who knew, too, from escape and evasion courses that pretending to escape often bred opportunity, I made a serious mistake. With no difficulty, that night I scrambled unnoticed onto the hospital roof from where I watched with some glee but rapidly increasing alarm the palaver below as all and sundry ran in small circles trying to locate me. These natural high spirits to bolster my own morale ensured my next move to the RAF Hospital at Wroughton in Wiltshire. This had more serious implications. My heavy cold had progressed to a form of pneumonia and now a combination of drugs and disillusionment began to sap my spirit.

Over a period of two weeks I received more than a hundred letters, all of them positive except for one from an ex-Naval man involved in a national noise abatement campaign. A month followed during which time my morale continued to decline and bizarre events occurred. These included the drug conundrum which arose at a legal Summary of Evidence taken in front of four witnesses, a cancelled court martial which I had openly sought and for which I had been declared fully fit by medical specialists, and my copy of the five-day Summary of Evidence which was forcibly taken back and later 'destroyed' so it was never found again. In the press we were told the outcome of a medical board even before the board had been convened. Senior officials at Whitehall had decided that I should be medically discharged from the service. I asked to see my air-officer-commanding-in-chief, a permanent officer's statutory right under Queen's Regulations, but this, too, was refused. So it was that, with a heavy heart, I was drummed out of the service.

Most fighter aircrew either start or certainly soon develop hyperthymic (from my Greek: 'excessively spirited') temperaments, with irrepressible energy, buoyant, generous but competitive personalities coupled with firm ideas, lodged in flexible and reasonably self-assured heads but with fairly low boredom thresholds and less risk-averse attitudes, all as part of their job. We were all caffeine junkies then (free coffee rations in any RAF crew room after some earlier RCAF study) but what the RAF and civvy doctors' drugs really were (they were prescribed for my heavy cold that week and were supposed to make me sleepy but proved quite the reverse), we will never know. Part of any possible defence of my actions, they were taken away from me for analysis – or not! The effect of the drugs that week triggered four days of sleep deprivation and, as noted by some colleagues, a transition from one's normal 'hyperthymia' into a more hypomanic euphoria en route to pneumonia. In 1968 it would be years before any drug's downside effects were mentioned let alone understood through Andrew Herxheimer's pioneering work on drug interactions, elements of which had come out at my Summary of Evidence. After a difficult period, I took up a civilian career in exporting for which my aggressive fighter pilot training and my language skills paid dividends: I even wrote an article for the *Export Times* on how similar those ten principles of War and Export actually were.

*

On the positive side there was a distinctly unexpected silver lining to our family's clouded departure from the light blue RAF No.1 (F) Squadron community in Norfolk, although my dining out night was memorable. In early May, to my wife's and my despair, our fourth child's meningitis at eleven months had been misdiagnosed and our baby daughter, Ann, became blind, deaf and paralysed in King's Lynn; quite accepted then (and before later key NHS changes), was the amazing reality that her foreign doctor's English seemed little better than my own seventy words of Arabic to him. Shunning the earnest advice of the top Addenbrooke's consultant to leave our daughter in special long-term care for the sake of the three others, thankfully HMG/MoD thus forced us to come south. At Queen Mary's Hospital Carshalton, a superb consultant's alternative treatment meant that, six weeks after admission there, our Ann slowly recovered her sight, smiles and movement, still remaining mentally handicapped but such a valued and special family member. These joint experiences led to my becoming an active campaigner on a variety of serious issues.

Author's Note

At the present moment in 2014 one could speculate on what might happen four years hence. On 1st April 2018, assuming that this nation still has an air force, maybe we will be treated to some form of flypast to celebrate the 100th anniversary of the formation of the Royal Air Force. Perhaps, if you happen to walk on London's Tower Bridge that day, you might spot an apprehensive gentleman with a nostalgic air as he paces up and down in anticipation of action. If so, I trust that you will feel able to come up to him, to shake him by the hand, and to commend him on his single-minded, if contentious, initiative of fifty years ago. Maybe you will empathise with him as someone who, despite the pitfalls, despite the shocking consequences for his own future, was an honourable fellow willing to demonstrate as any good fighter pilot should do, that, if nothing else, at least he had the courage of his convictions.

CHAPTER 2

BORDER PATROL

NIGEL WALPOLE
RECOLLECTS THE
ADEN EMERGENCY

With a serious expression, Flight Lieutenant Anthony Mumford closed the door firmly behind him. He was a flight commander on 43(F) Squadron based in Aden and he now commenced a meticulous brief on the flight ahead – an operational sortie in two Hunter FGA9s (fighter ground attack), guns loaded, at very low level along the border with Yemen. Although I was serving as a squadron leader at HQ Middle East Air Force, Steamer Point, I was able to keep in flying practice on the Hunter wing at the Royal Air Force base at Khormaksar (motto: *Into the remote places*). As a bachelor I was happy to volunteer for the border patrol on that Christmas Day, 1963. During his briefing, my leader stressed that I was not to fly my aircraft below his.

After we moved to the pilots' crew room for ritual pre-flight mugs of coffee, Flight Lieutenant Mumford performed the honours as we waited for the ground crew (also volunteers) to complete their checks on our aircraft. When I gazed through the window I could not fail to be impressed by the sight of the mighty Jebel Shamsan, an extinct volcano situated a few miles south of Khormaksar airfield. Below its jagged rocks were the towns of Ma'alla and Crater with their minarets, anomalous shops and general backstreet hubbub amplified by ubiquitous goats that wandered the streets with impunity. Nearby, surrounded by seas with a multitude of shades of aquamarine, Steamer Point and Aden Harbour were located at the end of the slender strip of land which formed the southern tip of the Federation of South Arabia.

I imagined the December weather back at home where, no doubt, a thin quiet drizzle fell, street lamps shone yellow on wet, black streets and the hiss of car tyres could be heard on sodden surfaces – a vivid contrast to southern Arabia's high temperatures and predominantly clear skies. And on that day, because it was Christmas, rooms and tables were prepared for families to enjoy, simultaneously, copious quantities of food, carols, colourful presents and family agendas. However, I felt no nostalgia – there was work to be done.

The coffee arrived, as did a message that the aircraft would soon be ready, and while we waited I reflected on how the tensions and violence between tribal factions and insurgents in this British protected area had escalated throughout the year. A couple of weeks earlier, on 10th December 1963, a grenade attack by the communist-led National Liberation Front against a group of British officials gathered at the civil side of Khormaksar airport had killed one person and injured fifty. A state of emergency had been declared, the so-called Aden emergency had begun; a seminal moment after Britain's loss, in 1956, of the Suez Canal which had led to Aden becoming our main base in the region. A governor back then had declared that South Arabia would be held for 'as long as Britain remains great' but now, faced with new realities, Britain's aim was to stabilise Aden and the surrounding protectorate in preparation for eventual independence. Earlier this year, in January 1963, the colony of Aden was incorporated into the Federation of Arab Emirates of the South, but this was against the wishes of the communists of North Yemen. The federation was subsequently renamed the Federation of South Arabia.

Today our pair of Hunters was scheduled to patrol the border, including the Radfan mountains, some fifty or so miles north of Khormaksar. Our aim would be to detect and deter potential border infringements. The problems now spreading all over the federation were particularly prevalent in the border districts of Beihan and Lodar where communist agents had armed and encouraged insurgents. The British Army and the Royal Air Force were required to counter these border violations which, on occasions, had involved Soviet-supplied MiG fighter aircraft strafing local communities in cruel and intolerable acts which it was our duty to oppose.

I thought back to the circumstances earlier in the year when a friend of mine, Flight Lieutenant Roger Pyrah, had been posted to Aden to take part in these counter-insurgency tasks, one of which was to act as air liaison officer and forward air controller with a contingent of some 600 local Arab soldiers of the Hadhramaut Bedouin Legion. With a British Army colonel in charge and accompanied by a geologist and a medical doctor, the purpose of the operation had been to establish friendly relationships in the tribal areas before Britain's withdrawal from the federation. The contingent of troops had planned to build a fort, a hospital, a school, and to construct an airstrip suitable for use by Douglas DC-3 aircraft of Aden Airways. In addition, there was a plan to organise a form of administration for the Mahra people on behalf of their sultan who lived on the tiny and remote island of Socotra (*Suqatra*), several hundred miles east of Aden.

Roger Pyrah.

After an arduous 500-mile march of many days to the ancient fort in Thamud, the contingent had continued due east to make for the coastal town of Al Ghaydah. Ambushed twice *en route* by dissidents, the men had faced hardships in the desert stretches where, as well as dissidents, great areas of barrenness were occupied by scorpions, lethal snakes, the occasional lizard, fast-moving spiders and scavenging dung beetles. After a rigorous day, campsite fires could be lit when the air became sharp with the nip of nightfall. At night, temperatures would plummet – a severe and perilous contrast to the stifling heat of day. Huddled in circles around campfires, figures of men would throw up flickering shadows on adjacent dunes. Occasionally, camel spiders – large, hairy, yellowy beasts with massive jaws – would make an appearance. The creatures would run very fast towards the campfire, and quiver as they stalked around warily before they dashed off. Some of the younger troops might jump up in alarm but older hands normally remained seated, however this was not the case if a small but deadly desert snake slid up to the fire.

As the campfires began to die down, the men would seek refuge in their tents. Sleep, though, could be elusive. Individuals would describe how they'd listen to the sough of wind through nearby sand dunes, stare up at the celestial panoply if the night sky was clear, watch shooting stars that arced above – sometimes fast and bright and extinguished in less than a second, sometimes slow and deliberate as if choosing with care a course across the galaxy. In this Lawrence of Arabia territory, they might marvel at an existence that seemed to come straight from the forty-second psalm.

The next day, the slanted rays of a fast-rising sun would wake everyone early. Men would emerge from their tents, blink their eyes in the strong light and listen for the sounds of enemy activity. Night guards would be stood down if signs of dawn attack were absent, then the men could relax a little, and look down to observe the sandy trails that squirmed across the desert floor. All would speculate on the wildlife that had passed close by in the dark, and try to forget the dreams of wolves in the night. The desert dawn would offer a purity and freshness soon erased by the overwhelming blaze of summer heat and light. At breakfast and other mealtimes, flies and insects would have to be picked out of food and drink. The flies might have doted on the wounds of desert animals, laid eggs on raw lesions which then erupted into foul swarms of wriggling maggots. There was little wonder that dysentery, mastoid, a gippy tummy, and desert sores were as much the enemy as dissident tribesmen.

When required to wash, shave and clean their teeth in one small mug of water, men would receive stark reminders of the value of the precious liquid. Privations were not restricted to searing heat and scarcity of water but to a thousand other tortures. This could be a place full of emptiness, which wanted you dead, where it could seem almost impossible to exaggerate the miseries. It was a place which could exert a strange hold on people. Debilitating sandstorms could blow up suddenly; normally placid men could become bloody-minded, lose their tempers with their friends, with themselves, with life in general.

To help him cope with this desert life (not to mention the curious menu of Arab food cooked in the soldiers' own particular way), Flight Lieutenant Pyrah had taken quantities of whisky, ostensibly to ward off desert maladies, in practice greatly welcomed by the expedition's British members. He'd learned salutary lessons, not least when the contingent eventually reached Al Ghaydah and an attack by members of the Kedah tribe had killed two soldiers. The experience of working with Arab troops among and against local tribesmen in alien conditions had left him with a deep sense of respect for the Hadhramaut Bedouin soldiers. Following the Kedah tribe's attack, he had sent an urgent 'air request message' to headquarters. Two Hunter FGA9 aircraft armed with 60lb high explosive rockets and 30mm cannon fitted with high explosive rounds had been despatched to attack a building on the outskirts of Al Ghaydah. The Kedah tribesmen had been forewarned so the building's destruction had led to loss of face rather than loss of life and subsequently the Hadhramaut Bedouin soldiers had suffered no further attacks.

Following these experiences, Roger Pyrah had helped to devise an ingenious, if basic, system to expedite the delivery of air reconnaissance photos to army units in operational situations. A Hunter FR10 (fighter reconnaissance) pilot, having photographed an area with terrorist suspects, would hasten back to Khormaksar where the reconnaissance film would be rushed to a mobile film processing unit. The pilot, meanwhile, would remain in his Hunter cockpit while relevant prints were selected. Within minutes, these photos would be placed in a special sack weighted with four cans of beer, attached to a small parachute, then carefully positioned within the internal framework of the Hunter's airbrake at the rear of the aircraft. When cleared, the Hunter pilot would roar off again, return to the required area where he'd fly low and slow, then operate the Hunter's airbrake which, thus opened, would allow the photographs to drift down towards eager recipients. This system, which normally achieved a drop accuracy of around twenty yards, proved of considerable value to battle managers faced with terrorist activity.

I glanced outside again at the expanse of Khormaksar airfield with the dark surface of the runway set between grassy sand on either side. Conditions were bearable at this time of the year but matters were different at the peak of summer. When the sun was high and when personnel could feel the hot air touch the inside of their lungs, some found it best to breathe through half-closed lips and to inhale quickly; it could seem cooler that way. On occasions a heat haze would hang like a vapour over the airfield and the runway surface would shimmer. When the heat of the sun became like a close fire, and perspiration ran down necks, inside service-issue shirts, over chests to collect by belts pulled tight around the tops of trousers, prickly heat on the skin could cause endless, irritable itching. Some personnel, devoured by stinging insects and worn down by the outlandish heat, could develop alarming malaise.

The hazards may have been great, nonetheless important work had to continue.

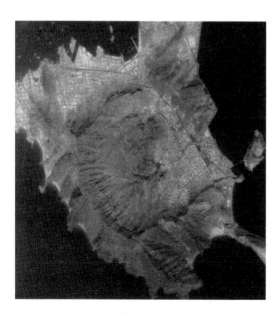

Roger Pyrah used his F95 oblique cameras for this vertical shot of Aden; Shamsan mountain in the centre. (Roger Pyrah)

In a few days' time, early in 1964, a British-run 'orders' group ('O' group) meeting will presage the start of a major offensive in the Radfan mountains, renowned as territory used by Egyptian-backed Yemeni intruders to stir up trouble amongst indigenous tribal factions. An army brigade headquarters will be set up at Thumier in order to run 'Radforce' – a British-led initiative manned largely by inexperienced troops of the Federal Regular Army. Royal Air Force Hunter FR10 pilots, experts at the detection of sand tracks and other telltale signs, would call up Hunter FGA9s armed with three-inch rockets and other ammunition to attack dissidents. The initial task, to secure the area and to re-open the strategically-important Aden to Dhala road, will be followed by the use of Hunters in daylight hours and Avro Shackleton aircraft for night patrols. The Hunters' firepower will prove effective in a variety of ways, including assistance with the rescue of a Special Air Services patrol whose position will be revealed by wandering goats. On a separate occasion, Hunters will provide air cover for the rescue of a group of men from the Parachute Regiment split from the main force during an assault on high ground. In another incident, the Hunters, despite heavy (if inaccurate) fire from the ground, will facilitate the recovery of an Army Air Corps helicopter crew shot down on the slopes of Bakri Ridge.

Three years later, in January 1967, mass riots in the old quarter of Aden town will persist for several weeks. The conflict between the National Liberation Front and the rival Front for the Liberation of Occupied Yemen will continue until mid-February 1967 despite the intervention of British troops. During this period there will be as many attacks on the British troops as by both sides against each other. The violence will culminate in the destruction of an Aden Airways DC-3 aircraft in the air with no survivors. At the end of November 1967 the British will withdraw from the area to leave Aden and the rest of the Federation of South Arabia under the control of the National Liberation Front.

*

All of this, of course, lay in the future on that Christmas Day in 1963. When, eventually, a telephone message informed us that our aircraft were ready, I followed Flight Lieutenant Mumford to the engineering line hut where we signed for our aircraft before we walked out to our respective Hunters.

One of the ground crew accompanied me as I carried out my external checks. He then manned a fire extinguisher placed to one side of the Hunter from where he would supervise the start-up procedure. Another 'liney' helped me to strap in to my Martin Baker ejection seat before removal and stowage of the seat safety pins. I began my pre-start checks in a methodical left to right routine and was soon ready to start the engine. After a 'thumbs up' from my leader, I raised one finger to the ground crewman, made a circling motion to indicate engine start and received a 'thumbs up' in return. I pressed the engine start button firmly; a shrill *wheee* confirmed that the Rolls-Royce Avon's start cycle had begun. I checked the engine instruments, found all to be in order and on the leader's signal instructed 'chocks away' before I followed him to the take-off point. When cleared by air traffic control, we moved rapidly onto the runway where I took up an echelon starboard position in close formation on the leader.

Flight Lieutenant Mumford now signalled with one finger to indicate 'increase engine power'. When satisfied, he glanced at my aircraft, saw that I was ready and, with a pronounced nod of his head, released his aircraft brakes. At once, both Hunters sprang forward and I concentrated on holding my echelon starboard position relative to the leader. My peripheral vision picked up a blur from the runway edge as the Hunters accelerated. Soon, I pulled back on the control stick to raise my nose wheel at the same time as the leader. Within seconds, the main wheels followed and both aircraft were airborne. Quickly, I went through my after take-off checks then applied bank to take up an arrow head formation as we headed north towards the Radfan mountains.

Now we remained, as briefed, at low level as we flew above flat plains, narrow winding wadis flanked by sheer rock faces, and over great sandy stretches. We crossed minor hills and valleys, bizarre conglomerations of sand and rock, thick walls of sand domed by forlorn-looking shrubs with rusty-coloured bristle and truncated spikes. Sometimes, clouds from sandstorms would blot out the sun as debris, darkened and spectacular, was whipped across the desert. When flying by the periphery of such storms, a sudden fusion of sun and dust could induce disorientation. If a pilot entered the heart of a sandstorm, visibility could reduce to a few yards, sand would blast cockpit canopies and penetrate aircraft systems.

The Hunters' reliability in these conditions had proved to be remarkably robust but not infallible, and I was aware of a local accident which had forced the pilot to eject after a catastrophic technical failure. Following his 'Martin Baker' let-down, the pilot had landed safely and – crucially – uninjured in the desert where his survival training, needed from the moment of touchdown, had contributed, no doubt, to his successful rescue. The basic priorities of survival, protection, location, water, food, were the same in the desert as in other parts of the world, although a desert survival situation could mean a further potential pitfall, that of an encounter with belligerent tribesmen. One time, a Hunter pilot had been painfully aware of this as he tussled with a difficult decision. Having used all four of his 30mm cannon to engage enemy tribesmen after they'd fired at his aircraft, his attention was abruptly diverted inside his cockpit by the engine fire warning system. With no external indications of fire, and reluctant to eject over hostile territory, the pilot opted to ignore the fire warning and return to base. His decision proved to be prudent: the warning turned out to be spurious.

As with other Hunter pilots I carried 'goolie chits' which promised rewards for my safe return in the event of an ejection, even so I was conscious that the tribesmen, hardy desert folk with lean hawk-like faces turned chestnut brown by the sun, had to be treated warily. With faces screwed up against the dazzle of sunlight, eyes twinkling with excitement, an attempt at communication with a mix of English and soldiers' Arabic could save a stranded airman's life. On the other hand, potential disaster lurked as was illustrated tragically when an Army Air Corps helicopter, brought down by enemy gunfire, had crashed in the desert and the two helicopter crewmen were believed to have been murdered by hostile tribesmen.

With the visibility remaining good on that Christmas morning, before long the vertiginous slopes of the Radfan mountains with the highest peak (Jebel Huriyah) at 6,125 feet came into view. Our maps of the area were poor but local experience helped as we flew up and down the border, peered into the caves and wadis from which dissidents were known to operate, and tackled the curious twilight zone of counter-insurgency operations. However, we spotted nothing amiss that day and after an hour and a half flew back to Khormaksar.

A thorough debrief followed which covered every aspect of the sortie and which went well until Flight Lieutenant Mumford reminded me of his order on low flying: 'never fly below me'. He had noticed a minor infringement of the rule and proceeded to tell me in no uncertain terms what he thought of this breach of flying discipline. He reminded me of the potential hazards of low flying in such diverse terrain. I could offer no excuse and soon, when we repaired to the officers' mess after the debriefing, the first Christmas beer was on me.

CHAPTER 3

FINE LINE

TIM THORN'S
SPLIT-SECOND TIMING

A tune wanted to rebound through my head, like Land of Hope and Glory or the Dambusters' March. I'd had a few scrapes in my time but this one, you might say, was exceptional. Outside, through a crew room window, I glimpsed my recalcitrant aircraft, Hawker Hunter FR10 XF428, as the machine was towed to a hangar for inspection by engineers. Painted on the Hunter's fuselage, the 4 Squadron crest appeared colourfully familiar set against the monotonous Dutch landscape that surrounded our temporary base at Deelen airfield.

Inside the crew room a buzz of conversation persisted as crews discussed planned routes, aviation charts, time and distance calculations, necessary fuel margins. All had been intrigued to hear about my recent experience but now the men had to concentrate on their own agendas as they prepared for the competition's next challenge.

Meanwhile, as I sipped at a mug of coffee to help calm adrenaline-charged nerves, I reflected on the eye-watering narrowness of my escape. With the memory triggered, perhaps, by a state of high anxiety, I seemed to recall particular events, including the moment four years ago when I'd had to eject from aircraft XM384, a Jet Provost Mk 3, which had just collided with another during a formation display rehearsal. Thoughts such as 'this cannot be happening to me' had wanted to rush through my head but I'd been too preoccupied for distractions. *"Eject...eject..."* I

Top: 8 Squadron FGA Mk 9s XF376-K and XG255-G on the line at Sharjah in November 1963. There being no hangar accommodation, aircraft servicing was being undertaken in the open on XF435 on the left of the photograph. (*Ray Deacon*)

Above: A team of examiners from the Day Fighter Combat School at Binbrook, part of the CFE, flew out to the Middle East in January 1963 to test the pilots and operational capabilities and readiness of the resident squadrons. This view, depicting the CFE aircraft shortly after their arrival at Bahrain in November 1963, comprises two F Mk 6s, XG204-B and XG209-C, with their distinctive yellow spines and tailfins, and T Mk 7s XL591-M and XL595-O. (*Ray Deacon*)

Below: Heading the 8 Squadron Hunter line at Bahrain in 1963, FGA Mk 9 XJ688-G was left behind as unserviceable by 208 Squadron after its two-month detachment to the Gulf State. (*Ray Deacon*)

Top: Course members at Hunter Operational Conversion Unit, 1966. Left to right: Ted Girdler, Tony Craig, Les Howe, Dave Carden, Roger Colebrook. Standing at rear: John Aldington. (*Roger Colebrook*)

Above:When 8 Squadron moved from Bahrain to Sharjah on a two-week armament practice camp in November 1963, the four CFE Hunters came too. In this view, CFE T Mk 7 XL595-O heads a line of eleven aircraft. (*Ray Deacon*)

Left: Beautiful lines of a Hunter in flight.

PS·1417·RAF·1315T·20AUG65·F/L JOHNS·REST'D

Top: Aden with RAF Khormaksar in the foreground, photo taken by 1417 Flight Hunter FR10. (*Peter Lewis*)
Above left: Group of local trucks in Aden. (*Peter Lewis*)
Above right: Eyes over Aden. (*Sandy Burns via Ray Deacon*)
Right: Hunter FR10 in flight. (*Tim Thorn*)

Top: Beautiful clean lines of the F4 as operated by 229 OCU at RAF Chivenor.
Left: Flt Lt Tim Thorn in Sharjah. (*Tim Thorn*)
Above: Radfan mountains, Aden, pre-strike. (*Peter Lewis*)

yelled at my student, Pilot Officer Sedman, who reacted with commendable rapidity. A crashing sound above my head and an abrupt wind blast indicated that the Jet Provost's canopy had been ejected. My student followed a fraction of a second later. I was aware of his ejection seat rising up close to my arm, then, without further ado, I pulled my own ejection seat handle.

I could still recollect, even many years later, the subsequent sensation as if it had happened only yesterday. There was a bang then a jolt when my ejection seat's primary cartridge shot me clear of the doomed Jet Provost. I tumbled forward and felt a sharp pull on my helpless body. Thrust into a weird, wayward world, one of whirling activity where time, vision and perspective became alarmingly topsy-turvy, I was left entirely in the hands of fate not to mention Messrs Martin Baker's magnificent mechanisms. When I realised, however, that my continued physical existence appeared reasonably assured, even if it relied on the parachute canopy that blossomed above my head, I experienced an overwhelming, almost other-worldly, sense of relief. There was further comfort when, having been deposited unceremoniously on *terra firma*, I learned that my student as well as the pilot of the other Jet Provost, Flight Lieutenant Henderson, had ejected safely too.

That accident had occurred just a couple of years after I'd graduated from the Royal Air Force College at Cranwell in Lincolnshire. I retained potent memories of my time at Cranwell. The three years that I spent there had begun in 1961 when a rather rag-bag group of individuals, some arriving by car, some collected from Sleaford railway station by a very basic air force bus, had assembled at the college. There'd been an air of appeal in all of our eyes as we gazed at each other in bewildered fashion. Suddenly someone said something amusing and everyone laughed and our expressions relaxed. Years later, the passage of time will have proved the enduring nature of friendships formed early in life.

As new recruits we were marched off more or less directly to the camp barber after which we started a relentless round of slave labour to bull up boots, prepare beds in the regulation manner, buff up linoleum-covered floors, polish brass taps and clean exposed water pipes in the flimsy wooden huts provided as accommodation by the Royal Air Force. We were hustled here and there by in-your-face sergeants, pestered with tiresome questions by members of the senior entry, and given tasks that seemed to have little to do with military duties let alone flying aeroplanes. I could recall how, one time, our drill sergeant looked up at the sky and tutted irritably when the noise from a Jet Provost aircraft passing overhead had interrupted his drill instruction. As a group we became immersed in unreality which, before too long, we accepted as eccentric but necessary. Nowadays our treatment would be regarded as bullying and, doubtless, would be outlawed. Back then, though, a huge and intransigent common sense had been the secret of survival. We'd learnt deep and thorough lessons which for most of us would provide invaluable tools for life.

Tim Thorn after gunnery firing.

The regime at Cranwell had helped, too, with cadets' sporting activities. Sport had always been an important part of my life; as a youngster, just after leaving Ipswich School, I had represented the county of Suffolk as a cricket fast bowler. At Cranwell I played a variety of sports, including hockey when, one time, an over-exuberant swing of my hockey stick might well have decapitated Flight Cadet Richard Pike but for the latter's quick reactions. In the sport of rugby I was honoured to represent the Royal Air Force then in 1968, four years after leaving Cranwell, I won a bronze medal at the European championships just prior to the Olympic Games...

*

Back to reality, I looked up at the sound of raised voices at one end of the crew room at Deelen.

When the hubbub calmed down, I glanced outside to observe hectic activity as engineers scurried about to refuel and make ready various aircraft types involved in the NATO Royal Flush competition. This annual aerial reconnaissance competition, hosted that year (May 1970) by the Royal Netherlands Air Force, was designed to identify the best NATO reconnaissance squadron and the best overall pilot. As one of four pilots representing the Royal Air Force, I had flown recently from my home base at RAF Gütersloh in Germany to Deelen where I'd joined the other competitors.

All competing crews had received copious briefings at Deelen: the competition rules, the types of targets, aspects of the local area, the airbase facilities; all were covered in great detail. We learnt, among other matters, that the airbase at Deelen had an unusual past. When, in World War 2, the Netherlands had surrendered to Germany, the Luftwaffe had expanded and upgraded Deelen airfield to accommodate an important day and night-fighter base. An enormous bunker system was developed from where all of the airspace over Holland and large parts of the Ruhr were monitored and defences coordinated using approximately twenty radar stations. Towards the end of the war the airfield had been bombed so extensively that flying activity was suspended and the base turned into a depot for V-1 flying bombs.

The world, though, had changed out of all recognition since those dark 1940's days. Just now, as I continued to look out of a crew room window, I could make out adjacent farmland with clusters of low trees beyond the airfield boundary. Some cultivated areas, not too distant from the boundary, had lines of immaculate stripes which contained, I assumed, colourful varieties of tulips for Amsterdam. The airfield's main runway, a slick black ribbon of tarmac, was orientated in a north-south direction; set back from the runway were the air traffic control tower and numerous engineering hangars. Inside one of these, squadron engineers had begun to work away, no doubt, to resolve the problem with XF428.

I reflected on the competition's incongruous start. For the first mission on, this, the first morning of Royal Flush, all personnel were in a state of high excitement. Having been selected to fly, I'd studied the assignment assiduously and anxiously. This task, set in the Ardennes area of Belgium, had covered a region of extensive forests, rolling hills and ridges close to the borders of France and Luxembourg. My mission had been to conduct a line-search over a forty-kilometre stretch in order to find and identify two static targets, hidden camouflaged military vehicles. The sortie would be timed precisely from take-off to crossing, on return, an imaginary line between Deelen's air traffic control tower and the Royal Flush umpires' tent. Unless this line was crossed at the stipulated time plus or minus five seconds, the umpires would deduct points from the overall total.

From the moment of task allocation, timing was critical. As speedily as possible, therefore, I read the task details, selected and studied relevant maps, folded them solicitously and placed them in my flying suit pocket. Then I hastened to sign the flight authorisation sheet and technical log before I walked briskly towards XF428. Soon, on completion of external checks and start-up procedures, I was ready to taxy out. The controller duly cleared me after which, as I headed at a fast pace towards the runway, I called for take-off clearance.

"You're clear to take off," the controller said in his lilting Dutch accent.

"Cleared for take-off," I acknowledged. With minor throttle adjustment turning onto the runway, XF428 rolled slickly towards the take-off point. I had a final check around the cockpit...*engine and flight instruments satisfactory...fuel contents sufficient... maps okay.* Approaching the runway centre-line, I brought the throttle back and squeezed the brake lever to bring the Hunter to a halt. Deelen, as a helicopter base, had a relatively short runway – less than ideal for fast-jet aircraft.With full external fuel tanks the Hunter would need all of the available runway length. Now, with my left hand, I advanced the throttle again. Behind me the low whine of the Rolls-Royce Avon rose and rose as it progressed from a cry to a scream; I increased engine power until the brakes struggled to hold the aircraft. Ahead, all was clear; I was set to go.

As I released the aircraft brakes, the Hunter sprang forward like a greyhound suddenly set free. I could picture the umpires' clock being pressed. I took off on Deelen's southerly runway so needed just a small turn to take me towards the target area. I carried out the after take-off checks and flew at low level while rolling out on the requisite heading.

The flat Dutch landscape facilitated navigation as I remained at low level on course for the Ardennes. Before long, however, the dense forests that typified the area came into view, as did the high ground which averaged around 1,000 to 1,500 feet in the northern areas but which rose considerably in the boggy moors of the Hautes Fagnes region of south-eastern Belgium. Once there, I had to concentrate on my maps as the Hunter flew across steep-sided valleys carved by swift-flowing rivers, including the prominent River Meuse. This was 'Battle of the Bulge' territory when, at the start of the infamous German counter-offensive in December 1944, foggy winter weather had thwarted the air reconnaissance efforts of my predecessors. For the Americans, with over half-a-million men committed and some 90,000 casualties, the Battle of the Bulge had proved to be the largest and bloodiest battle they'd fought in World War 2.

Just now, though, in my peacetime situation of twenty-five years later, fine spring weather helped me to identify the required targets within the stipulated timeframe. However, as I started heading for the return to Deelen, XF428's fuel contents were much lower than planned: either the Hunter had a fuel leak or the gauges themselves were faulty. Still conscious of the Royal Flush time restrictions, I opted to abort the planned low-level route and to commence a gentle climb to a more fuel efficient altitude. Now, though, there were restrictions of a different kind – the plethora of civil airways that criss-crossed the sky above.

I levelled off below adjacent airways and maintained a northerly heading for Deelen airfield when, suddenly, my attention was diverted inside the cockpit

Tim Thorn once he had landed back at RAF Deelen.

again as the fuel 'Bingo' lights illuminated. This confirmed my worst fears: the fuel gauges were reading correctly; the problem was one of fuel leakage. With just 600lbs of fuel remaining in each wing tank, a cold sense of dread touched the pit of my stomach. I realised that I'd be hard pushed to make it back to Deelen, let alone meet the Royal Flush time constraints. My pulse quickened as calculations began to work through my head.

With XF428 still at the most fuel efficient airspeed, Deelen airfield eventually came into view. Now, with the fuel tanks nearly empty, I spoke urgently with air traffic control. "You're clear for a priority landing on runway 19," came the reply. I judged the point from where I reckoned to glide the Hunter with minimum engine power, then commenced a steady descent approach. When confident that the aircraft could make the touchdown point, I selected the undercarriage down. The Hunter's undercarriage system, however, took some thirty seconds to lock down with the engine at minimum power, and as the aircraft crossed the runway threshold the indicator showed the right main wheel and the nose wheel locked down, but a single, dreaded, red light revealed that the left main wheel was still travelling.

At this stage I'd selected full flap, but the flaps, too, were slow with the engine at minimum power. As the Hunter touched down, I landed on the right wheel before applying full aileron to keep the left wing up. This worked for some three or four seconds after which the left wing started to drop. Then, a fraction of a second before the wing struck the runway, the left wheel locked down. If I breathed a sigh of relief, this was transient for with the slow flap operation, the Hunter had landed some twenty knots too fast. I operated the brake parachute at about 150 knots (the normal airspeed)...but the 'chute failed (this was its fiftieth time of use and it was due to be replaced – just my bad luck). By now the flaps had lowered fully but with such a short runway I realised that, with braking alone, the Hunter was unlikely to stop before the end. I passed the Royal Flush timing line (within, incredibly, the required time constraint) but had to make an instant decision: go off the end of the runway; raise the undercarriage; or overshoot. I chose the latter.

As I selected full power, a last, gloomy glance at the fuel gauges showed empty tanks. The engine, nevertheless, reacted to the demand for full power; the Hunter even achieved a height of 300 to 400 feet in a hard left turn before the engine flamed-out. With XF428 now transformed into a reluctant glider, I managed to turn the aircraft through 150 degrees back towards the runway. I flew above two Canberra aircraft at the marshalling point as they waited for take-off clearance (later, the crews said that they thought they'd 'bought it'). The Hunter passed over the runway threshold at an angle of about 40 degrees from the centre-line. It was at this point, with the Hunter now below stalling speed, that the aircraft started to drop. Just before plunging into the runway, however, a form of ground effect must have produced an ultimate, last gasp boost to the superb design of the Hunter wing which seemed to lift itself up as if by prestidigitation to land perfectly on the runway centre-line where I rolled to the turn-off point, and eased left to freewheel along a downhill gradient to my squadron dispersal where the machine ended up ten yards short of the required chock position.

I climbed out of XF428's cockpit with the required reconnaissance film, mission report and photographs of the target – and with no Royal Flush penalty points. However, rumours that I proffered a nonchalant, James Bond-type salute to admiring crowds should be treated with scepticism.

In the crew room later, amazement was universal as details of my experience emerged. The two Canberra crews who'd witnessed the event seemed pensive. My own feelings were philosophical. I waved cheerily at members of a Luftwaffe crew who I recognised from social events held in the officers' mess. They were good types, I reckoned, and efficient at their jobs although, for some curious reason, the notes of the Dambusters' March seemed to rebound patriotically through my head as I stood up, smiled and waved again at my German friends, then headed for the operations set-up. Once there, I planned to get down to the inevitable paperwork that followed the incident. As I strode along, I reflected on how, in the world of aviation, the division between success or disaster could turn out to be a fine line...a very fine line indeed.

CHAPTER 4

HUNTER TRAINING

ROGER COLEBROOK LEARNED SOME FIGHTER PILOT ARTS

Gun-cameras do not lie, and this one revealed that my fellow student, as he flew his Hawker Hunter astern the banner-towing Gloster Meteor aircraft, was dangerously out of position. Later, the Meteor pilot reported how he'd heard a sudden sound as ball ammunition had shot past his aircraft. His brain must have gone into overdrive while he struggled to digest the information; seconds, no doubt, had appeared to stretch into infinity. At any moment his cockpit may have been shattered and he might have been subjected to a clamorous increase in ambient noise as his canopy disintegrated. If this had happened, he would have tried to climb his bullet-ridden Meteor to take stock of his situation.

Fortunately, however, the shots missed, the Gloster Meteor remained unscathed, and the master pilot and his aircraft lived to tow another day. Nonetheless, in the incident's immediate aftermath a poignant silence dominated the air waves. At length the master pilot said simply: "Mister...go home!" At this dark and succinct instruction, my fellow student turned his Hunter towards RAF Chivenor and sneaked off to confront the wrath of his flying instructor.

From my point of view, and after what felt like an interminable pause, the Meteor pilot went on eventually: "Mister Colebrook, you may continue."

The sun was brilliant on that summer's day in 1966 and a lack of significant cloud was helpful as I worked to adjust my Hunter's position on the 'perch'. I peered anxiously ahead, above and below. I'd been briefed endlessly that accurate parameters – height, heading, airspeed – were needed when flying the perch position before 'tipping-in' to fire at the towed banner. I focussed on my flight instruments and I was conscious of the background whine of the Hunter's Rolls-Royce Avon engine. As though I was about to run an important race, I developed a sensation of queasiness in the pit of the stomach. Soon, though, I became too preoccupied to feel anything while I tried to concentrate on avoiding the errors just made by my fellow student.

I was, after all, an inexperienced pilot at that stage. Up to then I had flown the Jet Provost and the Folland Gnat as I'd progressed through the RAF's pilot training system, and at RAF Chivenor in Devon I was due to spend some six months at the Hunter operational conversion unit. On completion of the Chivenor course I would move to RAF Coltishall in Norfolk to attend the Lighting operational conversion unit. Although I was supposed to be officially delighted about my posting to the Lightning force and the air defence role, in truth my first choice had been to fly the Hawker Hunter in the ground-attack role. I'd harboured ambitions for a posting to the likes of 208 Squadron at RAF Muharraq on the northern tip of Muharraq Island, one of thirty-three islands in the Bahrain archipelago.

I'd read about the illustrious past of 208 Squadron (motto: *Vigilant*), including an incident that had occurred three years after the end of World War 2. At 0930 on 22nd May 1948 two Egyptian pilots flying their Spitfire Mk LF9 aircraft had taken off with the intention of attacking Ramat David airbase in the northern reaches of Israel. However, a 208 Squadron pilot, Flying Officer McElshaw in a Spitfire Mk FR18, had intercepted and shot down both of the Egyptian machines. This action during the Israeli War of Independence was the last formally recorded fighter aircraft air-to-air 'kill' using only bullets, not guided systems. From my perspective eighteen years later, and as a young man barely in his twenties, this activity was enthralling. I yearned to be part of such a world and its fascinating recent past. At the advanced flying training school at Valley, Anglesey, I'd been rather disappointed when told that I was to be posted onto the Lightning force with, as I saw it at the time, limited opportunities, although I had to admit that my chief objective in life had been achieved: I'd been selected to become a fighter pilot.

So it was that, once at Chivenor, I'd concentrated on learning the basic skills needed for my future role as an air defence fighter pilot. I'd had to learn about the air combat techniques employed by Battle of Britain Hurricane and Spitfire pilots – albeit in modified form. The fundamentals of good lookout, of spotting the 'Hun in the sun' before he saw you, of techniques used in a 'circle of joy' combat, had hardly changed. In a close air combat situation the fighter pilot, whether in the cockpit of a Supermarine Spitfire, Hawker Hurricane or a Hawker Hunter, even a missile-firing English Electric Lightning (unless the pilot was absorbed with his radar picture), would need to move his head ceaselessly from side to side, up and down, and all around until, from force of habit, his attention was directed almost entirely outside the cockpit. Occasionally, and without interrupting the movement of his head, the pilot would glance at his aircraft instruments, then he would look outside again to search persistently for a small speck in the sky that might turn into a life-size enemy aircraft.

And if that happened, if a fighter pilot was faced with an enemy machine closing up, the trained pilot would steel himself, prepare his aircraft, and continue to watch the other closely. He'd carry out pre-combat checks: still with eyes focussed in the direction of the enemy machine, his hand would move instinctively, delicately, around the cockpit. He'd ensure that his pilot attack sight was switched on, he might adjust the brightness, and be ready to flick his armament switch from 'safe' to 'arm'.

In the Battle of Britain, when a squadron's entire complement of serviceable aircraft might be ordered airborne, the leader would aim to gain as much height as possible. Eventually, a pilot in a Hurricane or a Spitfire might call "Tally ho" followed by key information, or he may even drop down in front of the leader to dive towards the approaching enemy. The leader, who now would spot the enemy machines at once, would call to the rest of his squadron: "Okay...line astern, go." The squadron pilots would react spontaneously. Aircraft would be repositioned as pre-briefed; mouths would tighten, nerves would strain while all prepared themselves for action. In 1940, a common Luftwaffe tactic was to form a protective circle of aircraft, a defensive formation which was hard for the fighters to break. Now the fighter squadron's leader might call: "Echelon starboard, go." His squadron members would fan out to the right. Then the leader would call: "Going down!" and one after the other his pilots would follow in a power dive.

In the descent, an experienced pilot would double check that his gun button was set to 'fire'. He'd pick out a particular enemy machine, aiming to have it in his sights by a range of around 300 yards. As the distance reduced to 250 yards, he might start to stroke his gun button. The palms of his hands could start to feel damp, though his mind would take on a startling clarity. He'd follow any evasive moves while he closed to a range of 200 yards at which point he'd press the gun button. A harsh vibration would rock the fighter's airframe; the pilot might sniff the sour odour of explosives. Now he would have to act quickly. If his aim had been good, if the enemy machine began to break up, the fighter pilot would have to manoeuvre violently to avoid debris. Later, Battle of Britain fighter pilots would report how, one minute surrounding airspace would be a mass of individual dogfights as foes tore into each other without mercy until, quite abruptly, the bedlam of machines would disappear. With dizzying speed an eerie silence with not an aircraft in sight would dominate the scene.

A quarter of a century on from those dark days, when the world had changed out of all recognition, the techniques learnt back then nonetheless continued to form the basis of our Hunter air-to-air fighter combat exercises at Chivenor. Typically, an instructor and a student, or perhaps two students towards the end of the course, would take off in their individual Hunters, climb to a pre-briefed altitude, select a suitable area then commence one-versus-one air combat training.

During my time at Chivenor, a particular incident highlighted the potential hazards of our activities. In mid-June 1966, two students took off in formation to climb through layered cloud before the Hunters split for one-versus-one above the cloud. However, as the pair climbed through the cloud layers, the number two aircraft's pilot, flown by an ex-V bomber man converting to Hunters, promptly called: "lost contact." The subsequent procedure should have been straightforward: both aircraft should turn outwards through thirty degrees for thirty seconds to avoid collision after which the leader would state his heading and airspeed. When above cloud, the aircraft would join up again. That day, though, the formation leader heard no further calls after the initial "lost contact". Before long, air traffic control advised the leader that his number two's radar trace had disappeared. The leader was instructed to return to base where he learned that a farm worker had telephoned to report that he'd witnessed a Hawker Hunter plunge in a vertical dive out of cloud and explode in a field. The pilot had not ejected.

I didn't fly that day but I remember vividly the fraught atmosphere when I entered the operations room. The duty operations officer's pale features were creased with concentration; I spotted uncharacteristic flickers of uncertainty in his gaze. Conversation was tense and lacked the usual ready-humour. Perhaps, privately, we all felt the need to ponder our mortality, to think about our own efforts, actions, and, hardest of all, a realistic understanding of our own weaknesses. Flying involved hazards, we'd come to terms with that; it was part of our mental make-up. We were young, of course, indestructible, and we knew that accidents normally happened to the other fellow, and we trusted the high quality of our training. However, when things went badly wrong, maybe then we felt the need to re-evaluate the qualities, so elusive, that defined the necessary attributes of a competent fighter pilot.

When, on that day, I walked across the room to glance at the flight authorisation sheet, I noted with a shudder that the relevant section was marked with a horizontal

Hunter T7 at RAF Chivenor, 1966.

line and the words 'aircraft destroyed'. That, apparently, was that: just a stark statement of fact. Later, a board of inquiry concluded that the pilot had become disorientated in the cloud and lost control of his aircraft.

A separate incident when I was at Chivenor ended, happily, on a less tragic note. This time the task involved four Hunters in two-versus-two combat – a complex scenario which was testing for both students and instructors. The normal practice in such exercises was to place the Hunter's flaps at 'combat setting'. This ensured the aircraft's improved manoeuvrability, although a pilot needed to remember a potential danger: if the Hunter was allowed to accelerate in a dive to transonic speed with flaps set, recovery from the dive became impossible even with the control stick held fully back. The drill in such a situation was to relax back pressure on the stick, retract the flaps, then pull out of the dive.

That day, while all four Hunters cavorted around the sky, judicious handling was crucial in order to cope with the machines' persistent shake close to the stall speed. If a pilot tried to raise the nose, the Hunter's airframe vibration became even more pronounced as the airspeed and rate of climb reduced further. More than once I found myself in a deteriorating situation...'nose up and nothing much on the clock'. The next moment, as I dived to pick up airspeed, the airframe might start to judder for different reasons if speed build-up was too enthusiastic. Like something out of a Wild West movie, air combat often turned into a yo-yo of fortunes. Paradoxically, smooth and accurate flying was the key to success. If the airspeed indicator hovered at a dangerously low reading I'd have to repeat to myself over and over '...*easy does it...watch the attitude...mind the airspeed...don't over-control...don't allow a spin to develop...'*

In the midst of our exertions that day, my fellow student evidently became carried away; he appeared to forget about the flap problem. Suddenly, a plaintive cry struck the airwaves: "I can't pull out!" A note of panic was all too obvious and when I glanced down I could spot his aircraft in a hard left spiral dive as the machine plunged earthwards. I could visualise his situation, how the cosily familiar cockpit had become instantly hostile. I felt very tired and very hot; I watched in horrified fascination – as if mesmerised – not a casual glance but something deeper, more intense. A prickly sensation on my scalp grew as the Hunter plummeted down ever faster.

Then, as though struck by a rush of cold water, I seemed to wake up with a jolt when I heard another voice – that of one of the instructors. The voice said just two words on the aircraft radio: *"flaps f***wit."* It was enough; my fellow student reacted. Now I saw the Hunter wrench itself from the by-then almost vertical dive into an almost vertical climb. He'd raised the flaps but forgotten to release the back-pressure on the stick. The Hunter's structural limits were grossly exceeded, the airframe suffered popped rivets and a broken engine mounting bracket, but the pilot survived.

Not long after this incident my connection with the Hunter ended and I began my Lightning course at RAF Coltishall. However, some two years later, in April 1968, Hunter memories were revived at the time of the fiftieth anniversary of the foundation of the Royal Air Force. By then I was a member of 56(F) Squadron stationed in Cyprus and on the morning of Friday, 5th April 1968 I acted as squadron standard bearer at a parade to mark the anniversary. With due pomp and ceremony the parade formed up, drill sergeants bellowed orders, tidy lines of airmen and airwomen stood to attention shoulder to shoulder. All remained rigid when the inspecting officer was driven up in a highly-polished car from which he stepped out to inspect the rows of personnel before he made his way to the saluting dais. Soon, the band struck up the tune of the Royal Air Force March and the parade began to move past the dais. The 'eyes right' was given; the marchers obeyed in an instant; the inspecting officer saluted severely. Meanwhile, families and friends, wives in posh frocks, miscellaneous guests, had assembled near the dais so as to admire the proceedings.

Eventually, the parade was declared an official success, participants were dismissed and in the afternoon, as tended to be the case in the swelter of a Cypriot day, personnel were stood down from their places of duty. Many would head for Ladies Mile Beach, a sandy stretch close to the town of Limassol in southern Cyprus. With shallow, clear water the area was popular with families, and safe for small children. That afternoon the beach was unusually busy. I recall looking around, blinking in the strong light, and noting the sound of portable radios on the beach as service personnel listened to the local British Forces Broadcasting Service. When a peculiar silence fell across the area, I screwed up my eyes in the bright sunshine and tried to pick up the drift of an announcement on the radio.

Suddenly folk on Ladies Mile Beach erupted in spontaneous reaction to some remarkable event when towels, hats, sandwiches, drinks, plastic buckets, toy spades, kids (no, not kids) were hurled into the air in acts of uninhibited joy. I hadn't heard details on the radio, so asked a neighbour what was going on. His distant look dissolved into a winning smile when, eyes gleaming, he said: "someone's done it!"

"Done what?"

"Flown a Hawker Hunter under the Tower Bridge."

"My God!"

"There's uproar," he went on. "The Houses of Parliament were buzzed and a parliamentary debate was interrupted before the guy headed for Tower Bridge. At last – at long last – there's somebody out there with the gumption to mark our anniversary properly. Bloody marvellous!"

Later, when more details emerged, I found out that all Hunter pilots from Chivenor and elsewhere had been placed under close arrest after landing. The authorities, anxious to figure out the culprit, had treated anyone flying a Hunter at the time as suspect.

In Cyprus, though, I merely grinned and gave a circle of approval with thumb and forefinger to my neighbour on Ladies Mile Beach. Before long, from a hard, clear sky the sun started to eat through the shadows of the afternoon and it was time to head back to the officer's mess at Akrotiri before the rapid onset of nightfall in that part of the world. It had been an unusual end to an unusual week. While I drove along, and while I pondered the implications of the Tower Bridge news, I thought back to my own time on Hunters and smiled quietly to myself.

CHAPTER 5

ANXIOUS MOMENTS

JOCK HERON EXPERIENCED ENGINE FAILURES

Although of rugged and generally reliable design, the Hawker Hunter's Avon Mk 203 engine nonetheless let me down on two occasions. The first failure occurred in March 1959 when I had about 300 hours on the aircraft. I was flying at 48,000 feet during a four-ship air combat training sortie with the throttle in its customary fully-forward position while I fought to outmanoeuvre my opponents. Suddenly, I heard a bang accompanied by a thump and airframe vibration with an immediate loss of engine power. The engine revolutions decayed quickly, irrespective of throttle position. At that point, the vibration reduced and the jet pipe temperature fell to about 200°C so the Avon hadn't actually suffered a flame out. Apart from a buzzing noise there were no other indications although it was obvious that a major mechanical failure had occurred, undoubtedly in the engine. Aircraft handling, however, didn't seem to be affected. With the advantage of high altitude I was not under any immediate threat, other than possible further cumulative failure of airframe systems. If necessary, I could have abandoned the aircraft so I was able, therefore, to follow the stipulated emergency procedures with the aim of recovering my unhealthy jet.

The initial step was to inform my formation colleagues and air traffic control that I had a problem and required assistance. Now I needed to make a judicious assessment of my situation. First things first, I knew where I was (at high altitude south east of Glasgow) and I appreciated that the weather was good. Next, I was aware that the engine had failed and I had stated my intentions to air traffic control. Additionally, I wanted my base at RAF Leuchars to know about the problem. I had the options of gliding to Prestwick, which I could see some thirty-five miles to the south west, or returning to Leuchars, about sixty miles to the north east. Despite the longer distance I chose the latter for several reasons. I had practised flame-out landings there as part of our routine training so it was familiar to me; it was a military airfield and the controllers would allot the proper priority to my approach and landing; I knew that salvaging the broken aircraft would be easier at the home base. So I settled down to a long glide at 210 knots, the recommended airspeed for maximum range whereby the Hunter would cover about two miles for every thousand feet loss of altitude. The friendly and reassuring voice of the air traffic controller informed me that my base was alerted and that full crash services were on standby. This I didn't need to know – I wasn't planning to crash! After about fifteen minutes or so I arrived overhead Leuchars at around 15,000 feet with time and altitude to spare, a comforting thought. I could see the airfield clearly through patchy cloud with the fire engines and ambulance at the runway edge. My aim was to spoil their day and to land without incident.

The classic successful flame-out approach and landing in the Hunter should commence with flying over the threshold of the runway at a height of 6,000 feet at 210 knots. The pilot should then turn through 360 degrees while descending. He should use his judgement to gauge the best point to lower the aircraft wheels and finally, just before touchdown, he would close the HP cock and lower the flaps to reduce the touchdown speed and the length of landing run.

That day, fortunately, everything went according to plan and I was able to turn off at the end of the runway before coming to a halt. I was rapidly surrounded by fire engines, support vehicles and senior officers, all of whom wanted to know what had happened. So, too, did I. A quick look into the jet pipe gave a partial explanation: the base of the jet pipe was sprinkled with tiny metallic fragments which resembled iron filings. When I looked into the intake I saw the reason. The fragments were indeed iron – or at least steel – filings because behind the inlet guide vanes the first stage of the Avon's compressor had vanished. Deeper into the engine, the stators and the remainder of the core had seen better days.

Later, it transpired after investigation that one of the first stage compressor blades had broken at the root and passed through the compressor so that the cumulative effect was to 'haircut' the core. However, when gliding the Hunter at 210 knots the ram-air effect had sustained combustion thus providing some cabin pressurisation and hydraulic and electrical power.

Some time afterwards I realised that the failure had occurred over East Kilbride. This was not only the home of my parents but also the site of the Rolls-Royce factory which overhauled our engines. Presumably, with the local area sprinkled with tiny steel fragments from my Avon, some of them had been returned to their manufacturer!

*

It was six or so months later, at the end of the long hot and dry summer of 1959, that trouble emerged again. Having been selected as the 43 Squadron Hunter display pilot, I was rehearsing my low level aerobatics sequence for the Leuchars Battle of Britain at Home Day. Half way through my routine, I was carrying out an inverted run when the engine flamed out. Positioned along the 1,500 yards length of the disused runway at Errol on the north bank of the River Tay, I was about ten miles due west of my base at RAF Leuchars. This time the emergency was much more serious. I was at low altitude, flying inverted at about 360 knots with little time to respond to the engine failure. The options, in order of preference, were to relight the engine, carry out a forced landing on the runway, or eject.

I rolled the aircraft upright and gained as much altitude as possible while activating the relight system. Meanwhile, I flew a vigorous dumbbell manoeuvre to realign the aircraft with the runway in the reverse direction – hardly the classic Hunter flame-out approach and landing! The jet pipe temperature continued to register zero and the engine was not responding to the relight attempt. I prepared, therefore, for a landing on the runway at Errol while transmitting an emergency call on the radio. Wheels and flaps were lowered on the emergency systems and I touched down at about 160 knots which was much too fast to stop on the short runway. At a speed of around 80 knots, I duly smashed through a hedge at the overshoot end of the runway and came to a grinding halt in the middle of a field. The dry summer weather had hardened the surface which undoubtedly helped to keep the aircraft upright. Having evacuated the cockpit quickly in case of fire, I remain convinced that my feet were running before they touched the ground. As I watched the dust settle around Hunter XF514 from a safe distance, I was conscious of a mechanical noise, quite unfamiliar to me but which seemed to come from my aircraft. Before long, though, the source was identified: from behind the battered Hunter appeared a tractor driven at speed by a very worried farmer who, it transpired, had been watching my display until the noise had stopped and he had carried on with his work. The next thing he knew was the sudden appearance of my Hunter, trailing smashed hedgerow and ploughing erratic furrows across his field. When, eventually, the machine had come to a halt he could see the aircraft

Jock Heron's battered Hunter.

but no pilot in the cockpit!

The cause of the accident was soon revealed. As the fuel system high pressure pumps on the Hunter's Avon could not operate under conditions of negative 'g', the system had been designed so that fuel was fed to the engine when inverted via the Hymatic pressure reducing valve. Apparently the valve had stuck thus preventing fuel from being fed to the engine. The only available fuel was in the fuel lines which allowed about five seconds of flight under negative 'g'. Thereby hangs an engineers' tale and I'd have liked to have had words with the designers.

I had become engaged to be married earlier in the year and my fiancée learned of the accident while on a train by glimpsing my photograph on the front page of the local newspaper with the caption, 'Stunt pilot's engine fails'. She assumed the worst, burst into tears and had to be reassured by fellow passengers that the pilot was all right. So it was that my future wife learned of the potential risks of marrying into the Royal Air Force!

CHAPTER 6

NO SWEAT!

HARRY ANWAR IN AN UNUSUAL SPOT

All stared in my direction. The onlookers were mainly local sheikhs from Saudi Arabia, I reckoned, overcome with curiosity as they'd gathered to observe the strange performance taking place in an obscure corner of desert in southern Jordan. The high ambient temperatures, sometimes up to eighty degrees Fahrenheit even during this winter month of November 1964, were apparently no reason for them to miss a spontaneous opportunity to foster a fine festive spirit. Some had driven up in jeeps, some had come on camels. The sheiks had brought their servants together with tents, cooking utensils, food, drink, chairs, rugs, all the necessary paraphernalia needed for an unscheduled yet seriously jolly party in the desert.

From my point of view, such eccentric behaviour was immaterial so long as no-one interfered with my planned take-off run. I had a job to do and even though the circumstances were highly unusual, nonetheless my efforts to sort out this bizarre situation were urgent and potentially hazardous.

As I glanced up at the sky, I squinted my eyes against the merciless sun. When I looked down again, I felt a needle of anxiety while I scrutinised the local terrain to assess the possible pitfalls. The surrounding area was generally flat, a useful factor in this tricky and temporary arrangement, and I was reasonably confident that my calculations would work out. Nevertheless, there were no guarantees, furthermore my status as a relatively new officer in the rank of major on contract to the Royal Jordanian Air Force heightened my sense of apprehension.

I suppose I was conscious that, amongst various background issues, of significance was the fact that the Royal Jordanian Air Force was still in its infancy. This, perhaps, afforded me greater leeway than might have been the case in other, more established, air forces. I was new to the RJAF, but the RJAF itself was new as was made clear during my introductory briefings. Then it was that I learned how Trans-Jordan, renamed Jordan after World War 2 when the country had gained independence, had begun to develop, in the early 1950s, a small air arm known as the Arab Legion Air Force. In 1955 the Jordanian air arm was expanded when King Hussein established the Royal Jordanian Air Force. Five years on from that, a fleet of Hawker Hunters was built up to form the RJAF's 1 Squadron based at Mafraq, an airfield in Jordan's northern reaches five miles from the Syrian border.

Mafraq, or King Hussein Airbase as it was renamed in 1959, was my home base when I commenced my two-year contract in April 1964. My job, as officer in charge of the training of all fighter pilots of the Royal Jordanian Air Force, often held onerous but intriguing responsibilities. As a Pakistani national, I'd had to adapt quickly to Arab customs when I arrived at Mafraq. After initial difficulties, over time I was treated on the whole with friendliness, and I was amused when told the story of a British army captain in neighbouring Palestine who, like me, had much to learn about Arab ways. As he was settling into the officers' mess, the captain was greeted by a smiling Arab boy who offered a smart salute and the words: "F*** off, sir." When questioned, he said that he'd been briefed by Australian troops that this was the correct way in which to greet British officers. The captain thanked the lad for the compliment but explained that he didn't really deserve such treatment which should be reserved for very senior officers only.

Later, the captain described how he and a colleague, while on a trip to Egypt, were suddenly and inexplicably apprehended by Egyptian police. Taken to a local police station, the two men were required to sign a form written in Arabic. When asked what they were signing, the policeman replied that it was a declaration that they were not looking for a brothel. The policeman then added that if they were, there was a good one just round the corner.

When I began work, I tried to devise training schedules which were at once realistic and flexible. I learned the need for diplomacy in the crew room and other discussions on the complex relationship between Jordan and Israel, in particular how King Hussein's western orientation and his modest territorial aspirations had led to a pragmatic approach in dealing with border and other disputes. I was aware of rumours that clandestine communications between the two countries often led to accommodation even though they had been at a state of war since 1948. However, on the occasions when border disputes flared up into military action, I felt as if the responsibility for the effectiveness of Jordanian air defence fell on my shoulders. The notion plagued me sometimes.

I had been in Jordan for some three or four months when I received an unexpected task. I was in the middle of a busy training schedule when someone called out: "Major Anwar, sir," he said, cradling the telephone receiver in one hand, "you're wanted on the 'phone." I walked across the room. "I'm not sure who it is," he said under his breath, "...but…" he handed me the receiver, "it sounds important."

"Hello?" I said to whoever was at the other end.

There was a pause before a rather deep voice said: "Major Anwar?"

"Yes," I replied, "I'm Major Anwar."

"Oh, that's good," said the mystery voice.

"May I ask who is speaking?"

I was aware of a brief hesitation before I heard: "This is King Hussein speaking."

Now it was my turn to hesitate. Eventually, I cleared my throat and said: "Your Majesty?"

"Yes, it's me. Now listen. I have a special task for you." The king went on to describe his need for a firepower demonstration designed to impress an important visitor.

"But the pilots aren't ready yet," I protested. "They've only just started firing practice."

"Anwar," said the King, "I need this demonstration."

This seemed to leave me little option but to reply: "As you please, Your Majesty."

After this, I stepped up our training programme as much as I could and two days before the demonstration was due, we carried out a rehearsal. That would allow us one day for aircraft maintenance before the demonstration itself. Unexpectedly, the king turned up for the rehearsal to judge for himself whether it was good enough. Evidently it was; the king declared himself officially pleased with our efforts and the firepower demonstration took place as scheduled.

Two weeks later, I was called to the telephone again and – lo and behold – there was His Majesty once more asking for another firepower demonstration. The normally impenetrable spheres of royalty appeared to loosen when the need arose. "This time," said King Hussein, "our guest will be Field Marshal Abdel Hakim Amer." I was aware that the field marshal had recently been appointed Egyptian vice-president and deputy supreme commander by President Nasser. I was not aware, of course, that in three years' time, following the Six-Day War, Amer would take much of the blame for Egypt's defeat and would be killed by poisoning.

I planned to make this firepower demonstration one like no other. When I

His Majesty King Hussein I, back to camera, introducing Harry Anwar to Field Marshal Abdel Hakim Amer, First Vice-President of the Arab republic of Egypt, February 1965.

briefed the details, a circle of pilots stared at me with looks of awe while I explained the plan. As with the previous demonstration, we carried out a full dress rehearsal but on this occasion the king did not turn up. Maybe he'd decided that I could be trusted.

For the opening scenes on the day itself, two Hunters, flying one behind the other, flew past the assembled spectators. The first Hunter towed the national flags of Egypt and Jordan, the second Hunter's banner displayed the word 'welcome' written in Arabic. The flypast was performed at low level – just fifty feet above ground level – as a result of which the sound of the banners fluttering in the wind could be heard. Overhead, a Hunter dived down at high speed towards the spectators in order to drop a sonic boom.

After this, four Hunters flying in close formation gave a rocket-firing demonstration. When hit, their target, a pyramid of ten empty 55 gallon fuel drums, provided the dramatic effect intended. Next on the agenda, three Hunters flying in close formation strafed a target, a ten feet by ten feet metal frame filled with balloons of all colours. A certain psychology went into this plan: spectators would think that if these pilots could shoot balloons they could shoot anything.

After the balloon bonanza, two Hunters conducted a napalm run against a simulated target made of wood and cloth with doors and windows painted to look like army barracks. I heard later that one of the spectators, a Jordanian general, had asked how a Pakistani officer on contract to the Royal Jordanian Air Force

His Majesty with the 'Hashemite Diamonds' team members.

had managed to obtain a napalm bomb. The general was evidently unaware that we even had it.

Following the napalm event, four Hunters carried out a skip bombing run against a cloth target. All of the targets had been placed at a distance of some 500 feet away from the spectators, and all of the targets were demolished.

After the firepower demonstration a helicopter dogfight had been organised. By this I mean a real dog chased by a helicopter. The dog, the squadron mascot, was called Whisky and had been trained to wait in one spot until the helicopter swooped down towards it. At the last second, the dog would scoot off to a different place to wait for the helicopter's next 'attack'. The dog, the helicopter pilot and the onlookers all seemed to enjoy the performance enormously and I heard later that there'd been much hilarity amongst the spectators.

The final spectacle was a solo low level aerobatics display by a Hunter pilot.

As I was flying a Hunter for the firepower demonstration I was unable to gauge the spectators' reactions. However, I'd learned later that King Hussein, as he watched proceedings, had sat anxiously on the edge of his chair. Every time a target was demolished, the king would give Field Marshal Amer a knowing look as if to confirm silently how good the Jordanian pilots were proving to be. The field marshal had been so impressed by the pilots' capabilities that he'd asked His Majesty if the pilots were British. "No," the king had replied, "all the pilots are Jordanian apart from one who is a Pakistani national." The field marshal had found this so hard to believe that he had asked to meet the pilots in person. The king consequently escorted the field marshal across the tarmac to watch the pilots disembark from their aircraft. I could recall clearly the field marshal's comment that each one of us was equal to ten of his pilots and he wished he could have us as members of his own air force.

Perhaps, in addition to air combat exercises, our intensive training for the firepower demonstration provided additional benefits. For it was a few months after this, in late 1964, that pilots of the Royal Jordanian Air Force achieved their first combat victory in the air against hostile targets. In the so-called Battle of the Dead Sea, four Jordanian Hunters shot down two Israeli Mirages (one Mirage according to some reports) and damaged others. When this action took place I was in the air traffic control tower where I was caught up in the atmosphere of excitement and suspense as intermittent radio transmissions revealed the progress of events.

*

Two years later, on the morning of 13th November, 1966, alert sirens sounded at King Hussein Airbase and a flight of two Hawker Hunters was scrambled to alleviate the pressure on Jordanian infantry positions under attack by Israeli forces. Three minutes later, another pair of Hunters was scrambled. This second pair was led by Lieutenant Zayyad whose subsequent combat report would be along the following lines:

> Arriving at the scene I found that Red Leader (Lieutenant Salti) was engaged in combat with an Israeli Mirage while his number two, Lieutenant Shurdom, was closely pursued by a hostile Mirage which was closing in for a kill. I warned Shurdom of the attacker and told him to tighten the turn. At the time I was pulling up taking advantage of my speed to attack a flight of four Mirages. As I was zooming up, the Israeli aircraft released one missile at close range. I called Lieutenant Shurdom to break left and watched the missile miss him and explode in the vineyards. Apparently, the four Mirages spotted my section because they split into two pairs. As Mirages number three and four turned right and down, I decided to turn inside and pursue for a kill. I was closing to less than 600 yards when the number four left his leader to break port. I told my number two to watch him but he mistook the order. I closed in to 380 yards and released a good burst of my Aden guns. At that instant I heard Salti give a call: "Hunter behind Mirage BREAK." I immediately broke without ensuring the fate of the targeted Mirage. Re-grouping at low level, our situation looked desperate as there was a whole squadron of Mirages in the air. As we were close to the border and far away from base, I ordered withdrawal and made sure Red Section exited ahead of my section. I lost radio contact with Lieutenant Salti and found out upon landing that he was lost in action.

The following year, during the 1967 Six-Day War, Hunters of the Royal Jordanian Air Force attacked and destroyed an Israeli Nord Noratlas on the ground at Sirkin airbase in the central area of Israel. The subsequent Israeli counter-strike, though, rapidly removed the Royal Jordanian Air Force from the war by destroying its aircraft on the ground. In spite of this, during the closing stages of the war Jordanian pilots operating from Iraq, and flying Iraqi Hunters, shot down an Israeli Mirage 111 and two Sud Aviation Vautour fighter aircraft for one loss. Israel said that it lost three aircraft and claimed to have downed three Hunters. This action was considered by Israel to have been one of their failures of the war.

By the time the Six-Day War took place my contract with the Royal Jordanian Air Force had ended. I had moved on elsewhere. However, as the dramatic events unfolded, people around the world watched with a mix of fascination and alarm – and no-one more so than myself. Shortly after the war had ended, I wrote a letter to a Hunter pilot, a cousin of King Hussein. In the letter, I admonished the pilots for not jettisoning their aircraft fuel drop tanks at the start of a dogfight: a clean Hunter would have been much more manoeuvrable. The cousin showed the letter to His Majesty who in turn wrote to me. This exchange of letters inevitably stimulated stark reminders of my time with the RJAF.

One particular memory involved the precarious occasion when a young Jordanian pilot, lost over the desert, ran out of fuel. The pilot, rather than eject from his aircraft, managed to land it on a flat area of desert. When the news of this came through, I was despatched with others to locate the Hunter and to help determine if the aircraft could be recovered. Following the pilot's rescue we knew that the Hunter had come down in a position bearing 140 degrees from Amman at a range of 140 nautical miles. Armed with this information, we drove down in a jeep to inspect the aircraft which was close to the border with Saudi Arabia.

It took some time to pinpoint the downed Hunter's exact location and as we drove here and there I was conscious that this desert, historically inhabited by Bedouin tribes, could present the unwary with uncommon hazards. At night, the winter sun would go down by about 6pm and the day's heat would transform quickly to conditions of bitter cold. Wanderers through the night could penetrate deeper and deeper into a weird, wasted world. Dawns would be heralded by the descent of a chill stillness. Someone could feel as if he was roaming prehistoric earth along sands that wore the aspect of an unknown planet.

When, at length, we came across the Hunter, we found that the aircraft was in reasonable condition although a level of ingenuity would be required to recover the machine. I continued to explore the local area until I came across a particular spot and as I did so my spirits rose. For this was just what was needed: a dry lake bed not too far from where the aircraft had landed. We therefore towed the Hunter to a position at one end of the lake bed hoping that a take-off might be possible.

I drove the jeep from one end to the other so as to measure the available take-off distance. After this, with calculations and potential schemes whirling through my head, I drove back to base.

At base, while I paced the tarmac this way and that as ideas persisted to touch the surface of my brain, I watched while engineers de-fuelled a Hunter to tanks empty. I then instructed them to refuel the aircraft in a particular way: full fuel in the rear fuselage tanks and just a small amount in the main tank. When this had been completed, I climbed aboard the aircraft for a test run. As I took off, I noted carefully the exact spot where the Hunter's main wheels left the runway surface. After landing, I measured the distance which proved to be well within the available distance at the lake. This looked as if it was going to work – amazing!

Now I returned to the downed Hunter and supervised the refuelling process to ensure identical parameters to my experiment at base. Next, I arranged for engineers to extend the aircraft's nose-wheel oleo and to deflate the main tyres. The normal air pressure at around 150 pounds per square inch made the tyres like solid steel wheels; with lower air pressure I reckoned that the wider aspect would reduce the tyres' tendency to sink into soft sand.

It was at about this stage that the commander of the Royal Jordanian Air Force, Lieutenant Colonel Saleh El Kurdi, arrived at the scene. As he watched the process with an expression of disbelief, he asked why, just before take-off, I should want to instruct engineers to deflate the tyres. I looked at him but did not reply. I did, however, ask the lieutenant colonel jokingly if he would like to see an ejection at the end of the lake. "Okay," he said, his eyes twinkling with amusement, "but don't take off until I've driven there in my jeep." At this, he jumped aboard the vehicle and sped off down the lake.

Meanwhile, local sheikhs had begun to assemble by the lake to observe the strange phenomenon taking place in their backyard. Many of them seemed to believe that we were on Saudi Arabian soil although in fact we were just inside Jordanian territory. I noted much pointing of fingers and nodding of heads. Discussions in high-pitched, high-velocity Arabic ensued as the observers, some of whom evidently had never before seen an aircraft so close-up let alone a fighter aircraft, debated this and that. Servants brought out chairs, rugs, tents, cooking utensils as serious picnic arrangements started to formulate. As the festive atmosphere developed, I felt like a circus performer about to try out a dangerous act for everyone's entertainment. Crowds swelled as folk continued to turn up in jeeps, even camels, to witness events.

Eventually it was time for me to climb aboard the Hunter. As I stood in the cockpit, I believe that I resisted the temptation to wave to the assembled admirers who, nonetheless, assumed a reverential hush while they watched me. I checked the ejection seat carefully then settled into the cockpit while a member of ground crew helped me to strap in. All appeared to be in order as I carried out the left to right cockpit checks and soon I was ready to start the engine. I signalled to the attendant ground crew who gave me a thumbs up. I glanced inside the cockpit again and pressed the engine start button. Now I heard the familiar sound of the reliable Rolls-Royce Avon engine as it began to wind up. Before long, the engine had stabilised, the cockpit readings were satisfactory, I was ready to take off.

I looked ahead to confirm that the take-off area remained clear of Bedouins, vehicles, camels, picnics, and general obstacles. I kept the Hunter's brakes applied while, gradually, I advanced the engine's throttle. The whine of the engine increased steadily. Now, with a final check of the area ahead, I released the aircraft brakes. The aircraft sprang forward. I had no problem as I held the Hunter straight for what initially felt like a normal take-off. At an airspeed of eighty knots, though, I realised that the aircraft had stopped accelerating. It seemed that the surface of the lake was softer in the middle than at the edges; the main wheels had started to dig in. I felt a sharp knot of apprehension form in my stomach; I hadn't allowed for this. An ejection looked imminent. Ahead, I could just make out the lieutenant colonel standing beside his jeep. The joke, I thought, would be on me after all.

However, suddenly struck with a brainwave, I decided to try a last gasp experiment before I pulled the ejection seat handle. Quickly, I shoved the stick forward – the nose went down a bit – then I yanked the stick back. The aircraft reacted: in an instant I knew that I had something going for me. Now I worked the stick back and forth in rhythm with the movement of the nose-wheel oleo. Soon, the nose of the aircraft began to rise and descend in a more pronounced manner and, quite promptly, I knew that I would make it. With the final jerk back of the stick and with just fifty feet to spare I was airborne – a close thing indeed, but as pilots are prone to say...NO SWEAT!

CHAPTER 7

SPRINGBOK SPIRIT

TIM WEBB'S EARLY HUNTER DAYS

I reached the Hunter world through a circuitous and, one might say, somewhat unconventional route. Born in South Africa in 1942 to a farming family, my one and only aim in life as a schoolboy was to join an air force of some description, preferably the Royal Air Force. When I reached the necessary age, I therefore wrote to three different air forces with a view to possible enlistment: the Rhodesian Air Force, the South African Air Force and the Royal Air Force. The latter responded first and I was summonsed to Pretoria, the country's administrative capital (South Africa has three capital cities). All seemed to go well with my medical check and with my initial interview after which I was fortunate to be awarded a Commonwealth scholarship. So it was that, together with one other budding pilot, I officially joined the Royal Air Force on 5th October 1960 – the day when a referendum was held in South Africa to decide if the country should become a republic.

Two days later, as the pair of us prepared for the trip from Cape Town to Great Britain, we bade farewell to our families before embarkation onto the *Capetown Castle*, a passenger/cargo liner built in 1938. My colleague and I were the last South Africans to be awarded Commonwealth scholarships and the last of a long line of the country's aircrew who had served with the Royal Air Force, including the legendary 'Sailor' Malan and over twenty others who had fought with distinction in the Battle of Britain and who had gained a particular reputation for fearless flying.

While the *Capetown Castle* progressed northwards across the high seas, perhaps I harboured thoughts about less turbulent prospects as I left behind South Africa's contrary and increasingly intractable situation (it was earlier in the year that over sixty black demonstrators had been killed by security forces during the infamous

Postcard of the Capetown Castle.

Sharpeville massacre). It was not long, however, before any notions of a more placid future were dispelled to the four winds.

At 0449 hours on 17th October 1960, as the *Capetown Castle* approached the Canary Islands, the ship was suddenly rocked by an explosion in the engine room. Claxons sounded, forward speed reduced, the vessel slewed and began to list as water was pumped into the engine room to extinguish fires. Within the engine room itself, several crew members lay dead. Passengers were ordered out of bunks and told to assemble at lifeboat stations immediately even though, because of the early hour, most people were still in pyjamas. The ship's list caused considerable difficulties during attempts to launch the starboard side lifeboats and evacuation plans had to be revised hurriedly.

During the consequent kerfuffle, I decided, together with my fellow recruit, that it would be improper for members of the Royal Air Force to be shipwrecked in their pyjamas. We resolved, therefore, to hasten back to our cabin, a journey which included sliding on our backsides down the ship's laundry 'chute as a convenient shortcut before a dash along a corridor to the cabin where we quickly changed from pyjamas to smart blazers and flannel trousers. Regretfully, the return to our lifeboat station proved more problematic. I had broken an arm playing rugby shortly before leaving South Africa and now my attempts to negotiate the laundry 'chute in reverse seemed less than straightforward. "Hurry," urged my colleague.

"It hurts," I said. However, with my remaining serviceable arm I succeeded eventually but only just in time for the two of us to board the last lifeboat to leave the stricken *Capetown Castle*.

The lifeboat took us to the Union Castle Line's RMS (Royal Mail Steamer)

Windsor Castle, the company's largest and finest passenger/cargo mail ship. Earlier, we two air force men had jested with friends that the *Windsor Castle's* captain had invited us to breakfast. To our astonishment and delight, though, the joke turned true when the *Windsor Castle's* purser, as he welcomed us aboard, noted our smart attire and cordially asked us to follow him for breakfast with the ship's commodore. We nodded gratefully although in truth we both wanted to hoot with laughter and we struggled to stifle our mirth. It was not until after the breakfast that the commodore, having worked out the true nature of our lowly status, pointedly directed us towards the long queue for second-class accommodation.

The subsequent week, spent in a luxury hotel on Las Palmas Island as guests of the Castle Line, turned out to be interesting. On our first day and despite the company of two young ladies from the ship, we air force warriors were approached by a local pimp who invited us to 'meet his sister'. Even though we declined the offer, the pimp, whose name was Luigi, popped up at regular intervals to repeat his invitation. In the end the situation degenerated into a huge joke and our tears of laughter were such that even Luigi himself began to giggle. Four days after our evacuation from the *Capetown Castle* we were allowed to retrieve our belongings. Before this, the poor passengers (apart, of course, from the air force contingent) had been obliged to wander through the town in pyjamas to the considerable amusement of all and sundry. As our time on the island was about to end, we decided that a drive around the locality would be appropriate. We therefore approached Luigi for help. When he took us to the offices of an upmarket tour guide company, we pointed out that we wouldn't be able to afford the costs. "No problem," said Luigi, "for you, the tour will be free." It turned out that the guide was Luigi's father.

The next day we embarked onto the RMS *Pendennis Castle* for the last leg of our trip to Great Britain. Voted one time by the shipping press as the 'ship of the year' this vessel broke with British ocean liner tradition by having female waiting staff in the dining room. Perhaps this eased our mood as the ship steamed towards Southampton where my colleague and I received instructions to make our way to RAF South Cerney in Gloucestershire to commence officer cadet training. At South Cerney we were called to the accounts section to be told that, having been shipwrecked, we were entitled to a 'hard lying allowance'. This came in the form of a lump sum equivalent to approximately one-month's pay each. No doubt this acted as a fine incentive during our time at South Cerney where we two South Africans, both very fit after a rugby season at home, more than held our own on the sports field despite my broken arm.

From South Cerney I went initially to RAF Tern Hill in Shropshire to start flying training on the Piston Provost before I moved with No 6 Flying Training School to RAF Acklington in Northumberland. The course progressed well until the evening of 5th October 1961, exactly one year after my enlistment into the Royal

Air Force, when a motor-car accident fractured my skull. This was a dark time in my life. I was sent to the psychiatric ward at Newcastle General Hospital where I'd listen with alarm to other patients' deranged moans mingled with indigent and terrifying outbursts. One moment the black interiors of a lunatic mind would try to express floods of kind gratitude before switching suddenly to violent attempts to bite attendants. Some inmates would try to hide as if in a smokescreen designed to conceal something unsightly or unsavoury. Individuals would remain doubled over, rock back and forth, clutch their fingers and make sounds like that of a wauling cat. A ridiculous and ragged chorus would echo around the room. Patients would creep about as if nursing hangovers; some would reveal inexplicable bruises on limbs; some would remain suddenly motionless apart from a rhythmic fluttering and trembling of the hands. In the night, I might wake abruptly to find an inmate staring at me from the foot of my bed. I began to feel very alarmed and vulnerable. Eventually, after visits from my course colleagues, the senior medical officer at RAF Acklington was persuaded to have me moved to the RAF Hospital at Wroughton where I became a much happier patient.

After three months, when I was allowed to return to flying, I was re-coursed at Acklington to continue my training on the Piston Provost. Following graduation there I was sent to the jet advanced flying training school at RAF Oakington in Cambridgeshire. I was considered to be too tall to fly the de Havilland Vampire so was moved across the airfield to join the Gloster Meteor flight. This seemed to suit me well. The Meteor with its all-metal construction, tricycle undercarriage, and turbojets mid-mounted on low, straight wings was enjoyable to fly even though the aircraft lacked many of the aerodynamic features recently discovered. There was no doubt that the aircraft was dated and my course turned out to be the last Meteor course in the Royal Air Force. I graduated on 5th October 1962, exactly two years after enlistment, and was sent to RAF Chivenor in Devonshire to commence Hunter flying.

The winter of 1962-1963, known as the Big Freeze of '63, was one of the coldest winters on record in the United Kingdom and caused havoc to our flying programme at Chivenor. As temperatures plummeted and as lakes and rivers began to freeze over, records showed that only the winter of 1683-1684 had been significantly colder. At Herne Bay in Kent the sea froze for one mile from shore, and snow drifts of eight feet were recorded in that county. Around Chivenor and other parts of the West Country, snow drifts of fifteen to twenty feet caused villages to become stranded, power lines to be brought down, railway lines and roads to become blocked. As Hunter flying ceased, some of our course members flew with the search and rescue helicopters to assist with food distribution and other emergency tasks.

Despite the hazards, a period of intensive flying when the weather eventually

The formation (with Tim Webb, second from left), was about to be flown for the Kenya Independence celebrations December 1963 by 208 Squadron recently stationed there.

eased meant that our Chivenor course graduated on time in the spring of 1963. At this point I was excited to be posted to 208 Squadron based at RAF Khormaksar in Aden. The squadron had moved to Aden in November 1961 and was one of three Hunter squadrons based there in the ground-attack role. At any one time, one of these squadrons was sent to Muharraq for a two-month detachment. This commitment had followed Kuwait's appeal for help in 1961 when, after Kuwaiti independence, Iraq had been observed to mobilise troops and equipment for what was clearly intended to be a military invasion.

It was at Muharraq that I joined 208 Squadron shortly before my twenty-first birthday. To this day I retain thrilling memories of that time, of my sense of pure, unadulterated *joie de vivre* as life revolved around a phase of rigorous, action-packed flying. While my mastery of weaponeering, air-to-air combat, low flying over the desert and other skills grew, so my self-confidence rapidly developed. The floodgates had opened; I'd felt delighted, almost overwhelmed, by the intensity and importance of our flying activities. It was as if I had gained power and significance at a level altogether different from anything I had known in life before.

After two months at Muharraq, when it was time to return to Khormaksar, perhaps I felt a small niggle of worry that all might have been a mere vapour and a dream. At Khormaksar, however, such feelings were rather quickly dispelled when an unexpected distraction entered the equation of my life. In the private museum of memories that each one of us carries within our heads, I have recollections of an exquisite, if impetuous, period for it was then that, before long, I could make no secret of the fact that, in the course of one of my secondary duties as the squadron's aircrew rations officer, I was attracted at once, indeed experienced the most prodigious extremes of emotion imaginable induced by the efficiency, enthusiasm, finesse not to mention a great many other attributes including the most delicate fingernails imaginable that belonged to the beautiful young lady with whom, as she was clerk of rations, it was my good fortune to have to deal with. In short, Sally and I were married within six months.

As both of us were under twenty-five years of age, my new wife and I were not eligible in those days for a married quarter. The arrangement was made, therefore, for Sally to visit me at Khormaksar for two months in every six. This less-than-satisfactory plan changed, fortunately, when 208 Squadron was posted in May 1964 to Muharraq on a permanent basis. The officer in charge of administration at Muharraq, a South African ex-Spitfire pilot from World War 2, informed headquarters at Steamer Point, Aden that he could not subscribe to the 'stupid rules' for under twenty-fives and told them that he wished all those affected to be offered married accommodation. Headquarters, it seemed, agreed with his sentiments and we were allowed to stay in married quarters at Bahrain airfield, adjacent to Muharraq.

*

One month before 208 Squadron's move to Muharraq, I had broken my arm (again) while playing rugby. As I was unable to fly, the officer commanding operations wing at Khormaksar decided that I should assist the Brigade Air Support Officers' team which was working in the heart and heat of the Aden Protectorate in the Radfan mountains. We lived under canvas, the ground was covered in sand to a depth of six inches, there was dust everywhere; washing facilities were basic and difficult to manage with an arm in plaster. Despite the discomforts, this proved to be a most intriguing episode.

Operation Nutcracker, which commenced in April 1964, was designed to penetrate the country east of the key Dhala road and to quell intransigent Radfan tribes. Within four weeks, British forces had driven rebel tribesmen away from the road and enabled the Royal Engineers to build another into the middle of the Radfan area. The advance into the centre of Radfan was greeted with enthusiasm by loyal tribes and the British brigadier in charge was presented with an engraved sword by the Emir of Dhala. During the operation, I was based at Thumier on the

Dhala road while I worked with the brigade air support cell. Together with an ex-208 Squadron member, we tasked Hunter squadrons which were kept at constant crew room readiness in case close air support was needed. In addition, we helped to organise the brigade's re-supply by air using Scottish Aviation Twin Pioneer and Blackburn Beverley aircraft.

One time, Hunter close air support was requested by a Special Air Service scouting party which had got into difficulties. Surrounded by a large number of dissidents, the SAS men needed help. It was decided to call in the Hunters although communication proved problematic: the SAS never carried ground/air radio equipment and spoke to their headquarters on a discreet ground net only. In this situation, therefore, the headquarters had to pass information to us and we, in turn, briefed the Hunter squadrons. It was a long-winded process but nonetheless seemed to work. At one point the SAS leader called for urgent Hunter back-up: enemy guerillas had been creeping up on them and could be heard but not seen: "would the Royal Air Force do something about it, please?" My blood ran cold when I heard this. The SAS men were notoriously tough; such a message would not be sent without good reason. As I relayed this information to my 208 Squadron colleagues who happened to be on duty that day, perhaps I was wide-eyed with anxiety and maybe a tremor of apprehension ran through my fingers.

A flight of Hunters led by one of the 208 Squadron flight commanders was soon airborne and reported that they could see the attackers but that they were extremely close – a mere twenty-five yards or so – from the SAS contingent. Despite the danger of 'friendly fire', the army cleared the Hunters to proceed. In the ensuing moments I could picture the scene: the whistle of air, the whine of the Rolls-Royce Avon engine as the lead Hunter streaked towards the target; the sharp crack as the aircraft opened fire, an almost imperceptible pause, then a *basso profundo* roar.

Now debris would rise up into the sky, observers with awe on their faces would discern rotating slithers of shrapnel, powdery storms of dust and dry sand, black smoke and orange flame. Soon, as the uproar subsided, all would squint up at a brilliant white sun while an ominous, momentary hush began to dominate the atmosphere. Breaths would be held. The silence would linger. Then, quite suddenly, the silent spell would be shattered as the next Hunter dived down for a repeat performance. When the attacks had died down a further, less transitory, pause ensued and it was at this point that I picked up on the radio an army officer's laconic voice declare: "Bloody good shooting!"

Shortly after this event, the Minister of Defence (Air), Mr Hugh Fraser, while on a visit to Aden, commented to newspaper correspondents: "I think it's amazing that the troops in the forward area have been calling down Royal Air Force fighters to strike dissident strongholds only twenty-five yards from their own positions. This not only emphasises the skill of the Hunter pilots but also underlines the confidence of our troops in our pilots' ability to press home attacks with pinpoint accuracy."

Regretfully, in spite of verbal accolades, the outcome of the episode was one of tragedy. When the SAS men finally tried to break out under the cover of darkness, their leader, Captain Edwards, and a young soldier, Signaller Warburton, were killed and decapitated. In a sickening and depraved act of conclusion, their heads were stuck on stakes to be paraded in Ta'izz, Yemen's third largest city.

A few days later, Hunters from 8 Squadron were tasked to attack a suspected arms dump concealed within a cave at the base of an extensive stretch of cliffs in the Radfan region. The Hunter pilots, faced with a thirty-degree angle of dive in an area some 5,000 feet above sea level, had their problems. Their skill, nevertheless, was evident as observers witnessed spectacular black clouds of smoke grow and spread as the arms dump exploded. The Hunters' attack caused the sun and the sky to be blotted out, craters many yards across to be created, and tangled fragments of rock, shrub and soil to lie in haphazard piles as the cave collapsed to render it useless as a future hiding place.

All of this was achieved by employing the Hunters' main offensive weapon at the time, a 60lb rocket developed in World War 2 for use by the likes of Bristol Blenheim, Bristol Beaufort and Bristol Beaufighter aircraft against enemy shipping. Originally fired at 240 knots in level flight from a range of 400 yards, the Hunters' parameters were rather different: 400 knots in a thirty degree dive at a minimum range of 800 yards. Initially, the aircraft fired rockets with high explosive heads but these proved ineffective against mud forts – the rockets would penetrate the mud walls to detonate on hard ground within the forts. Someone's suggested alternative – to use our practice rockets with concrete heads replacing the high explosives – proved highly effective as the rockets acted like 60lb supersonic sledgehammers with devastating impact on the mud-walled forts.

Shortly before Operation Nutcracker commenced, ultra-high frequency (UHF) radios were fitted to all aircraft in the Hunter force. However, in our Middle East theatre the extremes of temperature caused trouble. As the problems persisted, we had to borrow army radios, although we benefitted from an unexpected twist: the ground element of the UHF system was built into a refrigerator which now sat in useless unemployment in one corner of our tent. Useless, that was, until, in a moment of inspiration, our tame signalman managed to extract the UHF electronics but retain the refrigerator section. Before long, the refrigerator was stocked with cans of beer in place of UHF electronics and our tent's former white elephant swiftly became a centre of joyous relief in the harsh desert climate. One time we were visited by a brigadier who, as he entered our tent, briskly informed one and all that he had endured a very bad day indeed. At this, with theatrical aplomb, we made a generous gesture: "May we offer you, sir, an ice cold beer served in a frosted glass?"

The resultant reaction – the look on the brigadier's face – is something that will live with me forever.

*

After two-and-a-half years on 208 Squadron I was sent to RAF Chivenor to be trained in the art of fighter reconnaissance (FR) before a posting to a Hunter FR squadron in Germany. Because the start of my course was delayed I was required to fly in a limited capacity as a staff pilot at Chivenor. At that stage my future seemed bright; fighter reconnaissance was considered to be a plum job and all looked well in my world – until, that was, the chill finger of fate intervened.

Early one morning I flew a Hunter Mk 6 as a target aircraft for an instructor and student programmed to practise air-to-air interception techniques in a two-seat Hunter T7. The pair of them carried out a dummy attack followed by another then another after which it was time for them to return to Chivenor. I'd been briefed to fly back independently. At this point I could see, below and ahead of me, the T7 stooging along towards Chivenor. In a spontaneous reaction, I reckoned that an appropriate 'beat up' would remind the pilots of the need for good fighter pilot 'lookout'. My overtake speed was significant and I elected to fly under the other aircraft. I was aware of the T7's tendency to 'nose dip' when another aircraft flew underneath but never in my wildest dreams did I anticipate the amount that occurred that day. Perhaps my overtake airspeed was too high; maybe I misjudged the distance. Whatever the cause, and despite leaving what I estimated was plenty of room, my starboard (right) wingtip touched the T7's nose cone when I flew underneath. The forward section of the nose cone detached on impact.

A moment of excruciating suspense followed then a few seconds of confusion and agitation. A quick check of my flying controls revealed that the starboard aileron was flapping at an alarming angle in the airstream. In spite of this, I found that the aircraft was controllable. I carried out a slow speed handling check which showed that, with my airspeed down to around 160 knots, I appeared to experience few or no adverse effects. I reckoned, therefore, to be able to land safely at this airspeed when I reached Chivenor. Unfortunately, however, on final approach to the airfield, my Hunter's starboard wing began to drop as the airspeed reduced towards 175 knots. I touched down at this airspeed right on the runway threshold. I expected to enter the crash barrier at the far end but managed to stop with just 100 yards to go; a record, I believe, for landing a Hunter Mk 6 at Chivenor at such a high airspeed without entering the crash barrier.

The next few minutes heralded a black period in my life. As I closed down the engine then wound back the Hunter's canopy, I saw the station commander's car race up towards my aircraft. The station commander leapt out of the car and stormed towards me his expression one of undisguised rage and hostility. I felt my stomach begin to churn. I removed my bone dome (headset) and waited for the figure of fury to deliver his tirade. "I shall ensure," he said with a notable absence of introductory comment, "that you are court martialled and thrown out of the air force."

What followed caused different, difficult emotions to influence Sally's life and mine. Sometimes we felt shaken to the very core. Occasionally, as if inhaling and exhaling nostalgia for what used to be, we wished we could turn back the calendars of our lives. Our treatment by colleagues was at once revealing, remarkable, ridiculous and at times almost grotesque. Experienced members of aircrew appeared to go out of their way to chat with us and to offer help. Some of the younger pilots, though, even those who I knew quite well from training days, seemed to do everything possible to ignore us and indeed, in what felt like acts of implacable malice, some would cross the street in the local town of Barnstaple to avoid being seen with us.

It was a salutary experience on how to treat, or more accurately, how *not* to treat a 'condemned man' and something that I have never forgotten.

The subsequent board of inquiry was led by one of my 208 Squadron flight commanders. Also on the board was another ex-squadron friend. I found this difficult and demeaning. Finally, after a long delay, my court martial was held on 5th October 1965. (Why did key events in my life always occur on 5th October?) However, one positive aspect of the delay was that the post of station commander at Chivenor was taken over by a different officer during the extended time interval. The new man, happily, revealed different attitudes. When he summonsed me after the court martial, and I entered his office, his first act was to turn to his secretary and say: "I think that Flying Officer Webb could do with a stiff tot of whisky." The station commander advised me not to worry too much about the court martial – a bad experience, he said, but one from which I should learn a lesson or two. He went on to assure me that my original posting to the fighter reconnaissance job would stand.

After a while, the results of my court martial were published in the *London Gazette*. On the exact same day I received a letter from the Air Secretary's department to say that I was posted to the Central Flying School at Little Rissington in Gloucestershire where I'd learn to be a flying instructor. 'Records show,' the letter pointed out, 'that you are ideally suited to be a flying instructor.' Perhaps it was the pressure of work; maybe the desk officer had endured a bad day; he might even have suffered a brain storm. Whatever the reason, I was clear in my own mind that a more inappropriate posting and more incongruous comments, especially in view of recent events, would be hard to imagine. Despite the station commander's annoyance at having to renege on his promise, the Air Secretary's department won the argument and what ensued was for me a very unhappy spell in Training Command.

Following my course at Little Rissington I was posted to Acklington where I found the standard of supervision above flight commander level to be poor verging on the unsafe. It was with some relief, therefore, when I spotted one day an unusual opportunity to escape my unfortunate Training Command situation. A notice in the form of a Defence Council Instruction sought volunteers who wished to apply to serve in Iraq. The job would involve instructing on Hunters and successful applicants could be accompanied by their wives. Fantastic, I thought: a brilliant opportunity; an accompanied post, something completely different, furthermore I'd be back in the Hunter world! I hurried home at the first chance to discuss the prospect with Sally. She was soon persuaded by my evident enthusiasm and my application was duly and hastily despatched. To our surprise and delight, the application was approved quite quickly and within three weeks Sally and I with our fourteen-month-old son set off for RAF Lyneham from where we would be flown to Nicosia in Cyprus and from there to Iraq.

In Cyprus, after a change of plan, we joined a Middle East Airways flight in a de Havilland Comet bound for Beirut, thence to Baghdad. Somewhat bedraggled when we eventually reached Baghdad at midnight, we were soon caught up in an atmosphere of excitement and turmoil. It was 1967, the year after Captain Munir Redfa had caused shock-waves to reverberate through the Iraqi Air Force (IQAF) when he defected to Israel in an Iraqi MiG-21. At Baghdad airport that night we were met by the head of the RAF volunteer contingent, Jim Crowe, who told me that I was due to be introduced to Air Marshal Abdul-Razak, the chief of the Iraqi Air Force, first thing in the morning.

I appeared to get on well enough with the air marshal who, following our meeting, wished me *bon voyage* for the drive to our new home at Habbaniya, an airbase close to the River Euphrates some fifty miles due west of Baghdad. The drive through hot desert stretches was an intriguing contrast to the scene we'd left behind – the green fields of Northumberland, dog roses and brambles in crowded hedgerows, the stubble of harvested cornfields. At one stage Sally laughed as she cried: "Look!" and pointed out a signpost to Babylon.

At Habbaniya I received various briefings on operational and general aspects of our new environment. Originally called RAF Dhibban, the base was re-named RAF Habbaniya in the late 1930s when it housed the air headquarters of Royal Air Force Iraq Command as well as maintenance units, an aircraft depot, a Royal Air Force hospital, the Royal Air Force Armoured Car Company depot, fuel and bomb stores. The base was self-contained with its own power station, water purification plant and sewage farm. Water taken from the River Euphrates for irrigation systems enabled green lawns, flower beds and even botanical gardens to be established. As an aside, I learnt that the writer Roald Dahl was stationed at RAF Habbaniya in 1940 but that the descriptions in his book *Going Solo* were thought to be somewhat inaccurate and his opinions were unfavourable compared to those of most personnel who served there.

In the 1950s de Havilland Vampires, de Havilland Venoms and Hawker Hunters were delivered to the Iraqi Air Force (in those days the Royal Iraqi Air Force) and some of these were based at Habbaniya. During the Iraq revolution of 14 July 1958 when the king was overthrown, the country subsequently cut ties with the West while establishing relations with the Warsaw Pact. The Iraqi Air Force dropped 'Royal' from its name and the Soviets were quick to supply MiG fighters to the new regime. However, allegiances in that tenuous situation changed again in 1963 when an Iraqi *coup d'état* realigned the country with NATO powers. As a result of this, second-hand Hawker Hunters were delivered to the IQAF and it was some of these which I was now required to fly.

In crew room discussions I swiftly learned the need for discretion. On my first day at Habbaniya when I visited the squadrons, during polite conversation I enquired after a couple of Iraqi pilots who I'd befriended when training. My question was met with an embarrassed silence, then someone tactfully changed the subject. I heard later that the two individuals had been on the 'wrong' side in the 1963 *coup d'état* and both had died in flying accidents.

Soon, I began flying at Habbaniya. I enjoyed the mix of tasks – formation, low level and instrument flying – some of which proved challenging to my students. Another difficulty was the technique needed on final approach to landing at the airfield. Pilots had to negotiate high ground to the west and high walls to the east, the latter designed to reduce the chance of flooding from the Euphrates.

High ambient temperatures produced problems, too. One afternoon I was detailed to carry out a compass swing on a Hunter T7. The young airman allocated to check the ground readings had to stand still for the minute or so needed while I made adjustments to the aircraft compass. However, when he next tried to move, the day's heat had caused his desert boots to weld to the airfield surface.

It was not long before Arab/Israeli tensions began to escalate and we were required to ensure that as many aircraft as possible were made ready in case of war. This included a Hunter Mk 6 which had been hangar-bound for a long period but which I was now tasked to air test. The air test seemed satisfactory until I attempted to operate the undercarriage system: on 'down' selection the wheels went down then immediately started to recycle up. The wheels continued to cycle up and down of their own volition as I flew back to Habbaniya. When I approached the airfield I operated the emergency undercarriage selector to blow the wheels down and now, fortunately, they stayed down. After landing, the engineers discovered a large rat nesting in the wires of the aircraft's electrical system.

Not long after this incident, the Six-Day War of June 1967 erupted and I found myself, together with the other three RAF loan pilots, well out of favour with the

Iraqis. We listened avidly to the BBC World Service news but as the situation deteriorated, the jamming of the BBC became progressively stronger until we could hear nothing. Without newspapers, we became cut off. Before long we were informed that wives and families would leave with embassy staff by road convoy to Tehran but that the pilots, still under contract to the Iraqi Air Force, were to remain. We moved into one house in order to pool resources but the announcement that our safety would be ensured by the Swedish Embassy did little to ease our growing consternation. Then, four hours before departure, we were told that we four RAF pilots were to travel with the convoy and that if we refused we'd be arrested and condemned to death as Israeli spies. This seemed a perfectly satisfactory incentive.

When the convoy set off I counted around fifty cars interspersed with armoured cars and police protection vehicles. At the border with Iran the border guards noted that my green-coloured South African passport did not have exit approval or entry visas. All other members in the convoy had blue-coloured British passports correctly stamped. It took me some three hours to attempt to explain my situation to the border guards who appeared especially perplexed by the green versus blue colouring issue, but eventually they relented and agreed to give me an entry visa. Meanwhile my fellow travellers had become extremely concerned about my fate.

Twenty-four hours after the convoy had left Baghdad we drew into Tehran where the embassy staff fed, watered and accommodated some weary and highly stressed individuals. Early the next morning we were loaded onto a commercial aircraft bound for London via Frankfurt. We landed at Heathrow in a state of considerable exhaustion and when, finally, we were able to rest, I managed for the first and last time in my life to sleep for a full thirty-six hours without a break. When I woke up, my father-in-law showed me a newspaper headline stating that the Iraqis had just hung six of their own people who, it was alleged, were spying for the Israelis.

At the first opportunity I contacted the Air Secretary's department to report my return and to request a posting to the Hunter force. "Any chance of Hunters?" I blundered. "No chance!" he thundered. I was told to report to Acklington where I'd resume my old job. I could barely believe my bad luck. When we reached Acklington, I needed to talk through this dire turn of events with Sally. We wandered outside into the chill Northumberland air one evening. The contrast with Iraq was stark. "It's as if we've never been away," I said.

"What do you mean, exactly?"

"Well I'm back at Acklington with the same aircraft callsign, the same old aircrew locker, the same lousy reputation."

She sensed my uncharacteristic air of melancholy, glanced up and inhaled sharply. In the developing twilight she studied me with intelligent, discerning eyes. There was a long pause while we gazed at each other, then at the first stars over the horizon. We remained quiet now but our thoughts seemed to coincide: we had one another; we had our fine young son; we had talents and energy. A good future with positive prospects surely lay ahead. Time would prove this to be the case: after Acklington (which, fortunately from my point of view, soon closed as a flying training school), I was posted to Valley and from there to Chivenor as an instructor. During my two-and-a-half years at Chivenor I was very happy to achieve 700 flying hours. After this, I was posted to the Hunter Wing at RAF Wittering and from there as a squadron commander at RAF Brawdy, the new home of the Tactical Weapons Unit. A most interesting and varied career followed and at the age of forty-eight I returned to Brawdy as the station commander. My last tour in the service was in the Air Secretary's department where I was responsible for the postings of junior officers and airmen aircrew.

For that fateful night at Acklington, however, when prospects seemed so bleak, when an apocalyptic feeling of despair was hard to shrug off and when the tempest of events appeared transparent in their absurdity, I realised that the solution lay in many guises, including consummate professionalism and a positive outlook. I glanced again at my wife, at the clear eyes and undaunted air of trust in a fine future. Still we said nothing, unaware, of course, that in our unspoken surmise, events would prove over the years just how much our optimistic hopes were, indeed, entirely justified.

CHAPTER 8

TEAM LEADER

BRIAN MERCER'S AEROBATIC DAYS

Frédéric Chopin, one assumed, would have been less than amused. The same could not have been said, however, for a group of British and Australian officers congregated around the officers' mess piano at RAF Tengah, Singapore on that day in 1956. Based there as a flight commander on 60 Squadron, I had been inveigled with a colleague to play a duet on the mess piano. England had just won the ashes and celebrations were underway. I think that we were playing something like Chopin's Nocturne opus 9 number 2 in E flat major, as one does, (although, on reflection, it might have been 'chopsticks') when an enormous explosion rocked the room. Chinese firecrackers had been thrown into the body of the poor piano and the culprit, a large Australian, took cover while the pianists, regardless of blackened faces and singed eyebrows, persisted valiantly, if briefly. For as the piano began to disintegrate, half the notes stopped working and we realised that Chopin would have to be abandoned. This was on the same night, I believe, that the medical officer had to be carried to bed. Normally a placid man, he'd started to throw bottles at the ceiling fan, a potentially lethal activity which had to be stopped despite his vigorous protestations.

My posting to the Far East had been signalled the year before, in early 1955, by a precipitate message from headquarters: 'Flight Lieutenant Mercer to report to HQ Far East Air Force Changi, Singapore, for flight commander duties. To arrive Changi three weeks from today.' As a member of 111 Squadron at the time, my reaction was one of astonishment. Good grief, I thought, Treble One Squadron was expected to re-equip with Hunters soon and now I was to be sent from Acklington to the ends of the earth to fly bloody de Havilland Vampires.

The flight to Singapore in a Hastings aircraft of Transport Command took five wearisome days. When, at last, the Hastings landed at Changi the climate felt decidedly hot after a Northumberland winter. However, I was warmly received (literally and metaphorically) by 60 Squadron at Tengah where, on my first night, I was taken out to a local restaurant and where, regretfully, I fell for a popular ruse: "Try the green chillies, they're not a bit hot," said my new-found colleagues. In a perverse way, the experience seemed an appropriate initiation for a squadron whose motto was *Per ardua ad aethera tendo* (I strive through difficulties to the sky).

The Malayan Emergency (so named after pressure from the rubber and tin mining industries whose losses would not have been covered by Lloyds insurers if the term 'war' had been used) was still going strong. In addition to air defence duties, the main role of 60 Squadron was to carry out 'Firedog' operations against communist terrorists. I flew about fifty such operations during my two-and-a-half years with the squadron, but targets remained well hidden in the Malayan jungle's close-packed tree canopies and I knew of only a couple of occasions when we actually hit assigned targets. On 21st February 1956, Operation Kingly Pile, an action that was our biggest success that year, commenced when a jungle camp used by communist terrorists was attacked by fighter bomber squadrons followed by ground troops. As a result of this effort, the important Johore State, with boundaries to the Republic of Singapore, became a safe area.

A week before the start of Kingly Pile, a small aerobatic team of four de Havilland Venoms, which by then had replaced 60 Squadron's Vampires, flew to Bangkok to take part in an air display. As leader of the team, this, for me, was a judicious glimpse of the future. At the briefing we were joined by some US pilots, all of them with identical crew cuts, whose leader, when he heard of our planned display, declared that he and his men would do the same even though they had not worked out or rehearsed any form of display routine. This decision nearly proved lethal. Halfway through their display, the pilots in their Republic F-84 aircraft experienced the so-called 'dishing effect' during a roll. As the wingmen banked towards their leader I witnessed the nearest thing to a mid-air collision I'd ever seen although mercifully this did not actually happen.

Our own display, happily, proceeded as planned, even if enlivened by a Thai Air Force Grumman F8F Bearcat which landed, for some reason never explained, downwind with the wheels retracted. The consequent shower of sparks was impressive, as was a programmed mass paratrooper drop when a soldier's parachute candled. The man dropped through his colleagues to face certain death except that one of them grabbed the collapsed 'chute and clung to it grimly until both paratroopers were safely on the ground.

Later that year, in October 1956, our display team was tasked to fly to Saigon to take part in celebrations to mark the first anniversary of South Vietnam's independence. *En route* to Saigon's Tan Son Knut airport, constructed in the 1920s by the French Colonial government of Indochina, we night-stopped at RAF Butterworth (soon to be taken over by the Royal Australian Air Force). At Butterworth, we heard that the station commander, a stern and frosty character who was in the habit, of all things, of walking around with a pet monkey on his shoulder, had met his comeuppance in a most bizarre manner. One evening, when the group captain strolled past the officers' mess, he was unaware of some young fighter pilots enjoying a raucous game of billiards. Suddenly, a billiard ball sailed through the air, smashed through a window then – in a shot of remarkable timing and brilliance – struck the station commander on the side of his head. The group captain cried out in shock and pain. The monkey, loathed by staff because of the creature's tendency to wander into offices to create havoc with paperwork, became frightened and, in a frenzy of provocation, bit a large chunk out of his master's ear. This caused the said master to shout out even more. The end result was a group captain with a heavily-bandaged ear, some delighted administrative staff, and no more monkey business.

When we reached Saigon, the team was invited to a cocktail party the day before our display. This was highly enjoyable, although not good preparation for the next day's aerobatic event. On the day itself, the display was watched by South Vietnam's President Diem, a Roman Catholic and staunch anti-communist (he'd be assassinated in 1963). The main street of Saigon, a typically wide Parisian-style boulevard called Rue Catinat which ran in a straight line from the River Saigon to a palace-like building at the far end, was my chosen line of departure for the final bomb-burst manoeuvre in front of President Diem. After the bomb-burst, the other Hunters split away while I flew up Rue Catinat. I can still picture thousands of faces and big eyes staring up as the formation rushed past at about 400 miles per hour. A few minutes later we landed in a hot and clammy state, our flying suits soaked with perspiration. I noticed that one of the team members was leaning unhealthily against a wing and I wondered if he was about to be sick. Perhaps, I thought, he was a victim of acute dehydration, then I remembered the heady mix of cocktails and prawn curries consumed the night before. We were about to change out of our flying gear when a Vietnamese officer ran up to us and cried: "Compliments of President Diem!"

"Thank you."

"He liked your display."

"Good."

"He liked it so much that he wants you to do it again."

"What, right now?" I asked.

"Yes!"

Our debilitated member groaned and said that he needed a shower. He returned just as the Venoms had been refuelled so off we went to repeat our display at the end of which, oddly, he said that he felt much better. That evening, at yet another cocktail party, a senior US officer was heard to remark: "We move the whole of our Seventh Fleet, deploy hundreds of airplanes, spend millions, then the Royal Air Force turn up with a few Mickey Mouse fighters to steal the show."

We enjoyed that.

The team's return to Tengah was not without problems when one of our members experienced an engine fire warning. Eventually, though, we reached Tengah where we found that trouble of another kind was brewing. As Singapore and Malaya approached independence, local politicians had begun to jockey for positions of power and at one point a riot developed. A number of air force officers from Tengah, in company with Tommies and Gurkhas, were deployed in aid of the civil power.

In spite of the hazards, life was good at Tengah and when it was time for me to return home I faced dilemmas. The dreaded Duncan Sandys' Defence White Paper of 1957 had struck; big, ugly missiles were 'in' and aeroplanes were 'out'. White-faced station commanders had to assemble their men in station cinemas to tell them that their squadrons were disbanding with immediate effect. Sandys, ex-Eton, ex-army World War 2 colonel, ex-a-great-many-other-things, would be sacked in a few years time, but of all the affronts, the growing realisation of his chilling proclivity for poor judgement would be the most hurtful, the most egregious.

I flew back to England as a passenger in a chartered Handley Page HP 81 Hermes aircraft. It was a long flog and I was keen to learn my fate. At the Air Ministry I met Squadron Leader P Latham who was in charge of aircrew postings. "How would you like to go back to Treble One Squadron as a flight commander?" he asked me. I could barely believe my luck.

In October 1957, before my posting to 111 Squadron, I went to RAF West Raynham for the Day Fighter Leaders' course where I flew the Hunter F6 – the first really good Hunter in my opinion. The engine surge and gun-firing problems of earlier marks had been solved, and with 3,000lbs of extra engine thrust and a saw-tooth on the wing leading edge, the high altitude/high Mach number pitch-up problems had been cured. The latter issue had caused quite a kerfuffle recently when a friend of mine, a New Zealand pilot, had felt the Hunter 'tuck-in' violently during a hard turn. So violently, in fact, that one of his eyeballs had been forced out of its socket and the poor Kiwi had been obliged to land the Hunter gripping the eyeball in one hand, an extraordinary feat. Equally amazing, the 'stringy bits' were still attached and in good order so that the doctors were able to re-insert the eye into its socket. According to my friend's account, the Hunter's accelerometer had registered 14 'g' – over twice the allowable limit – yet the aircraft was undamaged, proof that the Hunter design of Sir Sydney Camm (who started life as a carpenter's apprentice and who, unlike Sandys, had an uncanny knack of getting things right), was, indeed, incredibly robust.

The course at West Raynham lasted for two months and in early December 1957 I drove down to join 111 Squadron at RAF North Weald in Essex. It was my fifth tour as a fighter pilot. Treble One Squadron (otherwise known as Tremblers) had received a great deal of acclaim over the previous year for its Black Arrows aerobatic team led by Squadron Leader Roger Topp, who had an unusual background. Commissioned as a pilot officer in 1944, he'd been seconded to the Glider Pilot Regiment, an outfit with which he flew a Horsa Glider on Operation Varsity, the crossing of the River Rhine in March 1945. After a shaky landing which ended up in a dyke, Topp and his co-pilot had joined the infantry to attack, and knock out, a German gun emplacement. After the war, he flew de Havilland Mosquito aircraft, attended the Empire Test Pilots' School at Farnborough and helped trial the de Havilland Comet after the aircraft had suffered a series of accidents. In 1955 he was promoted to squadron leader and posted to take over command of 111 Squadron which already had an aerobatics team. Topp soon started to develop the team whose Hunters were painted gloss black and dubbed the 'Black Arrows' by the French press, a sobriquet which stuck.

In the spring of 1958, 111 Squadron began to increase the number of aerobatic practice sessions. I usually flew in one of three positions – number two, six or seven. Roger Topp had introduced some innovative, commonsense ideas, for instance he wanted to display the formation's plan view as much as possible for only in the plan view did a formation look 'right'. He also tried to position the formation so that spectators need not crane their necks excessively to keep the team in sight. He ensured that due allowance was made for wind and for the effect of wind on the formation's use of display smoke: some teams would overdo the smoke and consequently end up concealed from view.

Shortly after I joined 111 Squadron we were moved from North Weald to North Luffenham for a temporary spell until, in June 1958, a new permanent base at RAF Wattisham in Suffolk became the squadron's home for many years to come. The squadron flew a number of displays at that time, and in July 1958 took part in an important event at Soesterberg, Holland attended by Prince Bernhard of the Netherlands. The following month Roger Topp was given permission to try out a twenty-two-aircraft formation for the Farnborough Air Show. He developed a

*This painting was based on a photograph of twenty-two Hunters of
111 Squadron over Farnborough in September 1958.*

constructive working relationship with the commander-in-chief of Fighter Command, Air Marshal Sir Thomas Pike, who made a point of visiting the squadron regularly. Years later, by-then retired Air Commodore Roger Topp wrote: 'Sir Thomas Pike had a unique policy of speaking to me one-to-one in my office while he left all the hangers-on, including the senior air staff officer and the station commander, quietly fuming in the aircrew coffee bar. We both spoke our minds frankly and comprehensively about plans and possibilities. It was from this kind of dialogue that 'The 22' emerged and was indeed the secret of our international success. Sir Thomas Pike understood and exercised genuine high order leadership and it was an honour to know him.'

To make up the numbers for the twenty-two-aircraft formation, 111 Squadron had to borrow some extra Hunters and volunteer pilots from other squadrons. These pilots flew in the line-astern position, usually the least demanding spot, which worked out better than expected. So it was that, in August 1958, amidst an atmosphere of considerable excitement and apprehension, the full Black Arrows team flew to RAF Odiham in Hampshire, our designated base for Farnborough week. It was a poignant time. Formation aerobatic displays were inherently dangerous; a sobering number of national aerobatic teams had come to grief and we were about to reveal altogether novel techniques. The concentration required was total; the mutual trust between team members had to be absolute.

On each of the seven display days for Farnborough, team members assembled in good time to receive meteorological and other briefings before walking out to allocated Hunters. The unsung heroes, the team's ground crews, had gone above and beyond the call of duty in Herculean efforts to ensure that all the Hunters were serviceable, lined up and ready to depart. Pilots checked their aircraft then climbed aboard before, on instructions from Squadron Leader Topp, engines were started. When all were 'turning and burning' the team followed the leader as he taxied out slowly towards the take-off point. For the take-off itself, the Hunters remained in sections before joining up in the air and, at the appointed time, flying to Farnborough for the display. This routine worked well for the whole week apart from the Wednesday when low cloud and rain caused the leader to restrict numbers to five Hunters.

The first display manoeuvre, a loop with all twenty-two aircraft, no doubt triggered gasps of astonishment from observers. It was unique; we were making history; the aviation world was stunned. That first loop was followed by a second towards the end of which five of the volunteer pilots broke away to leave sixteen aircraft. These sixteen Hunters then completed a barrel roll and a loop after which seven broke away. The remaining nine Hunters now carried out a loop which ended with four aircraft 'bomb-bursting' away to leave a nucleus of five that continued with further manoeuvres to complete the show.

The subsequent edition of *Flight* magazine, published on 2nd September 1958, reported that the 22-Hunter loop was '...the most wonderful mass aerobatic manoeuvre ever witnessed at Farnborough (or, we are moved to declare, elsewhere).'

After Farnborough, the Black Arrows performed at several more events, including Battle of Britain displays at four separate airfields, after which the aerobatic season came to an end. For the winter of 1958-1959 the squadron nonetheless continued with aerobatic rehearsals as well as fighter tactical training, which included a detachment to RAF Leuchars in Scotland for practice air-to-air firing. It was on the return from Leuchars that I went through an eerie sixth sense experience. Flying along quite happily in my Hunter at 40,000 feet, suddenly I felt that something was not right. I wasn't sure what the problem was, or even if there was a problem at all, but the hairs on the back of my neck began to prickle uncomfortably. It was as if I'd entered some form of inexplicable, physical twilight zone. However, the Hunter's instrument readings were normal; the aircraft radio was working routinely; everything, it appeared, was fine. Then I looked directly upwards. There, within wisps of high level cloud, I spotted an image strange and indefinite, as wavering as that of a ghost, which I promptly realised was an Avro Vulcan bomber no more than 100 feet away and on the verge of colliding with my Hunter. It did not take me long to move.

When the 1959 aerobatic season got underway, now under Squadron Leader P Latham as the new leader, the squadron experimented with some routines of co-ordinated aerobatics. We took part in a number of air displays across Europe including the Paris Air Show at Le Bourget in June. For the 1959 Farnborough Air Show we planned to use sixteen Hunters initially, then split into two teams, one of nine Hunters and one of seven, the latter led by me. The practice sessions proceeded well with one manoeuvre in particular, when my group broke away from the main formation to barrel roll around the remainder, evidently looking very impressive. Regretfully, though, the manoeuvre was inclined to look untidy and worked well only three times out of four so we decided to cancel it.

For the Farnborough Air Show itself, we used sixteen Hunters for the first few manoeuvres after which my seven machines broke away in a bomb-burst before re-joining the others. At the end, nine Hunters carried out a loop followed by a downward bomb-burst with a smoke trail. My seven Hunters then climbed vertically through the smoke trail and bomb-burst upwards. The timing was tricky and one day we got a bit too close which, although it looked spectacular from the ground, caused my pulse rate to increase considerably.

As 1959 drew to a close, so did my time with 111 Squadron. In December of that year, however, an unfortunate incident occurred at Acklington. One day, as I climbed into my Hunter to go air-to-air firing as part of the squadron's annual armament camp, I lifted the master electrical gang-switch after normal safety checks. Immediately, two 30mm Aden cannon opened fire. Before I could bang the switch down again about twenty cannon shells whistled across the airfield right through the dispersal of 66 Squadron. Miraculously, no-one was hurt and the shells merely buried themselves in Northumberland soil. It was not long, though, before the commanding officer of 66 Squadron, Squadron Leader P Bairsto, was on the telephone. "If you'll give us a few minutes, we'll arm up and fire back!" he said with commendable aplomb. A board of inquiry was convened whose members did not seem to believe my story that I'd followed the correct safety procedures. Eventually, an electrical problem was discovered by engineers and I was exonerated.

This somewhat sour end to my tour with 111 Squadron was assuaged, however, when I received some good news on 1st January 1960. I received two letters, one of which announced my promotion to the rank of squadron leader, the other declared that I was to be awarded the Air Force Cross. Then I was told about my posting as a schools' liaison officer in Yorkshire, news that brought me down to earth with a very big bump.

When I exchanged my fine Hunter cockpit with all of its attendant excitement for a gloomy, Dickensian office in Leeds, I felt, to say the least, distinctly underwhelmed. A bit like a travelling salesman, my job entailed driving to schools across Yorkshire in an air force Standard Vanguard motorcar loaded with a film projector, lots of films and several boxes of pamphlets. Some of the headmasters and headmistresses were quite enthusiastic, although some were pacifists and reluctant to let me through their doors. One time, I faced a daunting task when I had to address the whole body of a girls' high school in Scarborough. The formidable headmistress shared the rostrum with me and I felt quite intimidated by the sea of young female faces gazing up from the floor of the hall.

A good aspect of the new job was that I was allowed to fly with 111 Squadron during school holidays. I therefore spent all of August 1960 flying out of Wattisham, and in September I flew four of the Farnborough Air Show displays. The number sixteen slot at the back of the Black Arrows was a novel experience for me, but the relative lack of responsibility was quite relaxing, even if noisy: the fifteen Rolls-Royce engines in front made a surprising din despite my Hunter's pressurised cockpit.

After Farnborough, and despite the irony of advertising the Royal Air Force when politicians seemed determined to wreck the service, I was mentally preparing to return to my job in recruitment when, out of the blue, an intriguing telephone call came through. I was told to report forthwith to Bentley Priory in Middlesex where the commander-in-chief of Fighter Command, Air Marshal Sir Hector McGregor who had taken over from Sir Thomas Pike in July 1959, wished to see me.

When I entered his office, the commander-in-chief was at his desk surrounded by grand figures including the senior air staff officer, the senior technical staff officer and the senior administrative staff officer. "Right, Mercer," Sir Hector said without further ado, "I've got a job for you." I gazed at him, determined to read, mark, learn and inwardly digest every word. "As you may have heard, 111 Squadron is re-equipping with Lightnings. I want you, therefore, to take command of 92 Squadron who will retain Hunters at Middleton St George. We're sending the squadron out to Cyprus shortly for a couple of months and we expect you to come back with an aerobatic team. Now what do you need?" I swallowed hard, scarcely able to take in the enormity of what he'd said. It seemed too good to be true.

"Need, sir?" I said hoarsely, struggling to hide my astonishment.

"Yes."

I hesitated before going on: "Could I have a few pilots from 111 Squadron to form the nucleus of the team?"

"Okay," said the commander-in-chief, "what else?"

"If there are any new, inexperienced pilots on the squadron, could they be posted elsewhere?"

"I suppose so."

"We don't want any 'second-class citizens', sir. It's important that every pilot should be involved because that's the key to high morale."

"Fair enough. We can do that. Anything else?"

I thought about this for a moment or two, then went on to ask for an engineering officer who'd be able to cope with the demands of the very high serviceability rates needed.

"What about that?" the commander-in-chief asked his senior technical staff officer, "who'd be the best man for the job?"

"Probably John Griffiths, sir. He's currently up at Duxford."

"Okay."

"Also," I persisted, "I think it would be a good idea to have a couple of senior NCOs from 111 Squadron who'd be imbued with the necessary spirit."

The commander-in-chief nodded and the result was that I got John Griffiths as requested, and two excellent NCOs from 111 Squadron. Sir Hector then went on to discuss the aircraft colour scheme – "let me know your ideas as soon as possible" – and concluded the meeting with these words: "Right, Mercer, we've given you what you asked, so go and do the job and don't have any accidents." He spoke in a different tone and gave me a penetrating stare.

I left at once for 92 Squadron whose previous commanding officer had led a small aerobatic team as a back-up for 111 Squadron. Now, though, 92 was to become the 'first eleven' and we all looked forward to it. New squadron members began to arrive and from October 1960 to January 1961 we flew a mix of aerobatic practice sorties and tactical training. The finalised colour scheme, a deep royal blue with a white lightning flash down the fuselage side, was painted on all the squadron's Hunters over the next few months by Marshalls of Cambridge.

In early January 1961 the squadron left for Nicosia in Cyprus. As we flew above the Mediterranean Sea at 40,000 feet, we produced dense white condensation trails against a brilliant blue sky. The resplendent scene was, for me, a moving one and somehow indicative of the way my life had taken such an unexpected turn for the better – preferable, anyway, to driving around Yorkshire in a Standard Vanguard motorcar. Our welcome at Nicosia, however, was a little lukewarm; it seemed that visiting fighter squadrons were not popular. The whole place exuded a stuffy atmosphere and the accommodation left much to be desired with all of our airmen and some of the officers having to live in tents. At a party in the officers' mess one time the station commander kept trying to find me to complain about the noise made by members of 92 Squadron. His efforts, though, were thwarted by a system of squadron scouts: every time he approached I received warning to leap out of a ground-floor window into the garden until given the 'all clear'. The fellow never did find me.

After a month we left, fortunately, for Akrotiri where the station commander,

Group Captain Andrew Humphrey (a future marshal of the Royal Air Force and chief of air staff), actually seemed glad to have us. Soon, as we continued with serious practice, squadron morale soared. Every display rehearsal over the airfield was filmed on 16mm cine which was usually developed and ready for assessment within forty minutes of landing. We performed three aerobatic displays during our time in Cyprus, one in front of the headquarters at Episkopi, one at Akrotiri itself and one at Nicosia where we evidently covered Archbishop Makarios in dust during a low pass. We were told that the display at Episkopi looked dramatic when, between manoeuvres, we disappeared below coastal cliffs.

In early March 1961 the squadron left Akrotiri to fly home to Middleton St George, and towards the end of the month we gave a display for the commander-in-chief who declared himself well satisfied. The problem of a suitable name for the team was resolved by a German journalist who referred to us as looking like 'blau diamanten' in the sky. The name stuck and from then on we were the 'Blue Diamonds'.

The following month, when the display season started, the squadron took part in several events in the UK and Europe. On one occasion we found ourselves in the company of Colonel Erich Hartmann and his German pilots. Hartmann, credited in World War 2 with an incredible 352 aircraft destroyed, mostly Russian, was renowned as the fighter pilot who had achieved the most number of victories in history. A slight, fair-haired figure, he looked much younger than his years and was clearly revered by his pilots. At an evening get-together in the officers' mess, Hartmann ensured that everyone had a glass of schnapps before he turned to a portrait of the Red Baron and cried: "Gentlemen, Herr Baron!" The German pilots repeated the toast, clicked their heels, downed their schnapps then hurled the empty glasses into a fireplace.

For the Farnborough Air Show of 1961, the squadron was based at the Hawker airfield at Dunsfold. The Farnborough week went well apart from one of the days when some cloud moved awkwardly across our approach line. As I pulled up into a loop, I realised that we would enter the cloud for a few seconds. Normally, this would not be a problem but the cloud was unusually dense and for several seconds the pilots could see nothing apart from the white wing tip of the adjacent aircraft. The pilot in the number sixteen slot, however, could see nothing at all and instinctively reduced the back pressure on his control column. At this point the sweat-soaked concentration which was an integral part of formation aerobatics suddenly seemed to multiply exponentially. To gasps from the crowd, the detached Hunter popped out of the cloud ahead of the other fifteen, although he managed to return to his position quickly. However, on landing at Dunsfold the poor pilot was almost in tears as he felt that he'd let down the team. Of course, he had not; if there was any fault it was mine.

Sixteen Hunters of 92 Squadron formed the flypast at the inauguration of the Trenchard Memorial by Prime Minister Harold MacMillan, in Whitehall, 19th July 1961.

One year later, at the 1962 Farnborough Air Show, the squadron experienced another problem but of a rather different kind. When he selected undercarriage 'up', one of the pilots found that his Hunter's nose wheel was cocked through ninety degrees and stuck outside its doors. As the aircraft was in the key 'Blue One' position, the use of an airborne spare would not have been appropriate. My mind went into overdrive as I tried to compute possible changes to the display routine, then the pilot said that he'd attempt a 'touch and go' landing at Odiham to see if he could bounce the nose wheel straight. Meanwhile, time was getting very tight and timing at Farnborough was crucial; even a thirty-second delay was unacceptable. Suddenly, when back on our radio frequency, the pilot called to say that the problem was fixed and that he could rejoin the formation. I was just starting the run-in from the north of Farnborough so I asked if he could rejoin in time. After a brief hesitation the answer came back: "Yes!" Within moments he came rushing in from the formation's rear left, dive brake out as, with notable *éclat*, he decelerated and slipped into position. I heard the call: "Blue section in!" and about three seconds later I announced: "Diamonds looping now!" Even James Bond would have been impressed.

Following Farnborough, the team did a few more displays but at the conclusion of the Battle of Britain events in September 1962 it was the end of formation aerobatics for me. I'd become, I suppose, a bit of an 'adrenaline junkie' and I realised that my life was about to become a lot tamer. From now on it would be up to the Yellow Jacks and later the Red Arrows.

Over the next three years I did various ground-based jobs until, in 1965, I decided to retire from the service and seek a future in civil aviation. I took the necessary licence exams, then applied for, and was offered, a job with Cathay Pacific, an Anglo-Australian airline. In May 1984, by which time Cathay Pacific had expanded greatly and lost the original 'family feeling', I retired from the airline to my new home in Western Australia. It was six years later when I ran into an old friend who had just joined Air Hong Kong and he persuaded me to do the same. Then, in April 1994 I retired from Air Hong Kong until, two years later, I spent time as a simulator instructor on the Boeing 747 before retiring for the last time.

Now, as I look back, I have a sense of gratitude for the fates have been good to me. It was a wrench when I left the Royal Air Force but I liked my flying and the prospect of manning a desk for evermore did not appeal. As leader of the Blue Diamonds I'd experienced fear now and again for there was no doubt that our activities were dangerous at times. Nonetheless, I'd enjoyed a period which must assuredly count as the highlight of a life spent in aviation.

CHAPTER 9

TEST PILOT

NEVILLE DUKE
DSO, OBE, DFC AND
TWO BARS, AFC,
CZECH MILITARY CROSS,
HAWKER AIRCRAFT
CHIEF TEST PILOT

I had just parked my car at Farnborough airfield. Stepping out of the car, I was keen to witness the display of a DH110 flown by John Derry with Tony Richards as his observer. I had no inkling, of course, of the horror that was about to unfold. Having watched Derry's performance every day so far at this 1952 Farnborough Air Show, I'd admired the way he had handled the de Havilland prototype. It was, in a manner, the aviation equivalent of a musical masterpiece – the likes, say, of Mascagni's *Cavalleria Rusticana* with the subtle first violins leading the way towards a huge *crescendo rallentando* ending *fortissimo* which, in the case of the DH110, came in the form of supersonic bangs. On that day, John Derry had been over to Hatfield to pick up the DH110's first prototype (WG 236) because the second prototype, which he'd flown in the earlier part of the week, was now, regretfully, unserviceable. He and his observer, having hastened to Hatfield, had flown back to Farnborough in WG 236 only just in time for their display slot.

The weather was good that day – a lovely afternoon – and it was shortly after John Derry had made his supersonic bangs that we could see a couple of puffs in the clear sky. The DH110 then came down towards the airfield where he would continue his display routine. Derry carried out a normal flypast and on completion of this manoeuvre he began to reduce airspeed and turn back over the airfield. In the next few moments, which would live with me forever, I seemed to have difficulty

Curtiss P-40 Tomahawk of 112 Squadron.

in absorbing the implications of what was happening around me. I was about to display the Hawker Hunter but now, suddenly, I faced terrible, tumultuous decisions.

I suspect that in times of high stress the mind plays tricks with reality. And if I looked back, such times in my own life had certainly played a trick or two. I suppose that one of the more potent of these seminal moments, so to speak, came in late 1941 in North Africa when I was a Curtiss P-40 Tomahawk pilot with 112 Squadron during the Western Desert campaign. Then it was that I was shot down not once but twice in less than a week.

*

The first occasion was on Sunday, 30th November 1941, a day which commenced with an early morning brief for a dawn wing patrol over the Western Desert's el Gobi area. Twenty-four Allied aircraft, we were told, would make up the wing and twelve Tomahawks from 112 Squadron would join forces with twelve Australian aircraft. I'd not long been a member of 112 Squadron, which was among the first Royal Air Force squadrons to operate the Tomahawk aircraft in North Africa, and the first Allied squadron to feature the distinctive 'shark mouth', the emblem boldly painted below the cockpit similar to the Luftwaffe's Messerschmitt Bf 110 twin-engined fighters. We took off in boxes of four that day and climbed to an altitude of 10,000 feet on course for the battle area. There was some anxious chatter on the aircraft radio, and no doubt all in the wing felt on tenterhooks when suddenly, ahead and below, we spotted a gaggle of thirty to forty enemy aircraft. The mix of

German and Italian machines consisted of Junkers 87s with escorting Messerschmitt Bf 109Fs with some Macchis and Fiats. Within moments, on instructions from the wing leader, we began to peel off and dive towards the enemy.

With adrenaline pumping through my system, there was not one thought in my head except for that of battle. If I felt close to entering some sort of strange psychological time zone, there was no time to be frightened or even to think of being frightened. As I homed onto a Fiat G50 aircraft, my mind was cool and precise; I was braced to react in an instant to the other pilot's next move. The symbiosis between attacker and attacked, the way fortunes could turn within seconds, even micro-seconds, could induce a sense of the surreal. Now the Italian pilot promptly entered a steep dive. Evidently determined to escape, he levelled his Fiat G50 just above the desert sands and streaked along at an altitude of just a few feet taking no evasive action apart from the occasional violent switch-back manoeuvre. With full power applied to my Allison engine, I sat upright in my cockpit and flew the Tomahawk with finesse – not with my hands so much as with the tips of my fingers. It was as if the Tomahawk became part of my own body; machine and man in subtle symmetry. I stayed with the enemy machine but found him extremely hard to hit. Every time I squeezed my firing trigger I used up a considerable amount of ammunition. Then, quite suddenly, my frustration ended when I saw him crash-land on the desert sands.

There was no opportunity, however, to congratulate myself on a combat success; I swiftly became aware of a new and immediate danger. The chase had been watched by some of the Fiat pilot's friends and now, in this dog-eat-dog environment, they had me to themselves. By 'they' I mean three or four Messerschmitt 109Fs and the odd Fiat G50. I forget how many attacks I dodged – probably four or five – and I managed to fire a few shots at a Messerschmitt 109F which then started to spurt glycol, but now it was my turn to bolt for home. I zoomed down to ultra-low level across the desert sands and applied full boost of fifty inches to my Allison engine. I was aware of at least one Messerschmitt 109F giving chase and I knew that his machine was faster than mine. Furthermore, I soon began to realise that the pilot was no ordinary pilot, that he was a very good shot and that, unlike me, he was not short of ammunition. (I speculated whether it could have been the German ace Hans-Joachim Marseille who, despite his apparently Bohemian lifestyle, was nicknamed 'Star of Africa' with, by the time of his death in September 1942, over 150 claimed victories. I discovered later, however, that my adversary was another German ace – Oberfeldwebel Otto Schulz of Jagdgeschwader 27.)

I could feel the perspiration break out on my forehead. There's still time, I kept telling myself. Then bullets began to smack into my aircraft's wings and into the rear fuselage. I carried out a violent vertical left-hand turn a few hundred feet above the ground, but with a good shot from fully ninety degrees of deflection the

German ace hit my left wing and I heard the tremendous bang of an explosive shell.

What happened next remains a blur in my memory. There's little doubt, though, that I came within a whisker, as they say, of meeting my creator. The Tomahawk turned on its back and I could see the ground far too few feet below – or rather, above – the cockpit. Entirely by impulse, I kicked the rudder and pushed the stick over as I saw the sand rush up towards me. There was a whirl of sky and desert until, abruptly, the world came the right way up and, as if by a miracle, I had some measure of control of my aircraft again. The Tomahawk hit the sand with its belly and bounced. Up we went…and down again…down in a crash landing. As the dust and debris subsided, I assessed myself hastily for injuries but luckily I appeared to be more or less in one piece.

I knew that, as rapidly as possible, I needed to jump clear and dash for cover. I scrambled out of the cockpit and found myself instinctively closing the cockpit hood; maybe I held some sort of hope that Marseille, or whoever it was, would reckon that I was still inside the cockpit and not hiding behind a bush. I jumped down onto the sand, ducked under the Tomahawk's engine and searched urgently for some kind of cover. I suddenly realised that the Tomahawk was on fire and I could recall thinking that it had probably been on fire when I was still airborne. I squinted my eyes while I glanced up at the sky. The Messerschmitt 109F had started to swing round as the pilot prepared to shoot me up. About twenty yards away I spied some scrub. Now, in what felt like world record time, I sprinted towards the scrub and flung myself down. I wished desperately that the scrub had grown higher than a mere one foot.

Above me I heard the snarl of the Messerschmitt. I was aware of the machine diving towards me then, as I listened to the horrible crack and whine of bullets, I tried to cringe into the sand and make myself as inconspicuous as possible. The Messerschmitt's cannon shells exploded as they banged into the Tomahawk after which I heard the 109F's drone start to drift towards the horizon.

Now, as if by some form of divine intervention, a weird silence descended across the scene apart from the crackle of flames as the Tomahawk was consumed by fire. In the distance I could still hear the drone of the Messerschmitt's engine and wondered if the machine would return, but it did not.

I sat by the scrub for some time. I tried to figure out what to do next, and as I watched my aircraft go up in smoke I listened to the rattle of the last few rounds of ammunition exploding. I felt almost mesmerised by my new and peculiar circumstances. One moment I'd been in the centre of noise, action, drama, but now I was squatting in the middle of nowhere with everything silent and static and where the desert seemed a very big and lonely place.

It did not take me too long to realise that I couldn't continue to sit there for evermore. A thick column of black smoke had begun to ascend above the Tomahawk and the wrong people might soon become curious. Before I set off, I made a hasty check of my equipment: I had my service revolver, a water bottle, a good pair of desert boots, and an escape compass built into one of my uniform buttons. I unscrewed the compass from the button and checked an easterly course. I had a vague idea that I was somewhere south of El Adem and on the wrong side of enemy lines. But I knew there was only one thing to do and that was to start walking.

Feeling hot, slightly dazed and very thirsty, I plodded on for about thirty minutes over the sand until I chanced across a desert track. I halted, checked in both directions and decided to follow the track. I kept a crafty eye on the horizon and was not altogether surprised when, after a while, I spotted a lorry in the distance. The vehicle appeared to be travelling quite fast as it bounced along the track towards the cloud of black smoke which marked my Tomahawk's funeral pyre. While I agonised about whether the lorry would be one of ours, I scuttled behind some scrub and rocks. The whine of the vehicle's engine grew gradually louder until, just as the lorry drove past my hiding place, I had a quick peep. It was one of ours! Immediately I stood up and yelled: "Hi! Wait a minute!"

As the lorry driver slammed on his brakes, the vehicle skidded to a halt. Out jumped four or five figures who gripped rifles and revolvers while they ran towards me. For an awful moment I thought I'd made a mistake and that these were Jerries; by their clothes they could have been anybody. I soon recognised them as Desert Rats, though, in typically irregular uniform. "My name's Duke," I yelled, "112 Squadron and that…" I pointed at the smoke, "is, or rather was, my aircraft."

The men soon realised that I was Royal Air Force. "So you got out all right," said one. "We saw you from quite a distance away, upside down with a Jerry beating you up. Never thought you'd walk away from that one!"

I had a wonderful feeling of relief to be talking with them. I was among friends, no longer lonely, no longer left to my own devices. One of them produced a hip flask and gave me a good nip of whisky while someone else handed me a cigarette. I felt that these were, without doubt, the best chaps in the world.

As we chatted and as I told them about what had happened we picked up the sound of an aircraft. All eyes searched skywards until someone shouted: "It's one of ours – a Lysander."

"Let's wave," I said. "If the pilot sees us and can get down, maybe I can thumb a lift home."

At this, we all began to shout and wave. The pilot, though, seemed to hesitate as he circled before landing. At length he straightened up and commenced an approach to land just a short distance away from our lorry. The pilot closed down his Westland Lysander's engine and stepped out of the aircraft followed, no less, by an army general. The latter, it appeared, had been looking for advanced army headquarters but was not having much success in the confusion of the rapid advance currently underway. We pored over some army maps and came to the conclusion that we were in an area of no-man's-land. "We'd better be off swiftly," said the Lysander pilot, "before Rommel decides to have a shufti at your Tomahawk's smoky remains." He then invited me to hop into the back of the Lysander where I squeezed next to the general.

The pilot now made use of the Lysander's remarkable short landing and take-off abilities and soon I felt thoroughly happy to be flying over the desert again, so much quicker than walking! Eventually we found the advanced army headquarters where we landed so the general could deliver his talk after which he agreed that the Lysander could drop me back at my base airfield.

It was evening by the time I reached base and years seemed to have passed since I'd taken off early on that Sunday morning. Excited and delighted to be home again, I walked slowly over the soft sand. As I approached the mess I noticed a small group of personnel with the padre who was holding a Sunday church service. Suddenly, I felt intensely moved by the scene and experienced an overwhelming desire to join them. We were in the back of beyond, an isolated spot in the desert, yet here was home and a church service at the end of an all too eventful day.

While I continued to walk quietly towards the group, almost instinctively I moved on tip-toe so as not to disturb the proceedings. Then I noticed a few heads turn followed by some quick, curious whispering. I did not know it at that moment but I had been posted as missing. When I spotted my friend 'Hunk' Humphreys – I'd never seen him praying before – and when he looked up and saw me, the undisguised pleasure that promptly lighted his face somehow startled, then surprised and delighted me. I went down on my knees and joined the others in silent prayer.

That night I slept restlessly. I kept on waking up to see the desert rush towards me. The next few days, though, were reasonably quiet which gave me a chance to recover a measure of equilibrium. "Don't you go doing a thing like that again," said Hunk.

However, by Thursday, 4th December 1941, events began to hot up once more. On that day I was in a wing of twenty-two Allied aircraft (ten from 112 Squadron, twelve from 250 Squadron) which, having spotted formations of enemy aircraft, had immediately dived down to engage them. In the subsequent mêlée I managed to bring my machine guns to bear on a group of Junkers 87 aircraft in close formation. As the enemy group began to break up, I saw one of the Junkers enter a gentle dive with smoke trailing behind. Then I spotted a Messerschmitt 109 start to pursue me after which a Macchi 200 entered the fray. I soon became embroiled in a fierce dogfight with the Macchi until, abruptly, he broke off to head for home. I chased after him and was astonished at one point when he carried out a 360 degree roll in front of me, as if involved in some kind of aerobatic demonstration.

Meanwhile, my guns developed trouble until eventually, one by one, they stopped working. While I persisted to chase the Macchi, all I could do was to perform a number of vigorous, threatening dummy attacks. We flew very low over the desert and once over the sea until, at one stage, I noticed the town of Tobruk rush by underneath. The chase ended when the Italian pilot, evidently put off by one of my dummy attacks, promptly entered a steep turn…stalled…flicked over the other way, then plummeted down to crash into the ground with a tremendous burst of flame.

But now, after this dramatic conclusion, I was short of fuel so I headed for Tobruk aerodrome to refuel and to get my faulty guns fixed. At the aerodrome I befriended some members of the Australian army who invited me to a lunch of bully beef and biscuits. The lunch, if basic, was most enjoyable nonetheless. Perhaps this was evidence of how, despite having just killed a man, the ruthless nature of all-out war could brutalise the senses. Notwithstanding this, I always felt that I was fighting a machine not another pilot, an attitude which stayed with me throughout the war.

The following day, I was as surprised as the Australians when I turned up at Tobruk aerodrome again.

That day – Friday 5th December, 1941 – had begun with another ferocious clash between our wing and the Luftwaffe in which ten German aircraft were shot down. I was the leader of a section of four Tomahawks but I recall that I felt not particularly happy. On take-off, clouds of sand stirred up by the section ahead had caused my perspex canopy to become thickly coated with dust which restricted my vision. After a while my radio packed up and, unable to hear what was going on, I began to feel very isolated. However, as our numbers were few and as there was a good chance that we'd meet up with the enemy 'circus' again, I decided to stay with the formation.

The sun seemed particularly brilliant that day, almost blinding when I glanced up to search for enemy aircraft. This was not helped by my sanded canopy. As I blinked and peered, I felt a little blind, and altogether deaf without the radio. When I saw the wing leader break downwards to attack a gaggle of enemy machines, I duly followed. However, with the combination of my sanded canopy and the brilliance of the sun, I failed to spot a top cover of Messerschmitt 109s. One of them, though, had spotted me. There was an abrupt bang in the cockpit on the starboard side, my foot was knocked off the rudder pedal, I felt a vicious blow on my right leg and the cockpit filled with smoke.

My heartbeat began to increase as if in concert with persistent banging on the side of the cockpit: the Tomahawk shuddered and clattered and I knew that the aircraft had been badly hit. Despite this, with the Messerschmitt still on my tail I

The boys of 112 Squadron, Neville Duke third from left (front row).

had to take robust evasive action which, at an altitude of 10,000 feet, caused the Tomahawk to enter a spin. The machine's right wing was torn at the trailing edge, the right aileron control was shot through and the right elevator was completely shot away. I did my best to regain control but the spin went on and on until I reached the stage when I reckoned it was time to bale out. I undid my seat safety straps and opened the hood. I was just about to leave the aircraft when, at an altitude of around 2,000 feet, the Tomahawk suddenly recovered from the spin and straightened out.

With the unappealing prospect of another walk in the desert, I decided to head for Tobruk aerodrome. Still with a wary eye on the Messerschmitt above, I remained at low level as I nursed my Tomahawk towards what I knew would be a bumpy landing. Sure enough, when I reached the aerodrome my touchdown at around 150 miles per hour (well above normal landing airspeed) was hard to control with a damaged wing, only one aileron and just fifty per cent use of the elevators. Furthermore, I was too preoccupied to re-fasten my safety straps. As I rattled around the cockpit after touchdown, I used one hand to try to control the aircraft and my other hand to protect myself. When the Tomahawk finally stopped, I abandoned it very smartly in case of fire. In the event, the machine did not catch fire but was a complete write-off nonetheless. I did, though, manage to salvage the aircraft clock as a souvenir.

It was not long before I met up with my Australian friends from yesterday: "Strewth," said one. "You again? You must like this place." Unlike yesterday, however,

I had little appetite for bully beef especially as I was in pain from the injury to my leg from the Messerschmitt 109's bullets. I was driven to the emergency hospital in Tobruk for medical treatment but had to endure the German attack on Tobruk's confined streets with artillery fire and Stuka dive bombers. It was with a sense of considerable relief, therefore, when I was offered a flight back to base in a Bristol Blenheim bomber. The Blenheim pilot remained at very low level for the flight after which I discovered that, as had happened last weekend, I'd been posted as missing – without a radio I'd been unable to report what had been going on.

Still afflicted by the leg injury, I hobbled around feeling quite a little proud of my war wound especially when, during sympathetic conversations, I picked out splinters of Messerschmitt cannon shell as proof of authenticity. When I reported to the squadron commanding officer, Squadron Leader Morello, he said with a smile: "Making a bit of a habit of this, aren't you?" He authorised me to fly a Tomahawk to Feyum for repairs after which, having delivered the Tomahawk, I could remain in Cairo for five days of leave. I still remember the marvellous hour spent soaking in a hot bath when I'd checked-in to a Cairo hotel. This was followed by a delicious meal which, for once, was not dominated by ubiquitous army-style bully beef and biscuits.

*

It was some three years later, in March 1944, that I was appointed as the commanding officer of 145 Squadron flying Spitfire VIII aircraft. By then, having completed my tour with 112 Squadron in April 1942, I had spent about eight months as an instructor with the Fighter School at Suez before I joined 92 Squadron flying Spitfire V aircraft in support of the Eighth Army's ongoing North African campaign. After a relatively brief spell with 92 Squadron, I was posted in April 1943 as chief flying instructor with 73 Operational Training Unit at Abu Sueir, Egypt before, a year less a month later, I was moved to 145 Squadron.

When I reached 145 Squadron, it was at a stage in the war when Rommel had been driven out of North Africa, the Allies had invaded Sicily in Operation Husky and now they were chasing the Germans northwards through Italy.

I felt rather self-conscious when I first met the other pilots and officers of 145 Squadron. Every new commanding officer is regarded with critical, appraising eyes in the first few moments of his introduction; not a word or a movement is missed but noted carefully, and during the first few days he is usually treated with great reserve. I wondered how I should make out.

The squadron's main job at the time was to give air cover over the Anzio area south of Rome. My first patrol took place on 4th March 1944, the day after I took command of 145 Squadron whose score of enemy aircraft destroyed at that point was 196. It was a cloudy day and we didn't see much. After my long absence from operational flying I felt like a new boy again, nevertheless it was good to be back.

The following day might easily have been my last. A shell splinter punched a hole in my starboard wing the size of my head and just a few inches away from the Spitfire's cannon ammunition. Despite a radio peppered with debris and problems caused by the damaged wing I managed to fly my aircraft back to base. After what had felt like a form of re-baptism by fire, the squadron spent the next few weeks patrolling Anzio and Cassino as the Allied armies struggled to push past Cassino to link up with the bridgehead at Anzio.

On 7th June 1944, the day after we'd all been cheered by the news that the invasion of Normandy had begun, I led a strafing sortie in the Rieti area of central Italy. We located some enemy trucks and set them on fire but I suddenly found that my Spitfire's radiator had been hit, either by enemy flak or by ricocheting bullets from my own machine. Soon, as I pulled up to gain height, the engine began to vibrate and flames started to shoot out from the exhaust stubs.

I turned for home and managed to keep the Spitfire going by opening the throttle slowly then closing it quickly when flames began to shoot out. The aircraft, though, lost height steadily, the cockpit began to fill with smoke and I realised that I might have to bale out. Descending through a fortuitous break in the cloud, I discovered that I was 2,000 feet above Lake Bracciano, a large lake with a circular perimeter of about twenty miles. By now the smoke in my cockpit had become excessive and the engine was well on fire. The time has come, I thought, so I released my safety straps and oxygen connections, rolled the Spitfire on its back and, still travelling at 180 miles per hour, expected to fall clear.

Perhaps my mind had been preoccupied with the problem of smoke, but it suddenly dawned on me that, instead of jettisoning my cockpit hood, I had slid it back; my parachute had become snagged which prevented me from dropping out. Furthermore, I was at very low altitude and found that hanging there upside down, half in, half out of the cockpit with the nose of the Spitfire beginning to drop, felt, to put it mildly, quite unpleasant. The surface of the lake seemed to rush towards me at an alarming rate. With a concentrated effort to kick myself free, at last I fell clear of the Spitfire at which point my helmet and oxygen mask were ripped violently from my head by the slipstream.

The combined effects of relief at being free from the aircraft and the sensation of tumbling head over heels were so delightful that a few seconds passed before it occurred to me to pull the parachute ripcord. When I jerked the ring, the parachute opened quickly, so quickly in fact that one of the shoulder straps broke or came undone which caused me to fall half-out of the harness. I managed to pull myself back in and noticed that I was still clutching the parachute ring. My parachute now began to swing from side to side, an oscillation that induced a curious sense of detachment. I could see from signs on the surface of the lake where my Spitfire had crashed and noticed that I was drifting towards the lake's northern shore. With a feeling of dread, I reckoned that large numbers of enemy troops would be congregated there since the German retreat from Rome had begun already.

I had the impression of falling slowly now until I was fairly near the water when the surface suddenly appeared to accelerate towards me. As I splashed into the lake, I banged my parachute quick release box at which everything except for one leg strap dropped clear. This strap kept me fastened to the parachute which, caught by the wind, started to drag me across the lake. I was hauled along, initially over the surface, then under it. I swallowed a great quantity of water and began to thrash about thinking that I should drown. The parachute, though, eventually settled on the lake before it began to sink and drag me down. With a flash of inspiration, I operated the dinghy quick release mechanism and tugged at my Mae West lifejacket inflation device at which, coughing and spluttering, I bobbed back up to the surface.

The water felt quite warm and when I looked up I was heartened to see some of my colleagues circling above in their Spitfires. I waved at them before, having recovered my breath, I started to swim. After about twenty minutes I noticed a boat push out from the lake's shore and speculated whether the occupants were Italian or German. As the boat drew near I could see that two boys were in it and decided that, from the sound of their voices, they were Italian. Luckily they were and, having helped me to scramble into the boat, the young lads set off for the side of the lake as fast as they could go.

We were met by several peasant farmers at the lake's shore. After some eclectic use of sign language and broken English, we all started to scamper up a hill at a sharp pace as it was evident that the Italians were fearful that Germans might turn up. When we reached a wood, my new-found friends helped me to remove my wet clothes, hastily hid them, then, one by one, the men presented me with alternative garments. As I put them on, there were a few smiles and guffaws: the trouser legs reached nearly up to my knees, the coat came half-way up my arms and the hat perched on the top of my head probably looked quite peculiar. We all laughed a lot, shrugged our shoulders cheerily and decided to lie low for a bit in case any inquisitive Germans should arrive. Luckily, though, it turned out to be safe: the Wehrmacht had withdrawn a couple of hours before, Allied troops had not yet advanced, and we were in an area of temporary no-man's land.

When, eventually, the Italians decided that we could proceed safely we moved with a good deal of caution as we set off along the lakeside. As we reached a house, one of the Italians turned to me and grinned. "Vino?" he said.

"Grazie!" I nodded enthusiastically. Quantities of wine, bread, cheese and tea were now placed in front of me and while I munched away it seemed that half the

Top: 74 Squadron Hunter F Mk 6 XF511-P taxies out at Horsham St Faith in 1960. The squadron re-equipped with Lightnings later in the year. (*Aviation Bookshop*)

Above: Bearing 26 (AC) Squadron markings, F Mk 6 XF417 approaches the Gütersloh threshold in 1960, the unit's final year of Hunter operation.

Right: This head-on view of 8 Squadron FGA Mk 9 XF421-C at Muharraq in 1964, reveals the gun port, sabrina, rocket rail and 230-gallon drop tank configuration of the ground-attack version of the Hunter. (*Ted Lambe*)

Above: This 8 Squadron line up of FGA Mk 9s and FR Mk 10s at Khormaksar in 1961 includes XG136-C, XF455-T, XE599-X, XE655-H, XE654-E, XE581-D, XE651-M and XE649-S. (*Des Meek*)

Left: Looking north along the 208 Squadron line at Sharjah in 1963. The nearest FGA Mk 9 is armed with concrete-headed rockets in readiness for a practice sortie on the range. (*Les Dunnett*)

Below: Pre-flight checks are in progress in readiness for an exercise with the Royal Navy as the sun breaks over the 8 Squadron line at Muharraq in December 1963. (*Ray Deacon*)

Above: Captured from the open doorway of a Sycamore helicopter in 1962, an elevated view of the Hunter pan at Khormaksar with aircraft from 208 and 8 Squadrons in evidence. (*Keith Webster*)

Right: Having completed an air-to-ground shoot on the Jeb-a-Jib range, 8 Squadron FGA Mk 9 XF440-L drops over the threshold on its return to Sharjah in 1963. (*Ray Deacon*)

Below: A March 1964 view along the Khormaksar Hunter pan captures FGA Mk 9s from 8 and 208 Squadrons, and FR Mk 10s and a solitary T Mk 7 from 1417 Flight. (*Ray Deacon*)

Above: Armourers carefully load a 60lb HE rocket onto a 43 Squadron FGA Mk 9 at Khormaksar in 1965. (*Willie Marr*)
Left: Bearing the pilot's initials 'PL' on the fin, FR Mk 10 XE614 flies in formation alongside the 'camera-ship' during a sortie from Khormaksar in 1964. (*Peter Lewis*)
Below: In this view of a fire drill at Khormaksar, three Hunters are pushed back to enable foam to be laid over a fuel spillage. Note the SAR Sycamore helicopter in attendance. (*Ray Deacon*)

Above: Bearing the markings of 8 and 43 Squadrons, rocket-armed FGA Mk 9 XE530-O was the mount of Roger Wilkins for a period at Khormaksar in 1965. (*Roger Wilkins*)

Right: This photograph of 8/43 Squadron FGA Mk 9 XE530-O was taken in 1965, shortly after it made a wheels-up landing at Khormaksar. The drop tanks appear to have absorbed most of the impact. (*Roger Wilkins*)

Below: Station staff officers greet 43 Squadron pilots with a refreshing beer at the commencement of a detachment to a baking-hot Masirah in 1965. (*Roger Wilkins*)

Above: Nine 229 OCU F Mk 6 Hunters taxi in at Chivenor in 1965 after a formation sortie. An Anson and line up of Meteor F(TT) Mk 8 target-tugs can be seen in the background.
Below: The red markings on this F Mk 6A indicate that XF418-16 was used as a 'bounce' aircraft by instructors at 1 TWU. (*Aviation Bookshop*)

Bottom left: One of a handful of FR Mk 10s operated by 229 OCU in 1971, XF426-12 is seen on the line at Chivenor bearing 79 (Reserve) Squadron markings. (*Keith Watson*)
Bottom right: View looking north across the 229 OCU Hunter pans at Chivenor in the summer of 1966.

Above: An unidentified 229 OCU T Mk 7 bearing the markings of 234 (Shadow) Squadron, photographed on the pan at Chivenor in 1966.
Below: The evening sun sets over the Hunter pan at Chivenor in 1966.
Bottom left: 'Yusha', the squadron mascot, sits in front of a 229 OCU F Mk 6 at Chivenor in 1966.

Bottom right: This 1968 view captures 208 Squadron FGA Mk 9 XJ687-E on the pan at Sharjah. (*Aviation Bookshop*)

Above: FGA9 XG130-E was pictured at Waterbeach in 1969, shortly before 1 Squadron converted to the Harrier. (*Aviation Bookshop*)

Below: To make good the high attrition rate of Gnats operated by 4 FTS at Valley, a number of T Mk 7s were painted in light-grey with dayglo stripes as depicted here on XL591-82. (*Aviation Bookshop*)

Bottom left: Still bearing Training Command colours, T Mk 7 XL600-83 was issued to Laarbruch Station Flight in 1980 during a period of temporary grounding of the RAF's Buccaneer fleet. (*Aviation Bookshop*)

Bottom right: Three FGA Mk 9s from UK-based 1 and 54 Squadrons share the pan at Bahrain with a fourth aircraft from 208 Squadron, not long after the Kuwait crisis of 1961. (*Ray Deacon*)

local population hastened over to the house in order to check me out. There was a great deal of chatter as folk roared with laughter and pointed excitedly. At length, when I was replete, I was taken to a bedroom where I soon settled down to sleep.

My wakening in this utterly bizarre situation was rude. American voices now replaced Italian ones and I found myself staring at Tommy-guns. Bleary-eyed, I sat up and gazed in bewilderment at the barrels of the guns being waved around in a threatening manner by two individuals. "Hey, Bud, wake up!" they cried.

This turned out to be the start of a strange and hectic journey for the return to my squadron's current base at Venafro near Cassino. At various stages along the way the Italians fêted me with receptions, flowers, free-flowing wine as if I was some kind of film star. Finally, after a night spent sleeping under a United States Army lorry for the lack of anything better, I was flown in a Piper Cub to Aquino and from there to Venafro in a Fairchild aircraft. Apart from an enormous bruise on my right thigh from the recalcitrant parachute harness, and one or two twinges of cramp caused by wandering about in wet shoes and socks, I felt fine. As a memento of the whole remarkable experience I still had my parachute ring and the mild distinction of being one of the few pilots in World War 2 to bale out and land in fresh water.

In October 1944, just a few months after this episode, I was posted from Italy back to England. Three days short of three years since I'd left Plymouth for North Africa, I was now a passenger in a Douglas DC-3 Dakota for the flight home. I observed with interest as the DC-3 took off from Pymigliano, flew out over Anzio, crossed Corsica, Toulon, Marseilles, Le Havre to land at Lyneham in Wiltshire at around 5.30 pm. I was driven to Swindon railway station but missed the connection to London, consequently the journey from Swindon to Tonbridge, where my parents and my sister lived, took longer than that from Pymigliano to Lyneham. When, eventually, I reached Tonbridge, the local bus service had stopped so I left my bags at the railway station and walked. I planned to creep in through a back window but all the windows were locked so I had little option but to bang on the front door and whistle. Fortunately my mother recognised the whistle and in no time at all she, my father and sister, all in their dressing gowns, rushed downstairs to greet me and to ply me with questions. When I went upstairs I found that my room was unchanged from the day I'd left it; a dust sheet still lay over the model aerodrome which once had been my pride and joy.

It was good to be home again but now I had to think about the future. When I visited the Air Ministry postings people I told them that I was not interested in a 'chairborne' office job, neither was I keen to become an instructor again. I was treated with some sympathy and asked if I would like to be considered for a post in production test flying. I was told then about a scheme for service pilots on operational rest to be attached to aircraft manufacturing firms. The job would involve test-flying new aircraft off the production line. I reckoned that there was nothing chairborne about this so, yes, I said that I would be interested.

A few days later I received a note telling me to call on Philip Lucas, the chief test pilot of Hawker Aircraft at Langley in Buckinghamshire. The interview seemed to go well which was confirmed when I received a telegram from the Air Ministry to tell me that I'd be posted to Hawker Aircraft Limited based at Langley from 1st January 1945 for one year. My rank would be flight lieutenant, but I was quite content to drop from squadron leader. Another possibility was for me to take an air attaché job in the rank of wing commander but I preferred to continue flying.

My job at Hawkers began at a servicing school run by the company. I had to learn as much as possible about the Hawker Tempest Marks 2 and 5. While I gained a working knowledge of these aircraft and their engines, I soon found out that Hawkers employed two branches of test pilot – the production and the experimental test pilots.

It did not take me long to settle into the swing of production testing. We flew every day, whenever the weather allowed. When we were satisfied that the Tempests were ready for squadron use, the machines were collected from Langley by pilots of the Air Transport Auxiliary, many of them young women who flew the aircraft off with all the assurance in the world.

During my year with Hawkers I was introduced to Miss Gwendoline Fellows – Gwen. I found myself thinking a lot of Gwen, dark, petite and very attractive, although for a long time we did not talk much. Later she told me that I was usually pretty silent, listening to others who did the talking. This may have been true, all the same I knew that she was there and if, perhaps, I did not talk much it was good just to be there in her company.

In the summer of 1945 it was suggested that I should think of applying to take the Empire Test Pilots' School course. At about the same time the Air Ministry offered me a permanent commission in the Royal Air Force to which I agreed without hesitation. Shortly afterwards I applied for the ETPS course and was accepted. So it was that, not long after my twenty-fourth birthday, I joined No 4 Course of the Empire Test Pilots' School. Established in 1943 at Boscombe Down, the school moved in October 1945 to Cranfield where I did the course, then to Farnborough in 1947.

At Cranfield I flew a jet aircraft for the first time (a Gloster Meteor) and encountered new phenomena like Mach characteristics, compressibility effects in the form of airframe buffet, changes in aircraft trim with the nose going up or down, and the flight controls becoming much heavier. As part of the course we flew Vampires and Meteors, as well as a remarkable variety of different types: four-engined Lancasters and Lincolns, a Hamilcar glider towed behind a Halifax bomber, a Grunau glider, Mosquitoes, Seafires, Tempests, Dakotas and many other types.

I found that I preferred the jet aircraft and became increasingly interested in the problems of high speed flight. Towards the end of June 1946, on completion of the first half of the ETPS course, I was delighted to be told, therefore, that I would become a member of the High Speed Flight to be formed at Tangmere where we'd make another attempt on the world's speed record.

In many ways, the results of the High Speed Flight were disappointing. It's true that, with an average figure of 616 miles per hour (Mach 0.81) over a timed course, we increased the world record by ten mph, but we'd hoped to do much better. A positive aspect, though, was that we proved that the conventional type of aircraft had reached its high speed limit and that now, with the development of the turbo-jet engine from 1946 onwards, we faced a new problem – that of designing an aircraft that could make the fullest use of the greater engine power now available.

I enjoyed Tangmere enormously, not least because Gwen had been living nearby. When she had to leave, I realised that I felt lonely and lost. Meanwhile, after Tangmere there was the second half of the ETPS course to complete at Cranfield. The day I passed the course to receive the school's diploma was one of particular pride. Of particular pride, too, was the news which I broke to my parents at Christmas 1946 that Gwen and I had decided to marry.

After Cranfield, I was posted to the Aeroplane and Armament Experimental Establishment at Boscombe Down. I went to the Fighter Test Squadron where the experience I'd gained with the High Speed Flight at Tangmere proved most useful. I conducted research work with Meteor aircraft at high Mach numbers and high altitude. Some of these tests required straight stalls, stalls in turns or under high 'g' loads up to the highest possible altitude. The tests eventually gave us a complete picture of an aircraft's manoeuvrability, speed and handling characteristics up to its maximum height ceiling.

As the months went by I realised that experimental test flying interested me more than any other type of peacetime flying. One day, while I was driving back to Gwen at our home at Bray in Berkshire, I took a short cut over Salisbury Plain. I pulled up and parked by the side of the road and just sat there admiring the broad expanse of countryside – green, attractive, bathed in light, the sky mottled with cumulus cloud. I thought about many things, about how I liked air force life, the comradeship, the service flying but now, having tasted the greater freedom to be found working with a civilian firm, I felt the need to seek broader horizons. I was attracted by the idea of helping to develop the new and interesting types of aircraft coming along in the next few years. As I sat there in the car mulling things over, I resolved to speak to the air commodore in charge at Boscombe Down. I would tell him of my decision to leave the service.

When I broke the news, the air commodore was silent for a few moments before he said: "Well, Neville, I'm sorry – for personal reasons – to think that you'll be leaving the air force. But if that's what you want to do, well I wish you all the best of luck."

*

I left the Royal Air Force in June 1948. Two months later, when I arrived at Hawkers to begin a civilian career, the experience was at once novel and something of a return home: most of the people I'd known two-and-a-half years ago were still with the firm. We worked on the Hawker Fury, the Hawker Tempest and the new jet P1040, a single-seat fighter intended for the Royal Air Force (although the machine would end up with the Royal Navy as the Hawker Sea Hawk.)

After the first few weeks of initial excitement and fresh interest, I realised that my adjustment to civilian life would take a little time. I went through a period of mental reaction and a sense of regret that I'd left the air force. In truth, I became rather restless, a phase that ended, however, when I bought a Hawker Tomtit aircraft which I entered in several air shows to entertain the crowds with mock dogfights against a Tiger Moth. It was all good fun but eventually the Tiger Moth was sold and I found a new challenge as a member of the Royal Auxiliary Air Force. I learned that the commanding officer of 615 (County of Surrey) Squadron was leaving and he suggested that it might be possible for me to succeed him.

So it was that, in September 1950, I took over 615 Squadron whose honorary air commodore was none other than Sir Winston Churchill who maintained a close interest in the squadron's work and activities. One time I was invited together with the squadron adjutant to lunch at Chartwell where our honorary air commodore soon put us at ease with his friendliness and his good humour. When talking on a serious subject, Churchill would look grim and forbidding, but his face would light up with an almost cherubic expression when an amusing thought struck him. He told us about some of his experiences of aviation in the First World War, including a narrow escape when he was flying with Major Scott who'd had to carry out a forced-landing. After the landing, both men were covered in petrol and Major Scott was badly injured, nonetheless he managed to turn off the engine switches to reduce the risk of fire.

Churchill seemed to take great interest in the trends of future development and he showed an understanding of current progress in aviation. We discussed how, in certain respects, the P1040 was an unorthodox aircraft for the period as it had straight wings, a straight tail and a normal fin. He was interested to hear of our experiments at Hawkers with a rocket motor in the P1040 and he asked me to write him a short report with my views on rocket propulsion.

There was no doubt in my mind that the P1040 was a beautiful aeroplane to fly. When the Royal Navy took it over, the project became known as the N7/46 and

The red Hunter WB188 in which Neville Duke set the world speed record for a closed circuit, in September 1953.

was converted for deck landings with the addition of a tail hook, folding wings and other nautical refinements. After the P1040 came the P1052 with a number of important changes in design. Two of these aircraft were built for research purposes with thirty-five degree swept-back wings – the first used by Hawkers – and much the same engine layout as the P1040. Eventually, one of the P1052's was converted into the P1081, fully swept-back on all surfaces and with a different engine layout.

I flew the P1081 on developmental work for a period while Hawker's chief test pilot, Wimpy Wade, was in the United States to gain experience on American jet aircraft. Shortly after his return from the States, Wade flew over to Farnborough to check on progress with the P1081 project. We never knew what happened, but he was killed when his aircraft crashed at Lewes in Sussex (he'd baled out using his ejector seat from which he did not release himself). Together with the secretary to Hawkers, I broke the news of the tragedy to Josephine, Wimpy Wade's wife. It was a poignant moment, made doubly sad when one of their three children, Michael, died quite suddenly a short time later.

In the middle of April 1951 I was appointed to succeed Wade as the chief test pilot of Hawker Aircraft Limited. I regarded this as a great honour though any pride or pleasure in the appointment was marred by the shock of the accident.

With the pressure of work as chief test pilot, I found it impossible to be responsible for all of the flying at Hawkers as well as continue my commitment as commanding officer of 615 Squadron. With regret, therefore, I resigned my post with 615 Squadron.

Meantime, the flight test programme at Hawkers proceeded apace. Towards the end of 1949 the wooden mock-up stage of the Hunter (known then as the P1067) had been reached and construction of this aircraft had proceeded throughout 1950. By the spring of the following year the aeroplane began to take a very definite shape. As the weeks went by and the final jobs were started, such as wing and fuselage skinning, wiring, control system functioning, engine installation and fuel system tests, everybody began to get a little tense.

At last the day came when the Hunter was moved by road from Kingston to Boscombe Down where the long runway of some 3,000 yards was useful for taxi trials and initial flights. For about three weeks in June 1951 engineers spent long hours running the Rolls-Royce Avon engine for prolonged periods to check that the airframe structure around the jet pipe received sufficient cooling. Finally, the Hunter was ready for taxi trials. The aircraft was parked by a hangar and looked such a beautiful machine as I walked towards it. Painted a pale duck-egg with RAF roundels on the wings and fuselage, the swept wings and graceful sweep to the tail were especially pleasing to the eye.

I climbed up the metal ladder, settled myself into the cockpit, started the engine then commenced the first taxiing at slow speeds along the runway. After a series of pre-programmed tests, I opened the throttle a little more and began to move the aeroplane faster along the runway as I checked for signs of shimmy or snatching of the brakes. From the first I felt at home in the Hunter. As, gradually, I worked up towards the fast runs, I noted on my speech recorder the speed at which the nose wheel came off the ground and the speed at which the elevators and the rudder became effective.

At length the time came to try a short 'hop' to check the 'unstick' speed and the trimmer setting, and to gain a feel of the flight controls. The Hunter hopped satisfactorily and I was happy with the flight controls but after touchdown the end of the runway appeared to loom up rather swiftly. The Avon engine's idling thrust was far more powerful than anything I'd handled before and the Hunter continued to move more rapidly than I intended. I braked as hard as I could and just managed to slew the aircraft onto the airfield perimeter track, but by that time a fire engine had started to chase after me as the brakes were emitting clouds of bluish smoke. The engineers discovered later that the brakes had burnt right out.

After a few more taxi trials, the Hunter was ready for its first flight. I went daily to Boscombe Down from Langley expecting to take off but the experimental team were taking no chances: some three years' hard work had gone into the Hunter, the machine represented an enormous amount of effort and investment, and the engineers were determined to ensure that everything was as fully prepared as possible. There always seemed to be some detail that had to be fixed. At last, though, one day in July 1951, we were told that the machine was ready. Together with a number of senior members from Hawkers I flew from Langley in a de Havilland Rapide. We landed at Boscombe Down to be told, however, that there was still some work to be done on the Hunter. Disappointed with this news, I drove with a party of others into Amesbury for some tea while we waited. I had, however, little appetite for tea. My thoughts were with the Hunter and its maiden flight; I'd never before taken up a prototype on its first flight.

After the tea party, we returned to Boscombe to learn that the Hunter wouldn't be ready until evening. As the day dragged on, there seemed to be hundreds of people milling about, all of them keen to chat about this and that. I wished there weren't so many; I had no desire to chatter so much; I'd have preferred to fly the aircraft without anybody standing around. Finally, my heart must have missed a beat when I heard the words: "Ready for you now, Mr Duke."

Observers stopped talking as I walked out to the aircraft. I tried to look nonchalant but I couldn't help an air of self-consciousness; everyone stared at me as if I was a stage performer at the theatre. I glanced up at the sky and noted a bit of cloud at around 15,000 feet, otherwise it was a nice clear evening. Before long I was ready to climb up the Hunter's cockpit access ladder. While I settled myself into the cockpit and went through the pre-start checks, I seemed to forget about outside distractions. Soon, having started the Rolls-Royce Avon engine, I was ready to taxi out. As I moved towards the take-off point, I noticed a number of cars parked on either side of the runway, about halfway down. Now near the take-off point, I spoke to air traffic control. "Hawker Baker," replied the controller, "you're clear to line up and take off."

At the take-off point, I applied the Hunter's brakes and advanced the Avon's throttle. Simultaneously, I checked the engine revolution and jet pipe temperature gauges. I noticed quite a whine from the engine and the brakes began to slip as the aircraft, like an Olympic sprinter waiting for the starter gun, leaned forward eagerly. I made a last check of cockpit instruments, then released the aircraft brakes and pushed the throttle fully forward.

I was astonished by the Hunter's rate of acceleration – far greater than anything I'd known in the past. I used my speech recorder to chronicle every detail as the aeroplane sped along the runway. Within moments the Hunter was airborne and my senses were alert to the slightest fault; I was part of the aircraft in feel, sound, sight and smell. In case of significant trim changes, I delayed operation of the undercarriage until 500 feet at which point, as I raised the wheels, everything appeared to be absolutely fine. In fact, the aircraft handled beautifully while I climbed up through 5,000 feet, 10,000 feet, 15,000 feet. Soon, as the Hunter approached 20,000 feet, I initiated level off. With a sudden sense of exhilaration, my earlier tension began to ease. I turned back towards Boscombe to keep the airfield in sight while I went through pre-planned tasks. These included a simulated approach and landing when I noted every particular as I lowered the wheels and flaps, eased back the throttle and re-trimmed.

The hour or so I spent at high altitude seemed to go by remarkably quickly; in what felt like no time at all I had to call Boscombe for clearance to return. "Hawker Baker," said the controller, "you're clear to join for runway two-four."

At Boscombe I carried out a wide, gentle circuit in preparation for a long, smooth approach. I kept my airspeed deliberately on the high side aware that, with Boscombe's length of runway, there was no reason to fly too close to the Hunter's stall speed. At the touchdown point, I eased back the stick judiciously, closed the throttle and felt a slight rumble as the wheels made contact with the runway surface. The Hawker Hunter's maiden flight was over; an hour or so of airborne time had assuredly – magnificently – justified the seemingly endless hours of meticulous preparation.

As I taxied back to the hangars, I opened the cockpit hood to relish the rush of cool air. Numbers of cars now drove towards the Hunter's allocated parking spot and I noticed crowds of onlookers assembled there; all of them stood and stared as I brought the Hunter to a stop. When I applied the parking brake and closed down the engine, nobody appeared to say a word. I removed my flying helmet, stood up in the cockpit, and climbed down the access ladder. Everyone, it appeared, was waiting for me to say something, so I announced: "Jolly good!"

At this, a great hubbub erupted when all and sundry began to talk at once. I was asked many questions; excited chatter replaced anxious silence; smiling faces and relieved expressions substituted worried looks. A little overwhelmed by such a spontaneous and enthusiastic reaction I realised, nonetheless, that this was indeed a seminal moment.

*

Suddenly any opportunities for recollections were thrust aside when the sound of Farnborough's emergency vehicles startled me back to the present. As if rooted to the spot, I stood and gazed in helpless horror at the scene unfolding before my eyes. When the DH110 had turned back towards the airfield in a moderate turn, the machine had blown to bits. The outer section of starboard wing, followed immediately by the outer section of port wing, had broken off the aircraft. The cockpit and two engines had flown through the air and landed some distance from where I was standing. Many people on the ground lay killed and injured; the pilot, John Derry, and his observer Tony Richards had both been killed. There was nothing I could do but continue to stand there in a state of shock while the emergency services carried out necessary duties.

Standing nearby were a number of colleagues who I joined to discuss what could have caused the DH110 to split to pieces in such a way. Later, we discovered that the root cause of the accident was faulty design of the wing leading edge. At the time, though, the situation felt wholly surreal, especially as I had to decide whether to continue with my scheduled display of the Hunter which included supersonic flight above Farnborough. I was fairly clear in my own mind that the DH110 accident had not necessarily been caused by supersonic flight. I realised then that I had to stop thinking about my lost colleagues and concentrate instead on the Hunter display.

Before long, I was focussed on cockpit and other checks as I climbed into the Hunter and went through the engine start drills. When I called air traffic control for clearance to taxi, the controller said there'd be a bit of a delay while wreckage from the DH110 was removed from the runway. Eventually he said: "Please keep to the right-hand side of the runway on take-off and mind the wreckage." I had no difficulty with this and soon I had taken off and was in the climb as I mentally rehearsed my display routine. In order to allow time to climb up to 40,000 feet or so and to position for the supersonic dive on Farnborough, I always planned to take off about ten minutes before the display was due to start.

It was a lovely day for flying and at an altitude of 43,000 feet over Odiham I could see Farnborough airfield clearly. As I sat in my Hunter up there at such a great height the cockpit was quiet and warm; everything was in first-class order. I pondered the lonely environment around me, the brilliance of the scattered clouds below, the darkening canopy of the stratosphere above. It would be untrue to say that I was not disturbed by John Derry's death and worried about the implications; I reflected that so little was known about supersonic flight and that, maybe, it could have had something to do with the accident.

By now, though, the moment for action had come: it was time to commence a dive. I lowered the aircraft's nose and in the clear ambient conditions I had no difficulty while I aimed at Farnborough airfield. I monitored the airspeed indicator judiciously and as the aeroplane passed through the sound barrier, the Hunter behaved perfectly. On the ground at Farnborough, the supersonic bangs were heard by the assembled crowds whose eyes turned skywards when I flew over the airfield for the rest of my flying display.

When I landed I could see that ambulances were still in the area where the DH110 had broken up. I thought about my wife Gwen and about John Derry's wife Eve. I was greatly moved to learn later that Eve Derry had insisted on remaining at Farnborough to watch my display. I felt that she had shown tremendous courage. Gwen had not been at Farnborough that day but when she read newspaper headlines that an unnamed test pilot had been killed she rang the control tower at Farnborough to be told that I had just landed safely after my display.

It was later, too, that I was touched to receive various letters and notes, one of which was from Prime Minister Sir Winston Churchill. 'My dear Duke,' he wrote. 'It was characteristic of you, and of 615 Squadron, to go up yesterday after the shocking accident. Accept my salute.'

Perhaps, looking back, in the accumulation of detail about some of my experiences, the reader will conclude that my association with flying and with the world of aviation has been a deeply moving one. I have been given enjoyment as well as sadness. Test flying, like wartime flying, has its moments of danger, of apprehension, when skill, knowledge and experience can be the airman's only ally. The noise and bustle that must go, inevitably, with a test pilot's life should leave an echo audible to those who take the trouble to listen. If Homer's words – 'for wreaking havoc upon a strong man, even the very strongest, there is nothing so dire as the sea' – were to be modified to replace the realm of the sea with that of the air, then few should argue that this modernised version would seem more than a little appropriate.

Author's Note
Sincere thanks to Grub Street Publishing and Mrs Gwen Duke for allowing me to use the book *Test Pilot*, first published in 1953, as the basis for this chapter.

CHAPTER 10

GIBRALTAR GOINGS-ON

TIM THORN'S RACE AGAINST THE ODDS

A certain look crossed the wing commander's face. His expression seemed to emphasise that he knew well enough that I understood the tenuous nature of our presence here in Gibraltar, that small but significant landmass which covered just under three square miles on the southern tip of the Iberian peninsula. He maintained an awkward silence for some moments but his muteness nevertheless spoke volumes. And I had to admit that my actions had hardly helped to ease Gibraltar's lot in the contentious matter of Anglo-Spanish relations. His steady look was intended to remind me, no doubt, of the background situation – of the consequences of the referendum held five years ago in 1967 when Gibraltarians had rejected proposals for Spanish sovereignty. Gibraltar would continue to govern its own affairs, although the United Kingdom would retain responsibility for areas such as defence. Though unspoken, thoughts along these lines, as well, I suspected, as notions of mature conduct were disagreeably disseminated by the senior officer's intense, solemn expression.

"Well, Flight Lieutenant Thorn?" he said at length. "What have you got to say for yourself?"

"All I can say, sir, is that I'm sorry." I tried to adopt a look of woe.

"You are sorry?"

"Yes," I tried to look even more woeful, "sir."

"Is that the best you can do?"

"I'm really *very* sorry," I said but my state of virtuous woefulness had reached its limit and I was not the grovelling, hand-wringing type. The wing commander stared at me with disapproval; the tense silence resumed. I longed for him to adopt an air of forgive and forget, but I knew this was optimistic. Clearly he was in no mood for vapid chat or attempts to dispense gnomic with a serene, goofy smile. A bit like prodding a hippopotamus with a pin, I knew that further efforts or exhortations were unlikely to be productive.

In the ensuing hush, therefore, I could do little else but reflect on the unplanned, unfortunate – if intriguing – sequence of events that had led me to this moment. I was conscious, of course, of the truism that on the whole fighter pilots were only human, albeit in a very highly evolved form. So it was that, if I had transgressed when off-duty, I was confident that my on-duty performance had not been affected.

It was in mid-February 1972 that I'd been sent to Gibraltar, along with two other Hunter pilots, for a period of some three weeks. Detached from our base at RAF Chivenor in Devonshire, our job was to challenge any incursion of Gibraltar's airspace by the Spanish. In rotation with my colleagues, I would man one of two Hawker Hunters (plus a spare as back-up) held at a high state of readiness. These aircraft were fitted with fully operational gun packs for the aircraft's four 30mm Aden cannon with 150 rounds of ammunition per gun.

Much of our time was spent on duty, however when not on duty there were opportunities to explore Gibraltar and its unusual past. An inevitable focus was the Rock of Gibraltar which, at nearly 1,500 feet high, dominated the area. Hidden within the Rock were numerous tunnelled roads most of which were operated by the military and closed to the general public. I learnt how, in World War 2, General Dwight D Eisenhower had set up his headquarters in Gibraltar during the planning phases of Operation Torch, the Allied invasion of French North Africa. Within Gibraltar's 'underground city', masses of rock had been blasted out to form huge man-made caverns, barracks, offices, even a fully-equipped hospital complete with an operating theatre and X-ray equipment. As an interesting aside, I learned that Eisenhower had not fired a shot in anger at that stage in his military career. Later in the war he apparently fired at a rat in the bathroom of his Italian headquarters, but missed.

Above this underground complex, when I scrambled over the rugged terrain of The Rock I would watch the semi-wild Barbary Macaque monkeys (commonly and erroneously called apes) that inhabited the area, along with over 500 different species of wild flowering plants. It was said that if the monkeys ever left Gibraltar, so would the British. In the streets below, sidewalks, gutters, houses, grey concrete buildings and shops teemed with people who jostled, shouted, bargained, and

Tim Thorn at low level in a Hunter FR10.

cursed in the crowded space. There was a rare, pungent smell, at once sweet, salty, and bitter. It was the start of spring and on a cloudless day temperatures would soar as the sun bore down.

I'd been in Gibraltar for nearly two weeks when, in early March 1972, I was ordered to scramble in a Hunter and fly due east over the Mediterranean Sea. A Russian ship, the *Leningrad,* had been under NATO surveillance but the tracking system had lost contact. I was tasked to find the ship urgently, take photographs, and report the vessel's position along with other factors.

As I took off and headed in the required easterly direction, local visibility was poor. I decided, therefore, to remain at very low level while I flew above the grey surface of the sea. The conditions, inclined to induce a sense of disorientation, meant that a glance directly downwards could trigger an impression of falling. The smallest miscalculation would lead to – splash! – and I'd hit the water. As the sea rushed by at a speed of some 400 knots I tried to look well ahead but the poor visibility constrained normal techniques. It was fatiguing to fly in such conditions but by this stage in my career I was a reasonably experienced fighter pilot and my training paid dividends.

After approximately forty minutes on a steady easterly heading, a large ship began to loom out of the mists. At once, I reduced airspeed and positioned the Hunter for 'dummy' attacks against the vessel. Before long, as I carried out manoeuvres, I was able to confirm that the ship was indeed the *Leningrad*. I felt a fine sense of satisfaction at having located the vessel in such tricky conditions. During the dummy attacks I took photographs of the 189-metre long, conventionally-powered ship capable of speeds of up to thirty-one knots. I noted markings, flags, vessel heading and other details of this modern ship (I learned later that she was on her maiden sailing) designed as a helicopter carrier and intended primarily for use in the anti-submarine role. I was aware that the *Leningrad's* ship-borne armament included the possibility of delivering a 'small' nuclear warhead of five kilotons (by comparison, the Fat Man bomb dropped by USAF Major Charles Sweeney and his crew over Nagasaki, Japan in 1945 was a little over twenty kilotons). The ship's strategic role, to defend the Soviet ballistic missile submarines against incursions by Western attack submarines, meant that knowledge of the *Leningrad's* position was key information for NATO planners. My task to re-locate the vessel had been necessary and effective.

It was perhaps natural, therefore, that some form of celebration should take place after such a successful flight. So it was that, together with my fellow Hunter pilots, the three of us left the officers' mess after supper to head downtown to sample Gibraltar's bars and nightclubs. The drinks flowed, our spirits stormed, our stamina was tested. My memory may have become a little hazy, even so I could recall curious snatches of minor events. In one establishment, as I glanced around the room, a young woman smiled coyly while she held her not-so-youthful admirer's hand. At a separate table, occupied by a group of young women, one of them suddenly caught sight of me observing her. Another of the girls had a look of concentration as she applied lipstick to her lips. Her friend used a small mirror to check her hair. All of the girls wore shiny dresses, blue baubled or luminous green or glossy gold.

I leant forward to draw lines with my finger across the dew of my cold beer glass. The room was warm and airless. A girl, her eyes full of worldliness, walked up to the bar. "More beer?" one of our group asked. The invitation, if directed towards the girl, appeared to backfire. While the Hunter pilots nodded assent she merely looked pained, as if we had just earned ourselves a well-deserved international prize for philistinism. She strolled away from the bar while our Hunter contingent, with the hour now well past midnight, debated what to do next. We decided to finish our drinks and move on.

When we wandered outside, now struck by a distinct chill in the air, we tried to hail a taxi. No taxis, however, were available; we'd have to walk back to the officers' mess. Before long, while we three highly trained experts in the art of fighter reconnaissance followed the line of Gibraltar's Winston Churchill Avenue, we drew near to the airfield area where we'd have to be wary of night sentries. We attempted to stride confidently past the airmen's billets and married quarters, but occasionally found ourselves walking on the balls of our feet if we sensed trouble.

At one point, through the rawness of the night, I heard the sound of voices. We could not stop or hide or turn around, that would have been ridiculous. We had to persist, to brazen it out if challenged. I felt a needle of anxiety when we spotted some far-off figures but they disappeared in a different direction. Suddenly, beyond the area of the married quarters we spotted a 'JCB' digger beside the road. Excited by our discovery, we hastened to the machine. "Our taxi's turned up at last," I said.

"How do we start the thing up?"

"Should be no problem for someone with your talent and training," I said sniffily. This must have sounded like a challenge for the protagonist now began to rummage around the machine's innards. Meanwhile, the distant bark of dogs, the clatter of airfield activity, added to our already-heightened sense of tension. It did not take long, though, before the promising sound of an engine starter mechanism was followed by the roar of the engine itself springing into life. "Bingo!" said our tame 'expert'.

Quickly, the three of us jumped aboard the JCB as our driver, with engine revving, set off down a narrow road, in places less than open and accessible. There were concealments along the way, mysterious dark places as we weaved uncertainly this way and that. The machine, it seemed, was harder to control than a Hawker Hunter. Ahead we spotted a parked car that blocked our route. "Hold very tight please!" cried the driver. I thought he'd ask for our tickets next but such detail suddenly became secondary as the driver tried to negotiate his way past the car. The JCB wobbled, we gasped, the front wheels went into a ditch, the machine turned over onto its side. All three of us were thrown clear, fortunately without injury.

Our situation now assumed a whole new dynamic. We stood up, brushed ourselves down, then made ready to run or hide. I opted for the former. As I sprinted off towards the beach it was necessary to clamber through a number of gardens. Soon, though, I ended up at a beach but on looking back for the others, realised that they had not followed...I was on my own – abandoned, isolated. Somewhat disconsolately, therefore, I started to walk along the lonely sands and my thoughts began to churn trying to figure out the best course of action. It was not long before the decision was made for me. When the line of Gibraltar's east-west runway loomed, it was evident that the speediest way back to the officers' mess was to dash directly across the runway. Now I remembered that I was very suntanned which should provide good camouflage from the prying eyes of night sentries. I consequently removed all of my clothing with the exception of underpants, bundled the entire attire under my arm and set off quite slowly across the runway.

The mind can play tricks at times like this. I glanced up at the sky where the stars seemed to flicker semaphores of warning. I shivered in the night air for it was cold with no clothing. Ahead, rows of buildings and hangars with drab windows appeared to hide faces with disapproving eyes. In the distance, searchlights played back and forth in haphazard fashion but not in my direction. I must have been about halfway across the runway when a voice began to yell. "Stop!" it commanded, "who goes there?" My eyes darted here and there like a startled rabbit. I sensed a curious, semi-absent feeling. With a ferocity that trapped the breath in the chest, my mind began to race. "Stop!" shrieked the voice again. "Stop, or I will release the dog."

I heard the dog's bark and promptly realised that this was no idle threat. In an instant, I decided, as a fit rugby player who surely could outrun any dog, to break into a sprint. I commenced a diagonal rush across the runway in as direct a beeline as possible towards the officers' mess. However, it was at this point that my luck seemed to be scattered to the four winds. Sirens suddenly began to wail. Searchlights came on and started to sweep methodically from side to side, up and down along the runway and adjacent areas. I heard men being scrambled from their accommodation. Car doors slammed; vehicles were revved up; and the dog – damn the thing – was proving faster than anticipated. I dared not look back but sensed that the beast was gaining on me. The conundrum became more acute. I disliked the thought of the roughness of the Alsatian's tongue, the creature's capabilities, and began to suspect it of a string of fearful acts.

By now the officers' mess front door was within striking distance. With some 200 yards or so to go and with my heart pounding, I accelerated the pace. The dog, though, continued to gain ground. It was as if I'd been caught in some horror movie with the scene about to be played out in slow motion. At any moment a stable clock would chime; the small night hour would be struck; some repressed Gothic fiend would rise up, its dwarfish face red, its glaring eyes compact and mean. Suddenly, though, I had to leap over a low-ish hedge near the front of the officers' mess. I was a fraction of a second ahead of the Alsatian which, in its enthusiasm, soared past me, the creature's anguished yelps all too apparent. This slight delay allowed me just sufficient time to lunge at the front door, grab it open then slam it shut behind me. The dog, meanwhile, picked itself up, careered towards the front door and, apoplectic with rage, commenced to prance up and down and hurl itself against the door.

A peep through one of the door's windowpanes revealed more bad news. I spotted two military policemen as they ran down a path towards the officers' mess. To one side of the path, a Land Rover vehicle sped up, skidded to a halt and army personnel leapt out. I therefore turned round and headed as rapidly as possible for a nearby staircase, a peculiar, curving concrete structure. Two steps at a time, I scurried up the stairs, nodding a brief 'hello' to a shocked Gibraltarian member of the mess staff as we passed each other. At the top of the stairs a glance down showed the two policemen, their Alsatian in tow, conversing with the member of mess staff. The latter was pointing upwards in my direction. I looked behind me. A long corridor stretched ahead with a window at the far end. Once more, I broke into a run and dashed towards the window. I planned to climb outside and down a drainpipe to safety. Regretfully, however, when I reached the window, a quick check revealed no drainpipe.

Now, from the direction of the peculiar curving staircase, there was further kerfuffle as policemen, Alsatian, army personnel and mess staff raced upstairs. I turned around again, fumbled hurriedly with a couple of bedroom door handles until – hey presto! – one of the doors opened. I jumped inside the room, banged the door shut behind me and locked it. Then I climbed inside the room's wardrobe, pulled the door closed, and waited.

There was not long to wait. The racket of the dog scraping its paws at the bedroom door was accompanied by the animal's angry barks. I tried to breathe quietly but the effort made me gasp for air. I began to perspire profusely. There were muttered comments, clatters and ominous noises. Suddenly there was a loud bang as the bedroom door was forced open. I heard the dog rush towards my wardrobe before the creature began to paw persistently at the door. "Whoever you are in that cupboard," said a voice, "come out now with your hands on your head."

I decided that an innocent appeal for sympathy might be the best approach. I therefore opened the door and presented myself, still naked apart from the underpants, to policemen, mess staff, Alsatian and all. The assembled personnel stared as if they had seen a ghost. Sensing that it would be impolite not to make some comment, I said: "Good evening, gentlemen." I beamed. "I'm your friendly bank manager." I paused. "Can I be of any assistance?"

My subsequent arrest led to a two-hour spell in the police station before I was released and driven back to the officers' mess. In the mess, I fell exhausted into a sleep too deep for comfort. Nightmares raged as motley, raucous – indeed as feisty a bunch of out-of-control fighter pilots as could be imagined – hurtled through my dreams. I woke up early with a headache, at once confused by thoughts about the unsteady course between virtue and sin. Compelled, though, to face the multiple miseries created by the night before, the midnight manoeuvres now seemed too incredible to contemplate. A hasty glance in the mirror was not encouraging. 'You're not yourself,' I reckoned, 'it's over, it's a mistake and it's too bloody difficult.' The inevitable storm of protest, however, had to be faced. The invitation to present myself to the wing commander in his office at 0830 hours was not negotiable. This, I knew, would be no docile departmental meeting.

"I'm really *very* sorry, sir," I said at the meeting, a comment that was met with a wall of silence.

At length, the wing commander spoke. "Your generation…" there appeared to be a touch of venom in his voice but, just as he was about to deliver a lecture, he seemed to change his mind. "You see that Hercules aircraft out there?" he pointed.

"Yes."

"Well, Thorn, consider yourself a passenger on it for your return home."

I saluted, turned around, and left the wing commander's office. The interview, I realised later, had lasted no longer than two minutes.

CHAPTER 11

WAR DIARY

A HUNTER PILOT'S EXPERIENCES IN THE INDO-PAKISTANI WAR OF 1971

The statistics paint a bizarre and terrible picture. The 1971 Indo-Pakistani conflict lasted for just thirteen days yet in the preliminaries and in the wake of war, millions of civilians were killed, genocide and other atrocities were on a scale almost too vast to comprehend and people in their millions fled from Bangladesh to India.

The circumstances that led to this catastrophe were complex and were caused, at root, by the deep divisions between the traditionally dominant West Pakistanis and the majority East Pakistanis. Trouble escalated after elections in 1970, then in early 1971 the Pakistani army initiated mass arrests of dissidents, conducted acts of ethnic cleansing against the Bengali population of East Pakistan aimed particularly at the minority Hindus, and attempted to disarm East Pakistani soldiers and police. As the situation worsened, in March 1971 Bengali political and military leaders declared the independence of Bangladesh. The East Pakistan-Indian border was opened for refugees who sought safe shelter in India and the consequent flood of millions of impoverished East Pakistanis began to place intolerable strains on India's already overburdened economy. India's leader, Prime Minister Indira Gandhi, who had expressed her government's support for the independence struggle of the people of East Pakistan, began to realise that armed action against Pakistan would be more effective than continuing to accept endless lines of refugees.

Meanwhile, the mood in West Pakistan grew increasingly jingoistic and antagonistic against East Pakistan and India. An organised propaganda campaign resulted in stickers – 'CRUSH INDIA' – appearing on cars and elsewhere across West Pakistan. In November 1971 thousands of people led by West Pakistani politicians marched through Lahore and elsewhere to demand that Pakistan 'crush India'. India responded with a build-up of military forces in border areas. Within the refugee camps, exiled East Pakistani army officers and members of Indian military intelligence started to recruit and train Mukti Bahini guerrillas.

On 23rd November 1971 President Khan of Pakistan declared a state of emergency and warned his people to prepare for war. Then, on Sunday 3rd December 1971, in a series of late afternoon pre-emptive strikes, the Pakistan Air Force attacked eleven Indian air bases. That evening, Prime Minister Gandhi made a radio broadcast in which she held that the Pakistani air strikes were a declaration of war against India. That same night, the Indian Air Force responded with initial air strikes which expanded to larger retaliatory action the next morning and for the rest of the war.

Below are extracts from a diary kept during the conflict by a Hunter pilot, Flight Lieutenant H K Singh, of the Indian Air Force 7 Squadron (nickname: The Battleaxes – motto: *Vanquish the enemy*).

DAY ONE

The commanding officer came to our rooms with the news that the 'balloon had gone up' and so we were 'on' in the morning. Briefing would be at 5am. He told us that he'd be at the bar to ensure that nobody had more than three drinks and the bar would close on time. It went through my mind that some of us may not be there the next evening but I quickly banished the thought.

At the briefing an army major gave details of the FLOT (forward line of own troops) position; we would only engage targets beyond that. One senior guy, to our dismay, questioned the major's brief by quoting the BBC news thereby betraying his anxiety while others put on brave faces.

After the briefing we checked that all Indian tags on clothes etc were removed. We were issued with a revolver and twelve rounds each, a Bangladeshi flag to be shown to the Mukti Bahini if shot down, and a money belt with 200 Paki rupees.

I flew two missions on that first day; a life changing experience. My anxiety seemed to vanish when the Hunter's engine roared to life. The best part was firing a long burst at the air traffic control tower at Lal Minir Hat airfield in the north of Bangladesh. As the control tower's glass shattered, the boss shouted on the aircraft radio: "good burst laddie!" It felt like throwing a glass against a wall in the bar.

That day we lost two Hunters and one pilot: Flight Lieutenant Andre Da Costa. Squadron Leader Gupti, whose Hunter's hydraulics had been shot up, ejected safely at 10,000 feet over the airfield, although he suffered injury. In the evening we brought Mrs Sandra Da Costa and her children to the mess and clumsily tried to give them hope. However, her husband's body was never found in the marshy area where he went down.

Someone put the Pak news on a transistor radio and the announcer said that Pak troops had reached Siliguri in the Himalayan foothills not far from the border with Nepal.

DAY TWO

The second day started early too. I was to continue in the same formation led by the boss, Wing Commander Bunny Coelho. Our targets were ferries and bridges. Later, we learned that the few pilots left in the Pakistani Air Force had fled to West Pakistan via Burma so we faced no credible air power resistance.

When I fired a three to four-second burst against a train nothing happened for a second or so then the bogie suddenly flew off the rails. We swung around for a second pass which drew heavy small-arms fire, some bullet holes appeared under my wing but nothing critical.

An unforgettable sight was the mass of people who scrambled for cover if by chance we flew over a refugee camp (there were many near the border). To see the throngs of humanity trying to outrun a fighter aircraft told its own story. Maybe these hapless people associated the sound and sight of a screaming jet with imminent death but we would waggle the Hunters' wings to show our friendly status.

When strapping-in before flight I would leave my jacket with the airman who was helping me and say that I'd be back to claim it. This became a sort of ritual and the return of the jacket after a mission would be accompanied by claps and cheers.

That evening when I thought about my attack on the train I realised that some people may have been killed. Then I recalled the many flashes from the ground near the target and told myself that those flashes were real anti-aircraft fire. It was a case of one trying to get the other. Better to thank your lucky stars for being alive today, for tomorrow will be another round in this deadly game played by both sides for the honour and freedom of their countries. At least, that was what most of us felt.

We were told to pack our bags as the squadron would move to the western sector tomorrow.

The squadron did not lose any pilots or aircraft on this day.

DAY THREE

We ferried all available Hunters to Kanpur then to Hindon airbase on the outskirts of Delhi. Someone's brother came in from Delhi and drove a few of us to have a meal in the Moti Mahal restaurant. The drive was in blackout conditions. Still clad in our flying gear, the restaurant owners refused to bill us and with folded hands offered the Punjabi blessing *Jinde Raho* (may you live long).

DAY FOUR

Orders were received for us to proceed to the forward airbase at Bikaner, co-located with Nal airport. When we reached there by early afternoon, it turned out to be a pretty desolate place in the Rajasthan desert. A Mystère squadron was already operating there and the airfield had been bombed a few times recently. Our Hunters were parked in blast pens. Some of us were dispersed to the officers' mess in town while others stayed on base. The town group was given a requisitioned taxi driven by a local civilian named Jetharam. I wondered about his security clearance.

DAY FIVE

Jetharam drove me in early for briefing at base ops. No targets were allocated first thing but later in the morning two search and destroy missions were ordered: "Look for enemy tanks on the other side of the national border." These missions, though, had nothing worthwhile to report but secondary targets were engaged. It was the same for all missions flown that day, including one flown by me. At dusk an air defence combat air patrol was mounted.

DAY SIX

Our squadron boss was shot down this day. Early missions were 'search and destroy' but low-level navigation was difficult over the desert especially when weaving all the time for tactical reasons. Later we decided to change our tactics to operate at around 5,000 feet. This exposed us to enemy radar but we were keen to engage enemy fighters; all of us had practised plenty of dogfighting in the run up to this war. However, no enemy fighters appeared.

When he and his wingman were engaging a bridge with T-10 rockets, our boss was shot down. He was seen to eject from a burning Hunter by his wingman. Apparently he ejected very close to the India/Pakistan border but enemy troops got to him first and he was taken prisoner. When he was returned eighteen months later, he described how, after his capture, there was a heated argument amongst his captors: some wanted to kill him there and then to avenge the death of colleagues lost during the attacks; others wanted to hand him over to their superiors and claim a reward. Luckily for him, the latter prevailed. In the prisoner-of-war camp some of the Pakistani pilots' wives came to ogle at the Indian prisoners. One of our guys asked them loudly: "What do you expect to see? Monkeys? You should have brought peanuts to throw at us." The wives were embarrassed and left hurriedly.

I flew two useless missions today. I fired rockets on a factory-type structure and a power station, in both cases on the way back to base.

As squadron adjutant, I've had to deal with accommodation and catering problems. We've detailed some of the non-operational trades to handle the cooking while I try to get local help.

Yet another day behind me and a further one looming in this deadly scenario living from day to day.

DAY SEVEN

We got a new CO today, Wing Commander N C Suri, a very experienced Hunter jock. I'm to be his designated wingman. I flew one sortie today as leader of a tactical reconnaissance mission near the town of Bahawalpur in enemy territory. At one point, having spotted dust kicked up by vehicle movement, I manoeuvred for attack. In the dive, with the gun safety catch unlocked, my finger was ready to squeeze the trigger when I saw that the target was a black car. I held fire, made a low pass and told my wingman to do the same. Usually, vehicles would stop immediately at the sound of a jet aircraft but this one just kept going. I made another dive but could not get myself to open fire. A one-second burst would have blown the car to smithereens but I called 'disengaging' and told the wingman to join up as we headed back to base. To this day I wonder who could have been at the wheel of that car. Perhaps oblivious to death screaming above, maybe it was some pretty damsel on her way to a rendezvous and lost in her own thoughts unaware of the war raging around her.

The new boss, clearly unhappy with the task assigned to the squadron, has been in touch with HQ and tomorrow we'll move to Pathankot in north Punjab, close to the border with West Pakistan and the scene of the real action.

Some airmen have begun to complain about difficult work without proper food and it was my unpleasant duty to make everyone 'fall-in'. I pointed out that refusal to work in a war zone was a court martial offence punishable by firing squad.

In the evening Jetheram drove us back to the mess via a market place where a crowd gathered as Jetherem treated us to hot tea and kachuries – his way of saying 'thank you'.

DAY EIGHT

A sobering incident occurred today. As aircraft were made ready for the ferry to Pathankot via Hindon, a damaged Hunter needed to be flown to a specialist repair depot. Normally a junior pilot would have been assigned to this task but a senior operational pilot wanted to do it. He was the guy who had witnessed the boss eject from a burning Hunter a couple of days ago. The new boss let him go. The guy, though, never rejoined the squadron until the day after the war was over. The war exposure affected him so much that he committed suicide a few months later. As far as we were aware, he never received any medical help and no-one knew about post-traumatic stress disorder in those days. In fact, all of us could have used some post-war counselling but each had to settle down in his own style.

We reached Pathankot late in the afternoon to learn that the two Hunter squadrons operating from there since the start of the war had taken heavy losses: five pilots killed on one squadron, two on the other squadron. The base was being bombed multiple times a day so we had to follow a pilot dispersal plan of no more than six pilots in one building. I was among the lucky six detailed to stay in a hotel in town. We arrived late in the evening and ordered a good meal which was luxury after Nal. As adjutant I signed the bill and the six of us knocked off in comfortable beds in a heated room. It was unsaid, but surely everyone knew that tomorrow would perhaps be a more challenging day than any we had seen thus far.

DAY NINE

We left the hotel early; it was still dark when we reported to the squadron. Senior officers, who were huddled anxiously in the underground base ops complex, were at the nerve centre of all our operations. When a mission was ordered, the selected pilots would be driven there for briefing. After briefing, the pilots had to remain in a separate room and they were not allowed to speak with anyone not involved with the mission. A senior escort would be with them at all times and when ready to go, the pilots would be driven straight from base ops to the aircraft. Before this system was introduced, it seemed that enemy intelligence had infiltrated our security so had known our callsigns and frequencies. Enemy agents had given false radio calls to split formations thereby spoiling mutual cross-cover. We heard how enemy fighters had shot down one formation leader after his wingman had been told to turn the wrong way. Our boss decided that any manoeuvre ordered by a mission leader would use the pilot's short name, not mission callsign.

My only mission this day was a bomb attack against an enemy railway yard close to the national border. We struck late afternoon to give less time for repairs and encountered heavy anti-aircraft fire. It was as if they were expecting us. Our formation was escorted by two Folland Gnat aircraft to cover our tails, but we spotted no enemy fighters. We'd been briefed that, if bounced, we should jettison bombs and head for home. It was not heroic to run short of fuel in an extended dogfight over enemy territory. Our usual ordnance was two 1,000lb bombs and guns. Mission debrief showed a direct hit by the bombs and a punishing gun burst in the second pass. My aircraft had no bullet hits but my wingman's suffered some proximity damage by shrapnel from an anti-aircraft shell burst. Went back to the crew room when the debrief was over.

That evening, we returned to the hotel after dark in a covered one-ton vehicle to avoid being seen by the public. We had some good hot food, a couple of shots then off to bed privately thanking our stars to be back.

DAY TEN

I flew wingman to the boss today. The target was a heavily defended radar tower disguised as a water reservoir and key to the enemy's detection of army support missions in the 'chicken neck' area of fierce ground fighting. Yesterday a couple of Sukhoi Su-7 fighter aircraft had tried to neutralise the target but had taken bad hits with one pilot having to eject. A Hunter has the same firepower as a SU-7 but presents a smaller target to anti-aircraft batteries. We were briefed that our two-ship formation would be armed with rockets and guns, and escorted by two MiG-21 aircraft. We took off in sections and were soon on our way with the MiGs covering us. Visibility was pretty limited but the boss proved to be an ace navigator. We made a flawless run from the IP (initial point) where I moved to a tactical starboard position. At PUP (pull-up point) the boss rolled in and I followed. The target appeared bang on the nose; the MiG leader called 'tail clear' and we fired our rockets in sequence. Then my concentration was on the other Hunter so as not to lose sight in the poor visibility. We turned hard and pulled up for the guns attack; a perfect manoeuvre which meant that I could track the target with minimum correction. After the boss had pulled out, in a longish burst I was able to press home the attack with the pipper riding the target. After this, the boss made his only radio call: "Catch up!" he said.

"Contact," I replied.

As we headed for home the MiG leader called coolly: "With you Tiger leader. Tail clear."

Our recovery to base was uneventful; no hits on either aircraft, perhaps the poor visibility had helped. At debrief, when we'd checked the gun camera film, the boss looked at me and just nodded his head and said: "Go and relax!" Later, we were told that the radar tower had been rendered non-operational for a couple of days. Back at the squadron, when I asked the armourer how many rounds I'd fired, he replied 386. With four guns firing at eighty rounds per second that made a burst of a little over one second.

That afternoon a major from army headquarters came to ask me how I was. He said that my father in Bombay wanted to know. This was an illustration of the poor state of the country's communications.

Back at the hotel, the locals had found out that some pilots were staying there. People were gathered outside to offer us parathas (flatbreads), milk, lassi (yoghurt-based drink) and sweets. There was no guard and we mingled freely to receive their good wishes and blessings. It was a very moving experience to be shown so much affection.

DAY ELEVEN

There have been news reports from the east sparking rumours that the war may end soon. Our army has made good progress: Dacca (now Dhaka) has been attacked by Dakotas and Caribous used as improvised bombers.

I was wingman for the boss again today. We were briefed to attack a large railhead with a TOT (time over target) of around noon. Start up and taxi-out went fine but on take-off I had a problem when my Hunter lurched to the left. I suspected a tyre burst but, my mind racing, I made a split-second decision not to abort. Instinctively, therefore, I raised the undercarriage then concentrated on my formation position. Our attack against the railhead was executed with precision. My bombs hit one end of the huge yard and the guns ripped open what looked like storage sheds. On completion, the boss called 'buster' (full power) and we 'hugged the deck' flying at very low level on the way home. At base, our escorting MiGs set up a combat air patrol because an air raid warning had been sounded. Before landing I called 'suspected left tyre burst' and on touchdown was able to retain control of the aircraft. When just clear of the runway the air traffic controller cried: "Jump out and get away from the aircraft!" I managed to slide down over the nose and drop to the ground in front of the Hunter. With thoughts about my distinctly unhealthy situation by a runway during an air raid, I quickly broke into a run. Feeling like a sitting duck, I sprinted as fast as I could. Luckily, the raid did not happen and I was picked up by a jeep after the 'all clear' had sounded.

During the debrief the boss asked me if the tyre had burst during the take-off run. When I said 'yes' he went ballistic: "Are you a mission-crazy madman who retracted a burning tyre into the wheel-bay of a fully armed Hunter?" I nodded sheepishly at which he cried: "You could have blown up your aircraft!" He repeated this several times then told me to get the hell out of his sight. Looking back, I felt that this was no dumb display of bravado but a reflex action in the highly-charged atmosphere. Most of us just wanted to get the job done. Anyway, the boss put up my name for a *Vir Chakra* (VrC) bravery award though he did not tell me or congratulate me, he merely scowled at me. At least that was another day behind us.

DAY TWELVE

Today we heard from an intelligence report how one of our pilots, shot down while attacking a railhead, had been captured by a civilian mob. The mob had beaten him mercilessly, dragged him to the town square where he was tortured, mutilated and finally his throat was slit. After hearing about such cold-blooded murder some of us decided not to remove our ejection seat safety pins. It would be better, we reckoned, to go down with the aircraft. However, not all such tales ended in disaster. Another of our pilots, shot down after a dogfight over an enemy airfield, was taken by guards to meet the pilot who had downed him, a senior squadron leader in the Pakistan Air Force. They shook hands and our young flying officer's mistakes were debriefed by the squadron leader.

In the event of capture, we'd all been required to memorise a personal cover story. This, though, could be rather useless when confronted by angry people who you'd just bombed. Anyway, for what it was worth, I had decided to pretend to be a Parsi Bawa as I could speak Gujarati (an Indo-Aryan language) and believed that there were a few Parsi pilots in the Pakistan Air Force.

I flew two missions today, both of them against a railhead close to the national border. The first mission was uneventful but the second, at late evening with a dusk recovery, was more challenging. My number two was a Mumbai Bandra boy and I was from Khar on India's west coast. We were escorted by two Folland Gnats led by one of my course mates – 'son of rock Bedi'. As he circled above the yard, I remember him shouting encouragement on the aircraft radio: *"Chak De, Chak De!"* (Keep it up, keep it up!) On the first pass our bombs were on the button, then, for the second pass, I opened up with the Hunter's guns on some built-up structures. I saw flashes of anti-aircraft fire so gave a pretty long burst. My number two, however, called "no fire!" and caught up with me in the turn. When we 'hit the deck' for a low-level return to base, I must admit that, if I had any fear of being shot down, it was at this getaway stage. I would develop an overwhelming sense of 'get-the-hell-out-of-here'.

After landing I saw that my Hunter had taken hits under the wing and near the tail-cone from small calibre anti-aircraft fire. Thank God for self-sealing fuel tanks.

In the debrief, the boss asked my number two why he hadn't fired his guns. He replied candidly that he would not fire his guns unless he could positively identify a target as military. He added that some of the guys were fighting a personal war but in his own case he had nothing to settle with the enemy. The boss made no comment to this. We left in the sealed one-ton truck for the hotel where, as the days had rolled on, the crowd outside had swelled as people patiently stood in the cold while they waited to greet us. This evening we were blessed by an old lady who had brought Karah Prasad (sweet, flour-based food) for all of us to enjoy after she had offered prayers for our well-being.

FINAL PHASE

For the last couple of weeks no pilot on our squadron has been 'bounced' by an enemy fighter, perhaps in part because we'd not been tasked to attack airfields. Today, though, was different and, in a four-ship formation to be led by the boss, we were briefed to strike an enemy airfield. I was number two in this formation which, though we did not know at the time, would prove to be our last in the war. We took off in pairs, then the boss threw an orbit so the rest of the formation, including two MiG escorts, could get into position. The boss's TOT was spot on – to the second – and I pulled up with him for the single pass. We dropped our load at a height of 3,000 feet then turned hard to avoid debris damage. My bombs were aimed at a hangar while the boss went for an airfield intersection.

As we set off for base at low level, we kept our eyes peeled and, sure enough, after about twenty miles the MiG leader suddenly called: "Bogey...4 o'clock high...2,000 yards!"

"Hard starboard!" yelled the boss. The formation's vigorous reaction meant that the 'bogey', a single Mirage, would have been sandwiched. A six-to-one fight, no matter how good the lone aircraft, is not healthy even in your own airspace. The 'bogey' therefore did what was best in his situation. He turned through 180 degrees, slammed in the afterburners and vanished. The boss called "reverse" and the formation resumed a heading for home. The rest of our recovery was uneventful and back at base we received a telephone call from the air officer commanding. "Good job, boys," he said, "the bloody war is over!"

AFTERMATH

The Eastern Command of the Pakistani armed forces signed the instrument of surrender on 16th December 1971 following which East Pakistan seceded as the independent state of Bangladesh. Over 90,000 members of the Pakistani armed forces were taken as prisoners of war. It was estimated that more than two million civilians were killed in Bangladesh and that as discipline broke down, hundreds of thousands of women were abused and raped by members of the Pakistani armed forces. As a result of the conflict eight to ten million people fled that country to seek refuge in India.

Pakistani Major General Qureshi later wrote: 'We must accept the fact that, as a people, we had also contributed to the bifurcation of our own country. It was not a Niazi, or a Yahya, even a Mujob or a Bhutto, or their key assistants, who alone were the cause of our break up but a corrupted system and a flawed social order that our own apathy had allowed to remain in place for years.'

In announcing the Pakistani surrender, Prime Minister Indira Ghandi declared in the Indian parliament: "'Dacca is now the free capital of a free country. We hail the people of Bangladesh in their hour of triumph. All nations who value the human spirit will recognise it as a significant milestone in man's quest for liberty." For their conduct during the war, three members of 7 Squadron were awarded VrCs. In addition, one Vayusena medal was awarded, and three pilots were mentioned in despatches.

CHAPTER 12

KODAK KIDS

PETER LEWIS
RECALLS HIS FIGHTER
RECONNAISSANCE DAYS

The coincidence was barely credible. All around me the buzz of conversation, the convivial atmosphere, not to mention the pub's pleasing proximity in the lee of Dinas Island, induced a hearty, happy ambience within 'The Sailors' Safety' at Pwllgwaelod in the heart of Wales. I was enjoying a lunchtime pint, as one does, in this establishment said to have been in business for 500 years, when a voice called out: "It's Peter Lewis, isn't it?" I stopped dead in my tracks, as though I had walked straight into a stone wall. At once, I turned around to see who had called out my name. A man was looking in my direction, a fellow with vivid eyes that burned forth from above hollow cheeks, someone who, it appeared to me, displayed the bearing of a soldier.

"Yes," I replied a little cautiously for I did not recognise this individual. "Yes, that's me, but do I know you?"

"Probably," he said with a slight grin. "In fact," he went on, "you probably know me better than you realise."

"Oh yes?" My curiosity was aroused.

"Yes," he said. "Do you remember an incident involving camels in the Radfan mountains?"

At this, my brain went into overdrive. My participation in operations within the Radfan mountains had been in the 1960s; I had long since retired from the Royal Air Force. It had, though, been an intense, exhilarating period – worlds apart, so it seemed, from my life since leaving the service – and now, as if a door had suddenly been kicked open to reveal a brilliant light just at the point of nightfall, recollections of that period came flooding back. As I lingered there in the pub, my mind became preoccupied with memories.

*

It was in July 1962 that, having just completed the fighter reconnaissance course at RAF Chivenor, I was posted to 8 Squadron at RAF Khormaksar in Aden. Some nine months later, in April of the following year, I was summonsed by the officer commanding the tactical wing at Khormaksar. "It's been decided," said the wing commander, "to hive off the Hunter FR10s from 8 Squadron to form, or perhaps I should say to re-form, 1417 (Fighter Reconnaissance) Flight."

"Re-form, sir?" I said.

"Yes. 1417 Flight was set up originally in World War 2 – in 1941, I think it was – and employed in maritime patrol duties. Since then the flight has been disbanded and re-formed a number of times. Anyway, I want you to take command of this latest reincarnation, so to speak." The wing commander went on to explain that I would have five Hunter FR10s in the flight, two twin-seat Hunter T7s, five pilots including myself and a dozen or so ground crew, the latter drawn from the three squadrons based at Khormaksar (Nos 8, 43 and 208). "I think that your first task will be to ensure that the FR10s are knocked back into shape," he said.

In this last comment, the wing commander was not wrong. 8 Squadron, whose main role was day fighter ground attack, had concentrated the squadron's servicing efforts on their Hunter FGA9s. The FR10s were not equipped to fire rockets or to drop bombs, so these aircraft had been treated, one could say, as second class citizens. For a start, the reconnaissance cameras were in a mess; many had been polluted by sand particles and some of the nose camera lenses had been sand blasted because their protective shields had not been serviced regularly.

The ground crew allocated to 1417 Flight were all experienced on the Hunter, however they were chosen, so I discovered, largely because the other squadrons had found the men difficult to manage. Luckily, a wise warrant officer was in charge and he advised me that two weeks of hard work should be sufficient to bring the flight's five FR10s up to standard. During this period, the pilots could focus on training, check rides in the two-seat Hunter T7, and organisation of the squadron's offices and accommodation. During this period I acquired the nickname 'Prussian Pete' and after a while a small notice appeared on my office door which read: 'Be reasonable...do it his way.'

More recently Peter Lewis inspects his museum-bound Hunter.

One of the pilots devised an unusual but effective training aid to improve our visual reconnaissance techniques. In turn, he would stand each of us on a chair while he sprinkled mapping pins on the floor behind us. When instructed, we would turn around then, in fifteen seconds (about the time taken for a Hunter to run past a target) we were required to count up the number of pins and memorise the pattern they had formed. Before long, we amazed ourselves by our improvement in comprehension of the difference between looking and seeing.

Between us we designed a cardboard 'prayer wheel' – a device for aiding fuel calculations when airborne, and for airspeed adjustments to ensure an accurate time on target. We were re-briefed on the importance of a well planned IP to allow the best photographic run past a target as well as establishing, if possible, an element of surprise in order to allow a clean getaway. The desert was a quiet place, though, and the noise of a Hunter in the vicinity would normally be picked up long before the aircraft was spotted visually.

We were briefed by a man who had worked in the Lebanon and who had a good understanding of Arab culture. Inevitably, the question arose about the 'goolie chits' and gold coins issued to pilots as offerings to any Bedouin wanderers chanced across in the event of a bale out over the desert. "In my opinion," said our lecturer, "such offerings are liable to do more harm than good."

Surprised by this comment, one of the pilots said: "Can you expand on that, please?"

"If you land in the desert," said the lecturer, "food and water are far more important than gold coins and bits of paper. Offer food and water as a sign of friendship and submission and this, if accepted, will be a signal that the Arab sees you as 'on his face' and will be prepared to help you back to your own tribe. Gold coins, on the other hand, might tempt an Arab to keep the coins before he does away with the carrier."

As a final flourish before 1417 Flight was ready to start flying, we had to design markings for all of our Hunters. After democratic debate we settled on an arrowhead motif with a crinkly front end to represent camera bellows. With the station commander's agreement, the crest of RAF Khormaksar was used as a centre-piece, and we chose the colours of yellow, green and black because they replicated those of the Aden Protectorate. Each of the five Hunters was given the initials of one of the five pilots – a novel touch which we felt was more individual than the usual practice of allocating fin letters. I was especially proud of my own aircraft, XE614, with the letters PL painted on the nose-wheel door.

So it was that, at the end of the flight's makeover, we were ready to reveal our shiny Hunter FR10s to the world in general and to 8, 43 and 208 Squadrons in particular. With a sense of delight, the flight's members were not slow to note that their efforts caused a considerable stir all round, and quite right too! Our new sobriquet of Kodak Kids created a fair amount of banter but this did not bother us in the least.

To hone our skills when flying commenced, one of the pilots, a veteran from the Korean War, devised some rigorous training sorties. We were detailed to locate and photograph watering wells way out in the desert, derelict buildings at the base of steep-sided wadis, desert landing strips and, one of the hardest of all, complexes of caves recognisable only by black holes in the sides of hills. When he became aware of an army convoy driving to Dhala, due north of Aden, our Korean Kodak Kid would task us to provide photos and a vehicle count which had to include the convoy's various vehicle types.

An operational test was conceived which required each pilot to obtain a picture of a target at a predetermined time with another member of the flight flying in the vicinity ready to 'bounce' his colleague. Just one frame on the 'bouncer's' gyro gunsight cine film was all that was needed to represent a fail and a fine to be paid in beer. Cheered by our growing skills, we challenged the other squadrons to act as bouncers and, as far as I recall, only one managed to acquire the necessary cine frame.

The secret of success, we discovered, was to fly at very low level over the flattest terrain we could find on the run-in to a target. Nine times out of ten it was not the Hunter itself that was spotted from another aircraft so much as the shadow that skipped along uneven ground. In order to avoid this shadow effect, our pilots had to fly at a height of around twenty-five to thirty feet. This was very hard to achieve at an airspeed of 420 knots so we flew mutual buddy checks from time to time so that, when necessary, we could point out the common and natural tendency for the Hunter's height to creep up to around forty to fifty feet.

By the end of April 1963, I was able to tell the wing commander that 1417 Flight was ready for operations.

At that stage, our main task was to participate in Operation Ranji which involved surveillance of the coastline from the airfield at Riyan to the Straits of Bab-el-Mandeb (meaning 'Gates of Grief') at the entrance to the Red Sea. We were faced with an eclectic mix of vessels acting as gun runners to land weaponry for insurgents inland. We found a few of these, but not many. Operation Ranji, however, turned out to be a catch-all for other reconnaissance tasks including surveillance of Soviet warships. One time, I received a telephone call about a Shackleton aircraft on patrol duties over the south end of the Red Sea. The Shackleton had been up all night its crew having spotted and identified a Skoryy-class destroyer used by the Soviets as a submarine chaser. Now short of fuel, the Shackleton crew were no longer in a position to catch and photograph the destroyer so could 1417 Flight help?

I said that we'd try. The Shackleton managed to maintain radar contact on the Soviet vessel and gave us a course and speed to follow. With this information, I plotted an intercept about 180 miles out to sea. I scrambled in my Hunter XE614 and concentrated on accurate flying while I pursued the target. At a range of around forty miles from the vessel I let down to as low a height as seemed sensible, and was gratified when the Skoryy appeared on the horizon roughly where it should have been according to calculations. I lined up for a pass down the ship's port side, took the required photographs then turned for home. Later, when the pictures were developed, we spotted that every gun on the Skoryy's port side had been following the Hunter. The covers on the starboard side guns, however, had remained firmly in place. Evidently the Skoryy's crew, despite my low altitude, had tracked the Hunter's position from a long way out and had anticipated a pass down the ship's port side. This, for me, was personal evidence that in the event of hostilities against the Soviet Union we would face a most powerful and efficient adversary.

It was on a different occasion, after a scramble to search for another suspected Soviet warship, that I became embroiled in a wholly unfamiliar and unforeseen experience. I was in the vicinity of Hodeida that day and the weather was unusually poor with numbers of ominous cumulonimbus clouds scudding about. When I spotted a ship some ten miles from my position, I headed towards the vessel which turned out to be an innocent cargo carrier.

I'd become, perhaps, overly engrossed with the task in hand because suddenly I realised that the visual horizon had vanished. The cumulonimbus cloud bases, still storming across the sea, now looked like colossal inverted saucers which had begun to merge with the grey of the sea's surface. Without a visual horizon, I realised that I would have to climb up and aim to break out above the cloud tops.

The first 5,000 feet or so of the climb, although bumpy, caused no great difficulty. Then, quite abruptly, everything appeared to go mad. Of its own accord, like a puppet on strings, the Hunter started to pitch and roll violently. All around, dazzling flashes of blues and whites illuminated the scene. As if shaken by some creature afflicted by rage and distress, the Hunter was thrown this way and that. At once, I reduced my airspeed to 'penetration speed' (the recommended airspeed in severe turbulence) and clamped my feet firmly on the rudder pedals. Supported by both knees, I gripped the stick with my two hands.

At this point my situation began to turn even more pear-shaped when, in quick succession, the Hunter's flight instruments failed. My primary instrument, the artificial horizon, became useless when it toppled; the G4 compass rotated gently like a roulette wheel; the radio compass swung wildly from one bearing to another, sometimes through 360 degrees; the airspeed indicator fluctuated plus or minus thirty knots; the climb and descent indicator was bumping against the 'up' stop. On top of all this, the aircraft accelerometer ('g' meter) was swinging off-the-clock in both directions: minus four 'g' to plus twelve 'g' – about twice the allowable limits. My only reasonably stable instruments (and even these had their moments) were the turn-and-slip indicator and the altimeter, although the latter indicated that the Hunter was in an alarming climb.

With a real danger of spatial disorientation, I felt as if I had been caught within a veil of unreality; a shroud that dimmed the light and blurred the vision. As if in a storm-tossed vessel where time and motion became distorted in a world of imminent peril, I felt like a gambler destined to dice with death. A chasm of uncertainty appeared to grow ever wider while the Hunter was tossed about like a leaf in a gale, but if fear welled up inside me I was too preoccupied to notice.

I have no idea how long the Hunter was held in this, what might be called, tortuous no-man's land (it felt, indeed, like a form of medieval torture). I do know that, while struggling to maintain some sort of mental and physical equilibrium, I employed every ounce of skill that I'd acquired as a qualified flying instructor and instrument rating examiner. I know, too, that the episode appeared to go on for an interminable period. Finally, however, and by a means which ended the whole affair as swiftly as it had started, the Hunter was hurled like a giant's plaything into blue sky above a background of towering white mountains of cloud. Now, in a sudden display of striking beauty, the cloud tops flashed in the sun as if they were species designed to transform my sense of suffocating helplessness into one of hope. However, at least I was no longer a slave to the situation and there was relief rather than malice in my thoughts as, almost transfixed by the splendour of the new surroundings, I focussed on level flight while I tried to calm down and think matters through.

My flight instruments still looked untrustworthy and I could not see any signs of land. I therefore turned towards the sun as I knew that home was in that rough direction. It was at this stage that I noticed my altitude. The Hunter's official service ceiling was set at 50,000 feet, yet I was now over 5,000 feet above that limit. This felt incredibly high, an altitude that was perhaps almost unprecedented for the aircraft type. At once I initiated a descent during which the compass and radio compass decided to start working again, and the artificial horizon (now I didn't need it) re-erected itself. I opted for a gentle, straight-in approach and landing at Khormaksar for I knew that my aircraft, having been so severely and repeatedly knocked about, was likely to have suffered airframe damage. After landing, the Hunter went straight into the hangar for stress checks which revealed that the aircraft had endured a very rough ride indeed but that apart, the FR10 was just fine. Testimony, for sure, to the Hunter's rugged construction.

*

It was some six months after this experience that I became involved in an operation which followed a long series of incidents on the frontier between the Yemen and the South Arabian Federation, characterised by frequent Yemeni incursions into Federal territory. On 28th March 1964, after a decision made by British government ministers, an air attack by Royal Air Force Hunters on Harib fort, situated just inside the Yemen frontier, was authorised in retaliation for insurgent raids on Beihan state, a member of the South Arabian Federation.

I was woken at 4am by someone beating on my bedroom door. "Wake up," said a voice which I recognised as that of the wing operations officer. "We've got to start some nastiness. Get down to flights ASAP."

At 'flights', there was a buzz of activity as maps were studied, navigational routes discussed, plans formulated. Quantities of coffee and toast had been organised and it was not long before the wing leader commenced his briefing. Orders had been received from London, the wing commander informed us, that, as a first step, warning leaflets were to be photographed as they were dropped over the fort. Then, after an interval of about fifteen minutes, eight Hunters were to initiate air-to-ground rocket attacks. During the operation's attack phase, the leaflet-dropping aircraft, one of which was to be flown by me, would climb up to an altitude of 30,000 feet from where the proceedings below could be monitored and any signs of opposition reported. When the ground-attack Hunters had completed their strikes I was to zoom back over Harib fort to take post-strike pictures.

Before long, pilots began to walk out to their Hunters which had been armed (in my case with leaflets stuffed into the cavity above the aircraft's raised flaps), re-fuelled and checked over carefully before the operation commenced. A cold calm dominated the mood as we set about proceedings in an exact, well-practised way. An experienced group of aviators, every individual knew precisely what was required. That is not to say there wasn't an atmosphere where anxious thoughts were prevalent and where a sense of excitement was in the air.

When we two leaflet-dropping Hunter pilots had started our engines, we were cleared to taxi out and take off after which, when airborne, we maintained radio silence as we headed in a northerly direction fifteen minutes ahead of the others. Tension rose as, together with my number two, we approached the fort. As briefed, my colleague flew low across the fort and operated his Hunter's flaps at which the warning leaflets fluttered down to cascade across the area. Meanwhile, as the leaflets fell, I had positioned my Hunter in order to capture the moment on film. After this, I re-positioned to drop my own leaflets during which process I suddenly noticed up to three anti-aircraft guns on the ground just south of the fort. Now, in an agonising moment of uncertainty, I tried to work out whether to warn the attackers and thereby break the all-important radio silence. I figured, however, that as the attack Hunters planned to commence their strikes from an altitude of 20,000 feet, the defensive gunners were unlikely to be sufficiently accurate to bother our pilots. I said nothing, therefore, and just waited for the strike aircraft to begin their action. I did not have to wait long.

As planned, I observed from above when the eight Hunters arrived over this singular target deep in the desert. I sensed a tight feeling of apprehension as the machines lined up for action, and the leader promptly dived down for a 'pickle barrel' shot. Now I spotted a yellow flash followed by a mass of dirty brown and black smoke which began to form a haphazard-looking mushroom shape. I reckoned that the leader's salvo must have hit an ammunition dump or something similar for the explosion was far greater than otherwise would be expected. It was, in a way, a shocking sight; a vivid reminder of the brutal gulf between training routines and live operations.

When, at length, the attacks had all been delivered I instructed my photo reconnaissance colleague to join the others for their return to base. Clouds of smoke and debris persisted to pollute the area and I realised that time would be needed to allow – literally – the dust to settle. Indeed, some thirty minutes elapsed before I was able to take a clear photograph of the attack's aftermath. The fort, I discovered then, was a mess. Bodies lay scattered in the places where the anti-aircraft guns had been positioned; the southern end of the fort in particular seemed pretty much demolished; I could see where solid pieces of the fort's structure had rained down on the sorry souls below.

But now my task was almost complete. I had only to dash back to Khormaksar to hand over the photo reconnaissance film to members of the mobile field processing unit to work their wizardry. They managed in double quick time so that at the operation's subsequent debriefing I was able to produce, much to the wing leader's delight, good 'before' and 'after' pictures of Harib fort. The wing leader's face revealed a mix of pride and relief as he smiled and said simply: "Thank you 1417!"

The episode caused quite a stir at home, with questions asked in the Houses of Parliament, and internationally at the United Nations. In reply to a question from a member of parliament, the secretary of state for commonwealth relations and the colonies said:

> 'I would refer the honourable member to the prime minister's full statement on 9th April 1964. There was no attack on the township of Harib. We do not know how many casualties were suffered by Yemeni military personnel in Harib fort. We regret any loss of life which may have occurred despite the warning given by leaflet. Most of the upper storey of the fort was damaged and some damage was also caused to the lower storey and to certain guns. Representations have been received from the Yemeni Republican authorities.'

Notwithstanding the outburst of protest from the Yemen who took the matter to the United Nations, the attack achieved its aim: the border in the Beihan area remained quiet for an appreciable period after the attack.

At about the time of the Harib fort affair, I was tasked one day to fly out into the open desert to take pictures of an insurgent meeting. We were instructed on such occasions to fire our guns if fired upon so long as this did not interfere with our primary object which was to take pictures of the event. So it was that on this specific mission, when I became convinced that the Hunter was being fired on as it flew by (I could make out yellow flashes from guns pointed at the aircraft), I decided to return fire as briefed. Judiciously, I checked behind for the best approach path then applied a high angle of bank to turn the Hunter through approximately 180 degrees. Ahead, a number of personnel were gathered by four or so Land Rovers and a fair few camels. Now I ensured that my Aden gun switch was selected to 'fire' as I squinted through the gun sight. At the appropriate range I squeezed the firing trigger. Immediately, I felt the vibration and heard the racket of all four Adens as they burst into life. I did not fire for long – maybe around three seconds which would have delivered some 150 rounds of alternate high explosive/ball ammunition.

I was uncertain how effective my attack had been but the Hunter's fuel state was insufficient for me to check. At this point, therefore, I initiated a climb and turned towards base. All appeared well until, suddenly, disaster loomed in the form of an engine fire warning. At once I carried out the necessary drills (which amounted, in effect, to ejecting from the aircraft) then glanced down gloomily at the desolate area below. My throat tightened. The prospects seemed doubly uninviting in view of that last attack. The gold coins and 'goolie chits', I reckoned, would not cut

A typical wadi. Note the intelligence officer's marks to indicate potential trouble spots.

much ice, as they say, with those particular protagonists. An ejection here would mean a hideous walk over desert stretches with, at any time, the most barbarous of possibilities.

Fortunately, however, the sense of doom swirling through my mind was promptly dispelled when inspiration struck. An initial check in the cockpit's rearview mirror had revealed no signs of smoke or fire. A further hasty glance confirmed that there were still no signs of trouble. The engine's jet pipe temperature appeared normal and the engine itself was behaving properly. With care, therefore, I felt for the fire warning test switch located in the area behind my ejection seat. Now I experienced a surge of relieved thoughts: the aircraft's desert survival pack had been shaken loose by the guns' vibration and had fallen against the fire test switch. I managed to ease the pack away from the test switch at which – hey presto! – the fire warning light went out and remained out for the rest of the flight. My sigh of relief on landing back at base was, to say the least, quite considerable. After this incident it was decided to remove desert survival packs from all Hunter FR10s.

It was not uncommon for 1417 Flight to be visited by senior officers and politicians, especially when the flight had been engaged in high-profile activity. An esteemed member of the flight was an Arab man who had been recruited locally as a cleaner. In addition to keeping the flight's offices in immaculate order, this individual showed willing in a number of other ways including, over time, assistance with non-technical aspects of aircraft turn-rounds; he would push trolleys, help our ground crew to manhandle heavy fuel hoses, pass tools and other such general tasks.

One time, the flight was visited by some members of parliament who came, presumably, to bolster the morale of those charged with enforcing the will of politicians. One of the group, a portly fellow, walked up to our cleaner and asked him if he did not feel ashamed of himself for helping the Royal Air Force to fight his people. A momentary and icy silence greeted this remark. Taken aback by the frankness of the question, those in the vicinity who'd heard it looked down in embarrassment or stared blankly into space. All wondered if our cleaner might be utterly stumped for an answer. We should not have worried, though: the cleaner appeared quite capable of accounting for himself to this stout MP who bore, it seemed, liberal/pacifist tendencies. "No!" cried the cleaner. "Not at all." He glared fiercely at the MP and went on: "Boss Pete is fighting the enemies of my tribe!"

The incident, if trivial, nevertheless stimulated thoughts on some of the moral issues surrounding our activities. I found it odd, for one thing, to get up at dawn, fly missions in the morning which might involve shooting at – and probably killing – people, then return home to sit down with my wife and three children for a late lunch. As I sat down with my family, the morning's activities may well have left behind a scene of lolling corpses with blood trickling out from the corners of their mouths and their eyes fixed upon infinity. Such contrasts – their unspeakable enormity – did not rest easily upon the conscience and eventually I came to the conclusion that wives and families had no place in a war zone. By the time I left 1417 Flight in July 1964, I had flown 112 operations in Aden. The flight as a whole had been tasked with 601 operations, all of which had been successful except for one (the engine would not start). Towards the end of my tour I began to realise that our activities were affecting my psyche in a deep-rooted and insidious way. After an operational task, for example, I was unable to remember any details such as walking out to my Hunter, the transit to a target, or the flight home. In spite of this, from the target's initial point through to the breakout I could give a faultless, frame-by-frame debrief of every detail as if I'd been subconsciously converted into some kind of automaton programmed for perfection.

Notwithstanding all of this, it was on one such mission that I had to work with members of the notorious Special Air Service. Since the start of the Radfan emergency in February 1964, the SAS had been active in operations, including an infamous incident about a month after the Harib fort attack. When a local lad stumbled upon a nine-man SAS patrol, he was joined by other locals who started to shoot-up the patrol members. That night, as the patrol tried to break out, two of the SAS men were killed and their bodies had to be left behind. Later, the news emerged that the bodies had been mutilated and the heads displayed on stakes in the Yemen (see also page 66). British forces had no doubts about the ruthless nature of the insurgents and the army became increasingly adept at making use of 1417 Flight and other airborne resources.

So it was that I was tasked one morning to fly north and look out for a suspicious camel train spotted near the Yemen border. When I reached the area, despite being pretty sure that I was in the right place, I could see nothing. Then a voice on the aircraft radio said: "They're there." That was it: no preamble, no grid reference, nothing else. So I searched more carefully and found an irregular track which followed the dried-up bed of a stream towards an odd-looking pool of water. I noticed that the colour of the track above the pool was different to that below. Now I recollected a briefing about camels' wet feet washing sand off the path below and suddenly I realised that what had appeared as rough boulders was, on closer inspection, a number of crouched camels. I turned the Hunter sharply, selected 'fire' on my Aden guns and...

*

An outburst of laughter in the 'Sailors' Safety' pub jerked my mind back to the present. The soldierly fellow continued to gaze at me. Doubtless he expected a reply to his remark about the Radfan mountains. "Yes," I said eventually, for the lack of any words that seemed profound. "I do remember."

"You see," he went on, "I was a member of the Special Air Service back then and, as you know, we were a somewhat clandestine lot."

"Indeed," I hesitated. "But tell me – how do you know my name?"

"You were in charge of the photo recce Hunters, weren't you?"

"I was."

"We all knew who you were." He beamed.

"I see."

"And by the way..." now it was his turn to hesitate.

"Yes?"

"Do you remember the call: 'They're there' which someone made on the operational frequency?"

"It was a long time ago," I said, "but, actually, yes I do remember that call quite well. The message was the essence of brevity, but still effective."

"Good," he nodded. "I'm glad to hear you say that. It was me who made the call."

"You?"

"Yes, me."

At this, I grinned and said something like "well, well," then went on to ask him if he was still in the army.

"No," he said. "I left the service years ago."

"So what do you do nowadays?"

"Oh," he said, "now I serve the community in a rather different way to back then." He smiled and said simply: "You see, these days I'm the local postman around here."

CHAPTER 13

TESTING TIMES

HARRY ANWAR IN JORDAN

It was the strangest thing. As I stepped out of the jeep into the glittering, hazy brilliance of a fine spring day in the northern reaches of their country, the Royal Jordanian Air Force pilots greeted me with pained, distant eyes. I'd just arrived at Mafraq airbase where I was about to start work as officer in charge of the RJAF's fighter pilot training. As a Pakistani national I knew that I'd have to be adaptable and tactful, and I was eager to meet my new colleagues who I assumed would greet me with enthusiasm. I was hardly prepared for the reaction, therefore, when the pilots, one by one, began to slink away into the crew room without offering me any form of welcome.

To be fair, there was one officer who remained. I therefore introduced myself to this individual who turned out to be Captain Mohannad Al Khas, the new airbase doctor who had arrived just a few minutes before me. "What's up with the pilots?" I asked him.

He merely shrugged his shoulders and said: "Ya, ya." Before long, the good doctor would earn the sobriquet 'Doctor Ya Ya' because no matter what anybody said to him his response was always: "Ya, ya." Evidently he had been trained in Germany.

The pilots continued to hide that day, nonetheless I was anxious to get down to work and soon began to plan training schedules. This, though, proved harder than should have been the case. Whatever I suggested was met with negative response and endless disagreements led, in the main, by the senior pilot Captain Nasri Jamean whose arguments in high tones caused needles of irritation to pull through my mind. After two weeks of getting nowhere, a simple but effective idea started to formulate itself in my head. By then, I'd heard rumours that the pilots were behaving in this manner because they felt that, of all nationalities, it was insulting for a Pakistani to teach them. Surely, went the line of logic, the flying abilities of members of the Royal Jordanian Air force were bound to be superior to a pilot from other countries, especially the likes of Pakistan.

I realised that there was one way which would put a stop to this preposterous nonsense. I therefore briefed the senior pilot for a one-versus-one combat exercise with his Hunter pitted against mine. After the briefing, when the two of us walked out to our respective Hunters, there was tension in the crew room as the other pilots became aware of what was happening.

After engine start-up and clearance to taxi, the senior pilot, as instructed, followed my aircraft in a close formation position for the take-off. We climbed up to an altitude of around 20,000 feet at which stage it was time to split before our pre-briefed combat exercise got underway. I kept a wary eye on the other pilot's Hunter as we both turned away from each other for a set period, then turned back for battle to commence. Soon, when both aircraft were in close proximity again, each made a vigorous, aggressive turn towards the other. In seconds a so-called circle of joy developed with each pilot trying to outwit and out-manoeuvre his opponent. Inevitably, the airspeed reduced rapidly in this situation and soon the Hunters were being flown close to the point of stall. Experience as a fighter pilot combined with subtle, judicious flying now became the key to success. I knew that symmetry between man and machine would prove seminal: the fighter pilot's muscles in his arms and legs should be in the wings and tail of his machine; he should turn, dive and climb with finesse to apply techniques that would break the circle-of-joy deadlock. The body of the Hunter should be the body of the fighter pilot; there should be no difference between the one and the other.

As the struggle progressed, so the altitude of both Hunters unavoidably started to reduce. At one juncture I looked down while we circled and descended towards the desert sands; in the distance, a stretch of river looked grey-green and cold against the heat of the land. Gradually, as experience began to pay dividends, as instinct galvanised control of my arms and legs as if connected with the wings and body of my Hunter, I started to gain on the other pilot. Before long, when his aircraft came within firing range, I was in a position to squint through my reflector sight. Swiftly, precisely I moved my Hunter a little more here, a little more there; the aiming 'pipper' danced and jerked this way and that. My thumb in the leather flying glove felt for the cine camera 'firing' button. For added emphasis, I closed up to a distance of about 150 feet – far closer than normal. Then, with my pipper on the other pilot's helmet I pressed the cine camera button. After a few seconds I broke away and ordered the other pilot to follow me back to base.

After landing, having taxied-in and closed down the Hunters, I walked to the engineering set-up to sign in my aircraft. Unfortunately, I walked alone; I heard later that the other pilot had removed his flying helmet and just sat in the cockpit with his head down. He'd felt sickened and disgraced, apparently, when he should have felt pride. At length, he had to be talked down from the cockpit by members of the ground crew before, in a pitiful state, he had tried to make himself scarce. Later, his facial expression suggested that he had been consigned to the caprices of the dark.

If I had hoped that this incident would settle matters, I was wrong. The exercise had to be repeated with each and every individual pilot on the squadron, culminating in a four versus one exercise before, finally, attitudes changed. Then it was that I earned the title 'umruk seedee' ('umruk' is Arabic for 'anything you say is okay; anything you wish will be provided'; 'seedee' means to give the highest respect when addressing another person). Squadron members would come up to me and say: "Major Anwar, sir, would you like to have a cup of tea?"

"Yes," I would say.

"Would you like milk with the tea, sir?"

"Yes, I would like milk."

"Would you like cow's milk, sir? If not, shall we make the tea with goat's milk, or with camel's milk, perhaps?" The level of obsequiousness was painful.

I would state my preference after which a further protracted discussion would ensue about whether to have sugar in the wretched tea: if I wanted sugar at all; if so, how much sugar would I like and of what type. However, this did not bother me. The main thing was that I felt that the situation was under control; now everyone was listening to me with about four ears each. We had wasted a week for nothing, but at least I could go back to my training programme.

And a very necessary programme it was too. The first phase was to teach pilots how to handle their Hunters at, or close to, the aircraft's stalling speed. I knew that this first step was required to instill confidence in the pilots who, despite their outward shows of bravado, in truth were not only contrary but also deficient in their skills to an alarming extent. A great deal of proper, in-depth training would be required which, presumably, was the reason why the RJAF had hired me. My training schedule, though, did not always go smoothly. Evidently someone reported to King Hussein himself that I was trying to kill his pilots. The king, though, did not question my methods. He had already heard about the practice combat saga and, as a pilot himself, he was well aware of the shortcomings of the RJAF's fighter pilots.

As events turned out, I had around nine months in which to progress my training schedule before, in December 1964, the squadron pilots' dogfighting skills were tested for real. I was in the officers' mess on that December day when the base sirens went off to signal that all personnel should report to their places of duty. I drove at once to the air traffic control tower where I learnt that two Hunters, followed three minutes later by another two, had been scrambled in reaction to a border violation by Israeli Mirage aircraft. Amid much excitement, not to mention a fair amount of confusion, we monitored the action as intermittent radio transmissions indicated that a dogfight had started between the Hunters and the Mirages. In the control tower it was necessary to try to calm the storms of anxiety and speculation; in the Hunter and Mirage cockpits the pilots, no doubt, were focussed on their tasks. Meanwhile, my fingers remained firmly crossed that the lessons I had tried to inculcate over the last nine months were working out.

When, eventually, all four Hunters returned unscathed from what became known as the 'Battle of the Dead Sea', I watched with trepidation as the pilots climbed out of their aircraft. On tenterhooks to receive their reports, I could soon discern from the pilots' facial expressions that the outcome had been favourable. "Sir," they said, wonderfully eager to tell their stories, "in just thirty seconds it was clear that we knew what we were doing and they did not."

"Go on," I said.

"We shot down two Mirages and damaged another!" I grinned but said nothing. "And look…" they went on, "our Hunters are fine – untouched by Israeli bullets!"

It was not long before news of this encounter was flashed around the world. Commentators stated that they thought that this was the first time in the history of the Arab-Israeli conflict that Arab acumen had gained victory over the Israelis. Meanwhile, King Hussein, who was in London, sent a telegram to Colonel Saleh Al-Kurdi, commander of the Royal Jordanian Air Force:

21 December 1964-1635 hours

MOST URGENT – COLONEL S KURDI RJAF AMMAN

VERY PROUD TO RECEIVE GOOD NEWS OF OUR AIR FORCES
RESULT IN THEIR FIRST COMBAT ACTION (STOP)UNABLE TO
CONTACT YOU BY PHONE OR CABLE THROUGH EMBASSY PLEASE
CONFIRMBY URGENT REPLY CABLE TO ME DORCHESTER LONDON
PREFERABLY ONE CABLE FROM COLONEL KURDI (STOP)FIRSTLY
ENEMIES TWO AIRCRAFT DOWN IN JORDAN SECONDLY CABLE
NAME OF OUR PILOT IN ACTION THIRDLY DID THEY ENGAGE THE
ENEMY ONCE OR MORE (STOP)FOURTHLY NUMBER OF AIRCRAFT
INVOLVED AND IF ANY DAMAGE (STOP)CONFIRM AIR FORCE
ON COMPLETE ALERT FOR FURTHER DEVELOPMENTS (STOP)
CONGRATULATIONS
TO AIR FORCE TO ANWAR AND ALL PILOTS RADAR OPERATORS
AND CREW (STOP)

ARRANGE FOR ANWAR AND PILOTS INVOLVED TO BE AMONGST
THE FIRST PEOPLE I MEET IN AMMAN AIRPORT TOMORROW ON
ARRIVAL TO RECEIVE HIGHEST HONOURS AND DECORATIONS
TO BE READY FOR ME TO CONFER UPON THEM (STOP) THANKS
(STOP)
REGARDS (STOP) BEST WISHES (STOP)
AL HUSSEIN +

The king was as good as his word. The pilots and myself were waiting to meet
him at Amman airport where the honours mentioned in his telegram were duly
distributed.

Many years later I wrote to General Ezer Weizman, who by then had retired
as the President of Israel, to remind him of the Battle of the Dead Sea and to ask
him for a meeting to discuss details. There had been arguments about whether the
RJAF's Hunters had shot down one or two Israeli Mirages and I wanted to try to
establish the truth from, so to speak, the horse's mouth. General Weizman wrote
to me in reply:

26 November 2002

Dear Anwar

What a pleasant and appreciated surprise to hear a roar of an aeroplane
from the past!

First of all you are more than welcome. Whenever you can, let me know
and I will invite some of the old characters that took part in the air battle
which I monitored from my command post. It is never too late to compare
notes. Lots of things have developed since then. Some for better, some for
worse. I am still an ardent optimist who thinks that despite the Israelis and
the Arabs, we shall definitely come to an understanding and to an agreement
and live safely and happily ever after...it is not easy but the trends of the
world indicate that it is possible.

I am now retired trying to the best of my ability to occupy my time in
theoretical dogfights. I have just completed a book titled, of all titles, *Roger
and Out*, which I hope sums up objectively my part in this good world. Once
I have it translated to English I will keep one copy honourably for you.

Do let me know as soon as you can when you come over so I will get myself properly prepared for the meeting.

Yours sincerely

Ezer Weizman

I met General Weizman at his office in Tel Aviv. The office was in a high-rise building, his office door was unmarked and I had to ask people for directions. When we first met, the door between the general's office and that of his secretary was kept open but after about ten minutes he said: "Why is this door open?" He got up and closed the door; I guessed that he'd figured by then that I was not a threat. Our meeting lasted for around forty minutes during which time I found him to be a most pleasant personality. He made me feel at home, offered me strawberries (the largest I have ever seen) and described how they had come from his home town. When I showed him a copy of the telegram from King Hussein with the mention of two enemy aircraft shot down in the Battle of the Dead Sea, General Weizman looked at me and said: "Who is Anwar? You?"

I said: "Yes. Your Excellency." The general did not dispute the claim. He went on to talk about a number of matters, including the time when he was with the Royal Air Force on a course at the same time as Nur Khan. The latter was a Pakistani national who went on to become a high-profile air marshal in the Pakistan Air Force. One time, Nur Khan was angry and wanted to file a complaint because he had been served pork in the dining room. "Calm down," Weizman wisely said and the issue quietly blew over.

After my meeting with General Weizmann, my Israeli host asked if I would like to meet then-Prime Minister Ariel Sharon. As Israel's eleventh prime minister, Sharon remained a controversial figure. He had orchestrated his country's unilateral disengagement from the Gaza strip, but it was his involvement in a cruel incident during the 1982 Lebanon War which I'd found inexcusable. A commission established by the Israeli government in 1983 had found that Minister of Defence Sharon, by 'ignoring the danger of bloodshed and revenge', had born 'personal responsibility' for the massacre by Lebanese Maronite Christian militias (Phalanges) of Palestinian civilians in the refugee camps of Sabra and Shatila. Sharon, in other words, had looked the other way which was why, when I was invited to meet him, I grimaced and declined.

When I looked back, I realised that the Battle of the Dead Sea had been a turning point in a number of respects. For one thing, shortly after the episode, Jordanian radar revealed that Mirages of the Israeli Air Force had instigated daily practice air combat sessions. The loss of Israeli aircraft to Hunters of the Royal Jordanian Air Force must have astonished and shocked Israel's hierarchy. Word reached us of a

Harry Anwar with former President of Israel His Excellency Mr Ezer Weizman,
Tel Aviv, Israel 2003.

pledge made by General Weizman, at that point the commander-in chief of the Israeli Air Force. Not known for prevarication, the general's overall summary of the situation was a model of military brevity. He'd said simply: "Never again!" From a different perspective, it appeared to me as if the Jordanian fighter squadron I'd known initially had now sloughed away its skin and revealed itself as reborn with energy and expertise.

However, before this point was reached I'd had to face other battles too. Not long after I'd arrived in Jordan (but after the *'umruk seedee'* watershed), I became worried about ongoing poor air-to-ground and air-to-air weapon delivery results. No amount of briefing or debriefing with cine camera shots seemed to have the slightest impact. I took individual pilots up in the two-seat Hunter T7 in attempts to demonstrate the required techniques, but all to no avail. We were getting nowhere. It was as if the pilots were blindfolded, apathetic and unwilling to learn. I realised that continued cajoling was not the solution; a different, more radical approach was needed to motivate them.

I'm unsure what caused inspiration to strike but strike it did when it occurred to me to introduce a donkey – yes, a donkey – into the proceedings. It was a simple and outrageous idea, but I reckoned that the pilot who obtained the worst score of the day should be officially, and ceremoniously, handed the donkey to look after until a different pilot with the next day's worst score assumed the creature's reins.

I called a meeting of all the pilots to inform them of the plan, which did not seem to go down very well at all. We were on a slippery slope, I pointed out, confronted by a world of wild dogs and wolves and that if something was not done about the pilots' weapon delivery skills then the squadron would be in no position to defend its homeland. A bit of a hue and cry ensued, but eventually my plan was reluctantly accepted by the pilots.

Quite soon after this meeting, a local farmer, the father of one of the pilots, was asked to deliver the donkey in the back of his pick-up truck. The next day's weapon firing results were studied avidly by all the pilots who, by the end of flying, discovered that Lieutenant Salti had qualified as the 'donkey man'. Suddenly it felt as if the excitement that went with the tension of waiting had transformed itself into different feelings in the face of reality. At the handing-over ceremony, the other pilots laughed and joked at Salti who looked very meek and said that he refused to accept the beast. "But you must!" everyone cried with one voice, "it was agreed." At length Salti came to me, puffed himself up with indignation, and said: "Major Anwar, sir, I cannot accept the donkey in front of all the other pilots and squadron personnel, it is too shameful. I will accept it inside the crew room."

If Lieutenant Salti had hoped for a measure of catharsis, his aspirations proved ill-founded. As if grappling with the vengeance of the tormented, he continued to look downhearted while the donkey was led into the crew room and handed over. When, with a melancholy air of delicate pride, he left the crew room, donkey in tow, all the other pilots burst out laughing. That evening in the officers' mess, poor Salti was heckled and teased as everyone asked if he'd taken the donkey outside for a call of nature, whether he had fed the animal properly and where he intended the donkey to sleep overnight.

The next day, Salti came to me and said: "Sir, I have had a terrible time being in charge of that donkey. All night I did not sleep." I stared at his haunted eyes, his haggard expression laced with vexation. "One thing I can promise you..." he paused.

"Well?"

"Today," he went on, his voice full of resolve, "I will hand the donkey over to someone else."

Sure enough, Salti's score showed an impressive improvement that day. For him, honour was restored, his face was a picture of pride and gratitude when, as if about to greet a conquering hero, he went up to the donkey to untie the beast and hand it over to the next qualifying pilot. When, Arab-style, he relinquished responsibility for the animal, Salti's ear-to-ear smile, the accompanying chorus of boos and heckling, all generated a remarkable air of jubilation. I almost expected a series of fine and moving speeches but fortunately matters did not go quite that far.

The donkey experiment carried on for the duration of my weapon training schedule towards the end of which the hand-over ceremony seemed like a festival

*His Majesty King Hussein I on an impromptu visit to Mafraq airbase,
being briefed by Harry Anwar.*

with everyone looking forward to the event. There was much laughter and general
jollity, nonetheless all of the pilots became very serious about their performance
and studied the cine camera results over and over again. Perhaps practice alone
might have achieved the squadron's improved results, I'm unsure. But improve
they did and maybe the donkey episode helped a bit. It was not until later, when
the donkey had been returned to the farmer, that I was told that one of the worst
insults for an Arab is to call him a donkey. I had no idea about this and learned of
it only when the 'donkey business' had ended.

While my training schedule was progressed, King Hussein continued to show a
keen interest. One time, just as the squadron had ended flying at around lunchtime
that day, the king and his entourage suddenly arrived without announcement. I
asked him if he would like an aerobatics demonstration over the airfield. He said
that he would, so I chose the most experienced pilot available then escorted the
king to the air traffic control tower for a bird's-eye view.

The demonstration, though, did not go well. The king looked bored. His
entourage seemed unimpressed. I felt embarrassed. I therefore requested permission
to get airborne myself to run through an aerobatics routine. The king nodded assent
so, as hastily as possible, while the squadron engineers prepared a Hunter, I dashed
back to the squadron. I was soon airborne and ready to commence my routine.
As a first move, I turned hard left immediately after take-off and aimed for a gap

between the air traffic control tower and an adjacent building. Then, with my left wingtip just a few feet above the tarmac, I flew in front of the hangars. A sergeant on his bicycle saw the coming collision and instantly made himself fall sideways while still sitting on his bike. Excellent reactions, I thought.

After this, I climbed a little and accelerated before returning for a high speed run at about 450 knots. As before, I aimed for the gap between the air traffic control tower and an adjacent building. Still at low level, now I turned back towards the runway before pulling up for a series of upward vertical rolls followed by downward rolls. After the last downward roll, which I had left a little late, the radio crackled with a message from the king. He wanted me to land immediately. It appeared that he was worried that I was about to kill myself. Excellent judgement, I thought.

My reply, however, was along the lines of…kindly inform the king that my routine had only just begun. Next, I initiated a series of further manoeuvres which culminated in lowering the Hunter's undercarriage before a touchdown on the taxiway in front of the air traffic control tower. After touchdown, I applied full power to the Avon engine but the Hunter's acceleration was slow; the end of the taxiway loomed alarmingly. Fortunately, just as thoughts of raising the undercarriage started to run through my mind, the Hunter achieved lift-off airspeed in the nick of time. Later, I realised that I'd performed the 'touch-and-go' with the wind behind me; how important is the wind factor!

The next manoeuvre, a 360 degree steep turn above grass in front of the air traffic control tower, was at low level; so low, in fact, that I learnt later that the Hunter's wingtip had left a line in the grass (the grass was cut to a height of about six inches). To complete the display, I flew at low level towards the air traffic control tower and as I did so, I noticed that observers seemed to be throwing themselves onto the floor. I even spotted one individual – a cousin of the king, I believe – who appeared to be lying on his belly punching the floor with his fists. Strange, I thought. The king, though, remained standing ramrod straight as he continued to grip a railing with his hands. He did not move an inch. What courage, I thought.

After landing I stopped the aircraft opposite the air traffic control tower, unbuckled my seat straps, stood up in the cockpit and saluted the king who returned my salute. Then I taxied the Hunter back to dispersal and closed down. Meanwhile, the king was driven to the dispersal area where he waited for me to climb out of the aircraft cockpit. I saluted him again as he walked up to me and said: "Anwar, I have seen a few aerobatics in my time, but nothing like that."

"Thank you, Your Majesty," I said tentatively for I was still a little unsure whether to expect a rebuke for having ignored the instruction to land. I need not have worried, though.

"No, Anwar," went on the king. "Thank YOU!"

CHAPTER 14

GREAT EXPECTATIONS

ANTHONY HAIG-THOMAS
RELISHED HIS DAYS OF
FLYING

"There's one piece of advice that I give to all new pilots," said the flight commander. It was June 1958 and as the new boy on the Hunter F6-equipped 63(F) Squadron based at RAF Waterbeach near Cambridge, I was naturally keen to receive his words of wisdom. "If your hair starts to fall out," went on the flight commander, "or if you are not getting it regularly then get married. Otherwise don't." A pause ensued while I absorbed this philosophical triumph which, at the time, struck me as pretty reasonable. I wondered why it had not been advocated at Ludgrove Preparatory School or at Eton College where I'd been educated. "Why are you still standing there?" continued the flight commander brusquely, "what do you want?"

"I'd hoped to fly, sir," I said.

At this the flight commander yelled: "MIKE!" and someone entered stage left, a fellow who looked just like a fighter pilot ought to look but with a large hooked nose; later, I learnt that everyone called him 'Hooky' but never to his face. "Give this lad a sortie round the local area in the Meteor will you?" said the flight commander.

Before long, as I walked with Hooky to the two-seat Meteor, I felt a strong sense of *joie de vivre*. By then I'd picked up the odd rumour about Hooky such as the way he brooked absolutely no nonsense from anyone, and that he appeared to run the squadron even though his rank was stuck at flying officer because he'd never bothered to take the required promotion exam.

None of this, though, bothered me in the least. My primary interest in life, to fly jet aircraft, had remained undimmed from school days through to pilot training, including my time on the Hunting Jet Provost T1 aircraft as a member of No 120 (Jet) Course at RAF Hullavington. I'd always felt rather proud of the 'Jet' bit, especially as the other students, the inferior mortals destined to fly the Piston Provost, were denied some of the privileges afforded to *crème de la crème* jet aces like me. When you are eighteen years of age a certain pleasure can be derived from getting right up the noses of your peer group, and the combination of a free Penguin chocolate bar and an extra half-a-crown a day of 'jet' pay certainly got up their noses all right. I felt very happy.

I felt happy, too, on that day when I walked with Hooky for a 'sector recce' flight in the Meteor T7 normally used by squadron pilots for IF (instrument flying) training . Hardly had I strapped-in before Hooky was taxiing out to Waterbeach's runway 23. The sortie that followed remained a blur. With about ninety degrees of bank and 6 'g' more or less permanently applied from the moment that the wheels left the ground, I remained in a semi-conscious state sitting in the Meteor's rear seat. Dimly I remembered: "…*key point this*…" "…*vital to rendezvous here in bad weather*…" "…*Dog and Duck – once you have found it pull 6 'g' like this*…"

Three days later, when I was programmed for a flight in a Hunter F6, I was told to read the Pilots' Notes then go out and fly the machine. Superficially, the F6 was like the Hunter F4 I had flown in training at RAF Chivenor, but with thirty-three per cent extra engine power. I strapped-in and carried out cockpit checks before indicating to the ground crewman that I was ready to start the engine. At this, I was surprised to see the fellow take cover behind the external power unit. Undaunted, I pressed the start button which set in train a high-pitched '*whee*' followed by a huge detonation (well it seemed huge), the cockpit filled with fumes that made my eyes sting after which, through the noise and smell, emerged the smooth singing sound of the Rolls-Royce Avon 200 series engine. Later, when I asked the ground crewman why he'd ducked down and hidden during engine start, he explained that there had been several explosions of late caused by fume build-up within the starter system.

Taxiing out after engine start I did not feel particularly brave and hoped that I would not disgrace my squadron. I did not, but found that – oh boy! – did the F6 go well despite carrying, under the wings, an extra 200 gallons of fuel, although the latter could affect high-altitude performance. On my second sortie, for which I was briefed to conduct a high-level climb and high-speed dive, I attained supersonic airspeed but only just: unlike the Hunter F4s at Chivenor which, on my last two high speed runs there had managed Mach 1.1, the F6s were hindered by drop tanks and by blast deflectors on the gun muzzles.

I had arrived on 63 Squadron just as rivalry for the Fighter Command weapons trophy, known as the Dacre Trophy, was at its peak. Hooky was in charge of our squadron's effort and had decided that, come what may, we would win. The competition was judged principally on gun-sight film from one aircraft tracking another. The tracking aircraft, flying as accurately as possible, would close from a range of 800 yards down to 200 yards while compensating for range and deflection. Hooky was not pleased with my arrival on the squadron as my efforts would count towards the evaluation total and my lack of experience would let down the others. One day, Hooky sidled up to me in the aircrew coffee bar. "I don't want the squadron's Dacre chances wrecked by you, Haig-Thomas," he muttered fiercely. He stood intimidatingly close and persisted: "You'll be given three films to expose but when you land I want you to hand in these three…" he slipped them into my hand…"not the films with your own efforts. Understood?" I nodded deferentially at which he turned away and walked off. I did as I was told, 63 Squadron won the Dacre Trophy, the real squadron boss complimented me on my high scores, and no-one ever knew the truth.

As well as Hunter flying, I tried to take advantage of opportunities to fly the squadron's Meteor, or 'Meatbox' as it was known universally. On one occasion, when I flew with a qualified flying instructor in the back seat, we flew above the great Bedford drains dug by an early Duke of Bedford (well, not personally I suppose) to drain the Cambridge fens. Then, as we settled at an altitude of 10,000 feet with the airspeed down to 125 knots, he told me to bring both throttles to idle before opening up the port engine to full power. The foot-load in this asymmetric configuration became crushing as single-engine power was applied, then suddenly the Meteor raised its nose and rolled over onto its back. "That's bloody dangerous if you do it trying to land," said the voice from the back. His comment, if somewhat obvious, nonetheless remained imprinted vividly in my mind. When we subsequently practised asymmetric flying in the airfield circuit I was the very model of judicious accuracy.

After a further sortie in the Meteor T7, the instructor sent me solo. Following this, however, I developed a burning ambition to fly the single-seat Meteor F8. While 63 Squadron did not have a Meteor F8, Station Flight at Waterbeach did. One morning, when I was not scheduled for Hunter flying, I decided to take the bull by the horns, so to speak, and clutched my logbook when I walked over to ask for a sortie in their very good-looking, camouflaged, single-seat Meteor F8.

I smiled sweetly, spoke politely to the elderly flight lieutenant in charge, and pointed to the relevant pages in my flying logbook as evidence of previous Meteor experience. The elderly flight lieutenant, however, tutted and coughed and looked unconvinced. Eventually, unpersuaded by my entreaties, he showed me the door.

Walking back dejectedly to 63 Squadron I bumped into Hooky. "What's the matter, Haig-Thomas?" he said. "You look unhappy." I explained the situation at which he roared: "Wa'd'yer mean he wouldn't let you fly?"

"I'm afraid he wouldn't," I said.

"We'll soon see about that," he said and stormed off to the operations room. I followed obligingly and was intrigued by the subsequent telephone conversation. There appeared to be a number of contradictory comments, even the odd bit of shouting here and there before the phone was slammed down and Hooky turned to me with a serious expression and said: "Go and get dressed, Haig-Thomas. A Meteor F8 is ready for you at Station Flight." I could hardly believe it.

When, for the second time that morning, I reached Station Flight, the elderly flight lieutenant was stammeringly contrite. "I had not realised that you were the designated tug pilot for air-to-air gunnery practice," he said.

"Oh, um…"

"I thought that you just wanted to fly a new type."

"A new type?"

"Some people seem to treat the Royal Air Force like a flying club," he said stiffly.

"They do?" I said and went on to apologise for not making myself clear earlier. I was despatched to the Meteor F8 which, as promised, was ready and waiting and gleamed in the summer sun. Soon, I was airborne for an incredible flight which felt like seventh heaven.

The following day I was scheduled for Hunter flying. A routine sortie on 63 Squadron would typically involve a pairs take-off in close formation with sometimes just one pair of Hunters, sometimes two. In the latter case, the first pair would pull up into a steep climb while the second pair stayed low. As number two in the pairs formation, I tended to stay slightly low on my leader for, with a heavy aircraft at take-off weight, the machine felt close to its stall boundary. I was conscious of a friend of mine from Chivenor days who, when he was a member of 65 Squadron at RAF Duxford, pulled up to stay level with his leader but stalled, rolled and was killed when his Hunter impacted the ground just off the end of Duxford's runway 24.

The two or four-ship formation would climb to around 40,000 feet, then split for practice interceptions controlled by ground radar with each pair taking turns to act as target. When fuel state dictated the need to return to base, we would descend in a tail-chase which became progressively tighter until, in effect, we entered a dogfight. Air combat was marvellously gratifying but physically very demanding and I would find myself in a struggle to avoid the humiliation of the leader ending up in my six o'clock position.

In September 1958 came two pieces of news, one bad one good. The good news was that we were due to be detached to Acklington, north of Newcastle, for air-to-air gunnery practice. The bad news was that the squadron would be disbanded the following month.

All twelve of the squadron's Hunters flew in formation to Acklington – my first time in a formation of that size and it felt wonderful. As the most inexperienced pilot on the squadron, I flew as number two to the commanding officer. When the formation reached Acklington, the CO did an extraordinarily tight break and landing. The concept of: 'If in doubt, go round again,' had been rammed down my throat in training. I was in doubt, so went round again only to learn later that this was not the sort of thing expected on squadron detachments.

To cheer myself up after this *faux pas,* I decided with a friend to set out in search of fun. We found it in the small village of Alnwick where the pair of us ended up (to cut a long and rather sordid story short) one at each end of a caravan in a caravan park with two girls who seemed to understand the pressing requirements of fighter pilots on a gunnery camp. Confined to the councils of the dark, our passions were rudely interrupted by banging on the caravan's locked doors then torches shining inside. The girls' boyfriends began to shake the caravan which left two completely fearless fighter pilots, not to mention the girls, thoroughly alarmed especially when the cuckolds left to get help. Not wishing to cause injury to a bunch of enraged Geordie miners, the said fighter pilots hastily got dressed and left the girls with memories of the undoubted experiences of their lifetimes. Making record speed to the Alnwick bus station, we arrived just in time to see the last bus leave. The two by-now rather bedraggled fighter pilots set out on a very long walk back to base which we reached in the small hours. The next morning I scored a big fat zero on the air-to-air gunnery flag.

After the Acklington detachment, when the squadron flew back to Waterbeach, we had to endure a hectic, dreadful atmosphere as disbandment plans were progressed. Shortly before the squadron was wound-up I was declared 'operational' and allowed to wear the top button of my uniform undone, a WW2 custom which was still an accepted practice within Fighter Command in 1958. For me, the demise of 63 Squadron was a disaster. I was posted to fly the lumbering, four-engined Handley Page Hastings aircraft at the Hastings Long Range Transport Conversion Unit at Dishforth in Yorkshire. On my first day at Dishforth I was told to do up my top button as that sort of nonsense was not welcome now that I was a member of Transport Command. It seemed to symbolise the end of my life as a single-seat fighter pilot, a jet ace, star of stage, screen and caravan park.

Having packed my trusty little 1932 Morris two-seater (she was five years older than me), I drove up the A1 road to Dishforth to enter a world which, for me, was as grim as Waterbeach had been sublime. Instead of single-seat fighter pilot, jet ace, star of stage, screen and whatever, my crew status was now 'second pilot' – a misnomer if ever there was one. The second pilot had to raise and lower the Hasting's undercarriage and flaps when instructed to do so by the captain, and he had to turn the pitot head heater on and off. And that was about all. There was no opportunity for me to take off, land or even taxi the aircraft. If the captain happened to die, and most of them were so old that they looked pretty close to it, I certainly could not have handled and landed the aircraft safely.

One wintry night, as soon as the Hastings had landed, I raised the flaps to prevent damage from wind-blown ice. When the geriatric in the left-hand seat ordered "Flaps up" I replied that they were already up. Instead of admiration for my alert airmanship, his lordship let rip with a torrent of abuse – under no circumstances was I to touch anything without the captain's authority *blah blah*. I'm afraid that this was a tipping point. I'd experienced life as a proper pilot and my present wretched existence was enough to make a grown man weep. The situation was outrageous, mind-numbing, clearly intolerable. I resolved there and then to do something about it.

In company with my spirits, the winter weather worsened until, at last, a bright spot appeared on an otherwise gloomy horizon. The current Dishforth course was sent to Libya where the weather was good in January and February and where in those days, unlike now, there was no likelihood of having one's throat cut for upsetting the Prophet Mohammed (peace and blessings etcetera to you all). I loved Libya. It was my first flavour of Arabian life and in the evenings, when I gazed up at the stars, I relished the distinctive atmosphere, the smell of wood smoke, the barking of feral dogs, the night air that resonated with chirping crickets.

In March 1959, when the Hastings detachment returned to Dishforth, I was given a welcome opportunity to fly a Chipmunk aircraft to Acklington which by then was the home of 66(F) Squadron whose squadron badge, a rattlesnake, was intended to signify aggressive spirit and striking power. While I was admiring the squadron's live rattlesnake kept in a glass case in the pilots' crew room, I got into conversation with the commanding officer. Like me, the squadron leader couldn't understand why the top fighter pilot in the Royal Air Force should be stuck in a rut flying in the right-hand seat of a Hastings. He was most sympathetic to my plight and said that if I could get time away from Dishforth he would arrange for me to have some proper flying with his squadron.

That evening, when I'd returned to Dishforth, I spotted on a board in the officers' mess an advertisement for Fleet Air Arm pilots. The next day I wrote two letters, one to their Lordships of the Admiralty requesting a transfer to the Royal

Navy, the other to my present commanding officer to tender the resignation of my Royal Air Force commission. As an additional line of attack, I contacted my former commanding officer on 63 Squadron who by then worked in the Air Ministry's personnel branch. However, he was quite angry and made it clear that I was out of order just to walk in and demand an interview. He did not understand my tale of woe and said that to resign my commission was a very serious matter not to be done lightly.

As I was still on leave, I decided as a next step to follow up the offer of flying with 66 Squadron. This squadron looked after me very well. I flew the Meteor, the Vampire and the Hunter. I could recall what Utopia felt like, not just for the flying, but also for the life and spirit of a fighter squadron for a young man in the 1950s. To be released, even for a short spell, from the world of Hastings' old codgers was relief indeed.

On my first Hunter re-familiarisation flight with 66 Squadron I climbed to 30,000 feet then asked air traffic control for a radar let-down and approach. I descended to what I thought was 2,000 feet but suddenly realised that the Hunter was actually at 12,000 feet. It was a sobering reminder. The altimeters in those days had three pointers, the smallest of which indicated tens of thousands of feet. A recent confidential survey had shown that almost every pilot admitted that he had got the 10,000 feet reading wrong at least once. Later, when two pilots in a Hunter T7 misread their altimeter, they thought that their aircraft was at 20,000 feet whereas it was, in fact, at 10,000 feet. This was obviously a much more serious way round than my own error and resulted, tragically, in the death of both pilots when the Hunter flew into the ground at night in Aden.

After eighteen flights in ten days with 66 Squadron, flights which were entirely thanks to the kindness and sympathy of the commanding officer, Squadron Leader P Bairsto, I drove back to Dishforth. There, I was told of my posting to Colerne in Wiltshire where I'd fly Hastings aircraft with 24 Squadron. My pitifully small worldly possessions were loaded into the Morris motorcar and I set off for Colerne with a heavy heart. I checked-in with the squadron adjutant first thing on Monday morning and was dumbfounded by his reaction. "We don't want you here," he said. "You've been posted to 8 Squadron in Aden to fly Venoms and good luck to you!"

"Why good luck?"

"Very simple. There are fifteen pilots on the squadron and they have lost six in the last six months. You, dear boy, are on a twenty-four month tour and unless you are mathematically illiterate, by my reckoning you won't need a return ticket."

I didn't care. I had gone, in a matter of seconds, from the brink of the darkest, most abominable abyss to the prospect of prompt deliverance. I wrote to their Lordships to withdraw my application to join the navy, then re-packed the Morris and drove home for embarkation leave. I realised that flying could be dangerous but with the confidence of youth knew that I'd be all right in my 8 Squadron aircraft.

*

One of the last to step off the de Havilland Comet that had flown us to RAF Khormaksar in Aden, the blast of heat that struck me could have come from an Avon jet engine. Indeed, my initial thought was 'jet pipes' until I realised with a shock that this was no jet engine exhaust but Aden in the hot season. I wanted to turn round and go home; surely it would not be possible to survive in temperatures and humidity levels as high as this.

The following morning, 7th May 1959, I awoke early, breakfasted and hastened on foot in the heat to my new home, 8(F) Squadron. I soon learned that this squadron, which shared a hangar with the Arabian Peninsular Reconnaissance Flight and their four Meteor FR9s plus a Meteor T7, was equipped with eighteen de Havilland Venom aircraft and two twin-seat de Havilland Vampire T11s.

After three days I was scheduled for my first solo in the Venom, an aircraft whose origin came from the Vampire itself (the Vampire was the second jet aircraft after the Gloster Meteor to enter RAF service). I found the Venom to be a pilot's dream as, on that day, I completed my general handling routine which included a compressibility run to the limit of Mach 0.88. I then flew back to Khormaksar for a practice engine-out landing. The sky was blue and the visibility unlimited (unusual for that time of year). While I set up for my flame-out pattern I became aware of a pair of Venoms taxiing out for take-off. Shortly after the pair got airborne I heard on the aircraft radio: "Red leader turning downwind for immediate landing."

"Do you have a problem?" asked the air traffic controller.

"Negative," came the reply, "my ammunition door has come open. I'll land and have it closed."

Those were the last words he uttered. I watched aghast from above as the Venom flicked onto its back and plummeted earthwards from a height of about 600 feet. An abrupt feeling of dread caused my stomach muscles to tighten as I witnessed a great pillar of black smoke rise up towards me.

I flew round at an altitude of 10,000 feet for a while before deciding that, in view of the appalling scene I had observed not to mention 8 Squadron's loss of seven Venoms and six pilots in the last six months, a nice, wide and gentle circuit before landing would be quite a good idea. After landing, I learned that my flight commander, having heard about the accident, had run to the commanding officer's office to tell him that the new pilot had crashed and was definitely dead. The CO rang the wing commander who told the group captain at which point I taxied-in to the squadron's parking apron to everyone's amazed relief, especially mine.

Even today, I don't think that anyone knows whether that Venom pilot stalled in the turn at nearly maximum all-up weight or if the open ammunition door caused a breakdown of airflow over the tailplane. If I had to guess it would be the former as both the Vampire and Venom were prone to violent airflow departures at low airspeed.

Over the next few months I flew 100 Venom sorties at the end of which I was getting good scores on the firing range, had been declared operational and loved the flying. Then one day, when the commanding officer began to engage me in friendly conversation, my happy-go-lucky life was about to be subjected, yet again, to calamitous metamorphosis. I should have been more on my guard, I suppose. "Have you ever thought of applying for a permanent commission, Tony?" he asked lightly. I replied that I was certainly thinking about it. Now he beckoned me to his office where he went on: "It's important for regular officers to have administrative experience, you know."

"Yes, sir."

"It's our turn to provide an adjutant at RAF Salalah in the Oman," he said.

"Is it, sir?"

He gazed at me for a moment or two before he continued quietly: "I'm sending you there next week. The admin experience will look good when you apply for your permanent commission."

"How long will I be at Salalah?"

"Six months."

The news stunned me. This air force, so adept at doing everything possible to upset its pilots, was incredible. After Chivenor I'd had six months on Hunters, six months on transports, six months on Venoms and now I was to have six months as an adjutant on a small route station with no aeroplanes based there. I was not even asked to volunteer, just told to go. I was grounded immediately and ordered to report to Headquarters Steamer Point where I'd spend two days learning about cyphers. Cyphers, for God's sake!

I went to Cypher school, did not understand a word that I was told, then took the Thursday Vickers Valetta transport to RAF Salalah 600 miles up the coast from Aden.

Halfway along the coast of southern Arabia and at the bottom south-west corner of Oman lay the small town of Salalah. At least, it was small in 1959 but probably not now. As a location, it was very unusual for Arabia because for several months of the year the coast was brushed by the same monsoons that provided so much rainfall in India. It was then that the Salalah coastal plain and low hills to the north became alive with flowers and grasses. Had my soul not been left behind in Aden it would have been a great tourist resort for a sabbatical, especially as there were no tourists.

On my first day at work, my assistant, Sergeant Fox, came in with a pile of

Girls were in short supply in Aden! Members of 8 Fighter Squadron
enjoying a drink at Khormaksar, October 1960.
Anthony Haig-Thomas third from left.

files for signature. "What are all these for?" I asked. To this day I remember his reply word for word:

"Don't you worry about that Adj, you just sign and we will be all right."

I just signed and kept on doing so for six months and we never had any trouble. Sergeant Fox taught me how to decode signals using what looked like a typewriter operated by the German military in WW2. Everything seemed to be classified 'secret' even though virtually nothing was important. One night after the great Fox had sent me solo on decryption I was dragged out of bed as a 'secret' signal that required urgent decoding had come in. Thinking that war must have been declared, I ran to the signals section, worked my way hastily through the piece of paper with its five figure groupings, and decoded the text which I read with a sense of astonishment. The message said that, with effect from Christmas 1959, the Persian Gulf region of HM Armed Forces could expect a shortage of soap.

Some two miles north of Salalah town, RAF Salalah itself was a hutted camp which compared unfavourably with the grandeur of the palace of Sultan Said bin Taimur whose nifty little pad dominated the town. One of my jobs was to decode and deliver foreign office signals for the Sultan in his palace. Having, one day, decoded a signal, I set off in the Land Rover in my capacity as the Sultan's telegram boy. I parked the vehicle then walked through the souk to the palace gates where, suddenly, I was confronted by an elderly Arab who proffered all the usual greetings before he grabbed me by the more private parts of my anatomy. He clearly wished to get involved in a way that the love of my life back at home had not for he wouldn't let go and a curious crowd began to gather. Eventually, two of the Sultan's guards came to my rescue whereupon I delivered the signal and was escorted back to the vehicle while my admirer was marched off for an unknown fate.

There were eight senior non-commissioned officers at RAF Salalah and two commissioned officers – the commanding officer and the adjutant. The senior NCOs ran the whole place backed by about forty junior NCOs and airmen who did all the work. I did not like the commanding officer, a pompous little man and a navigator to boot. Shortly after I arrived the CO went sick and I became the boss. Occasionally some important people would visit as they 'did' the Middle East tour. I have, for example, a photograph of Field Marshal Slim looking enormously fat being welcomed by Pilot Officer Haig-Thomas looking very slim.

All the time I was in the Royal Air Force I was a regular correspondent with my family and some of the letters have survived. The letter below captures the flavour of life at Salalah and shows how, at the time, my pleasant holiday resort routine meant that I had more or less forgotten about flying:

Sunday, 28th March 1960

Royal Air Force Salalah
BFPO 69

Dear Mum

Today I have been at Salalah for five months and it is only a month before I finish here. I do not have an exact departure date as it depends on how long Ken Brooking takes to be briefed on cyphers, accounting, catering and all the hundred and one duties one has to perform in an administrative role.

Ramadan has ended here tonight as we could see the moon; if you can't see the moon, fasting must continue by day until you can see it. Up in Muscat it was cloudy so it is still on. This afternoon I went and took coffee with Hamood, a local sheik – I have become his shooting partner, not because of my markmanship but because I have access to a Land Rover! Last week we went out after gazelle (no luck) and ended up in the foothills at some caves at Gazes a few miles north of here where there is supposed to be an eighteen-foot cobra snake, jet black, however we did not see it, thank heavens!

I went down to Aden and managed to get a couple of Venom trips and when I got back to Salalah, Hamood had organised a guard of honour for me who fired their rifles low over my head in accordance with Arab tradition. The better the friend, the closer go the bullets. It was the nearest thing I can imagine to a firing squad. However, the CO was not pleased I think because, after he had commented on it, I made an unkind remark about his lack of communication with the locals.

Our Arab employees have given us a goat to eat, however it is so nice that we couldn't possibly kill it so we have christened it Charles and it is the new mess mascot as our tame gazelle has died of pneumonia. Not much more news, longing to see you all sometime during the summer.

Much love

Tony

My letter was wrong: my successor was a month late so I arrived back on 8 Squadron at the end of May 1960 to find a big turnover of pilots and the squadron re-equipped with Hunters.

Soon, I was caught up in the whirl of activity as the squadron prepared for a detachment to Rhodesia (nowadays called Zimbabwe). Before the squadron's departure, I flew a few Hunter re-familiarisation sorties, including one up to Sharjah in the Persian Gulf where, whilst turning overhead Salalah at 40,000 feet, I felt almost nostalgic. It was the first time I had flown a Hunter with four underwing tanks; the heavy aircraft, during any manoeuvre at high altitude, was very close to the Mach stalling speed. On one occasion, the Hunter lost 2,000 feet after my slightly rough pitch input.

A new face on the squadron was that of John Volkers, a Cranwell graduate who'd made headlines as a competitor in the London to Paris air race. He was great fun, irrepressible and hopeless with money – always, like modern governments, spending more than he had. He'd acquired a girlfriend at the highest levels in the colony and, as luck would have it, she had a friend, a senior officer's daughter who had just arrived from England. One time, we set off as a foursome in Volkers' car for lunch at Shuqra about forty miles down the beach from Aden (literally down the beach as this was the road). Regretfully, the car broke down after twenty miles leaving two young pilot officers with His Excellency's and the air commodore's daughters in the middle of nowhere. There was no other traffic until, at last, an Arab lorry staggered towards us, the vehicle's brightly coloured bodywork piled high with goods topped by a dozen or so local Arabs who had hitched a lift. The lorry ground to a halt and took us on board (we promised to avert our gaze as the girls climbed ten feet up a ladder to reach the top) after which the Arabs chanted and sang happily as we continued to sway along our way. Eventually, when we reached the army camp at Shuqra, there was something of a hiatus when our mode of transport was seen as inappropriate for His Excellency's daughter. We were driven back in an army Land Rover which, *en route,* stopped to attach a tow rope to the car and drag it back to Khormaksar.

The preparations were prodigious but finally the squadron was ready to depart for Rhodesia. Together with two junior pilots, I flew the 2,000 or so miles in a Blackburn Beverley. We were in a poor state of mind as we droned down to Nairobi in this extraordinary flying box at 145 knots instead of around 500 knots in a Hunter. We had to be cautious, too, about the lavatories in the tail, tactically and tactfully placed beyond the paratroop doors. They had once been the cause of a fatality when a serviceman, as he exited the lavatory, fell to the ground because he was unaware that the paratroop doors had just been opened while he was ensconced inside.

For my first few Hunter sorties flown from our Rhodesian base at Gwelo, approximately 150 miles south of Salisbury (now called Harare), I found that I felt very disorientated with the sun in the wrong place as we were currently south of the equator. After my third sortie, with the weekend ahead, Volkers and I decided that we needed a little action on the romantic front while the rest of the squadron drank beer. When I explained our requirements to one of our most hospitable hosts, a young pilot who later became chief of the Rhodesian Air Force, he nominated two sisters who lived in Salisbury, over 100 miles away. Ever helpful, he drove us there, introduced us to the girls then went on his way. Our squadron CO had said that he wanted a pair of Hunters at Salisbury airport to be flown down to Gwelo on Monday morning, so the problem of our return transport was resolved.

Not resolved, however, was the problem introduced by a heady mix of jets and girls and twenty-one-year-old pilots. We took the girls to a dinner-dance at Meikles Hotel and after a bit I asked mine, the prettiest of the two, if she would like to dance. Her reply made me go weak at the knees. She said that if people wanted to dance they should dance, if they wanted to make love they should make love, but that they should never try to mix the two. We saw little of Salisbury that weekend.

On Monday morning, 18th July 1960, the girls drove us to Salisbury airport where the weather was as good as it gets for flying, which in Africa is very good indeed. We kissed farewell after which, looking as casual as possible, the two Hunter aces climbed aboard their machines. The girls promised to wave us goodbye and we promised them a flypast. Trouble was coming to the boil in the witches' cauldron.

After a pairs close formation take-off led by John Volkers, I touched my Hunter's

Top: The Black Arrows aerobatic team of 111 Squadron, 1959. Rear left to right: Stan Wood, Frank Travers-Smith, Dave Edmondson, 'Chas' Boyer. Middle: Dick Clayton-Jones, Paddy Hine, Pete Latham, Matt Kemp, 'Oscar' Wild. Front: 'Oakie' Oakfield, Roger Hymans, Brian Mercer, Norman Lamb and Tony Aldridge. (*Brian Mercer*)
Left: Fourteen Hunters of the Blue Diamonds in 1962. (*Brian Mercer*)
Below: Blue section of 111 Squadron, 1958. (*Brian Mercer*)

Top: 'The office' – cockpit of the Hunter.
Above: Seaside road in Aden. (*Peter Lewis*)
Left: Blue Diamonds over Middleton St George
in 1961. (*Brian Mercer*)

Top left: Typical desert rendezvous. (*Peter Lewis*)
Above left: Harib Fort. (*Peter Lewis*)
Left: A post-strike picture of Harib Fort, 1964.
(*Peter Lewis*)
Above: Hawker Hunter in RAF 'warpaint' – ready
for squadron service.

Above: Soviet trawler – in reality an intelligence gatherer (note how far back the bow wave goes indicating considerable speed for a mere trawler).
Left: 63 Squadron, Waterbeach. Three junior pilots – Mike Seymour, Trevor Philips, Anthony Haig-Thomas, aged twenty. (*Anthony Haig-Thomas*)
Below left: FR10 Hunter at low level. (*Tim Thorn*)
Below right: Tim Thorn (centre) having just won the best fighter recce pilot in Europe competition, 1971. (*Tim Thorn*)

brakes to prevent the main tyres from rotating in the wheel bay, and I used my left hand to push the undercarriage 'up' button. Now, sliding down and under the lead Hunter, I moved my aircraft into a low level tactical position for freedom of movement. Air traffic control cleared us for a flypast for which, as we turned in, I noticed a figure of 0.9 on the Machmeter (i.e. just 0.1 Mach below supersonic airspeed). The explosion of sound at ground level must have been impressive. I never saw the girls waving; I was too busy worrying whether the lead Hunter was about to hit the ground. I had not seen a jet aircraft as low as that before, other than when landing.

We headed now for Salisbury's Pearl Assurance building which dominated the skyline and from where we commenced a long, gentle curve to line up with palm trees that lined Kingsway at the end of which was the Caltex building where the girls' brother worked. We had promised him a flyby. Our two Hunters flashed past at the same height as the top of the building (well, a little below, I suppose) still at Mach 0.9 which was probably not a good idea. After this, as the leader set heading for Gwelo, we followed a convenient railway line along which, in the distance, the telltale signs of smoke and steam from a train could be spotted. As the magnesium sun hovered and blazed high above the horizon, surrounding vegetation stepped out of modest shadows while we flew lower and lower and headed directly for the train. When we flew past, still at Mach 0.9 (the Hunters, not the train), the driver, subjected to a sudden stereophonic eruption as two fighter jets flew past on either side, suspected that an engineering catastrophe had occurred. He consequently performed an emergency stop that, we learned later, caused the trains' wheels to 'square off' as a result of which the Royal Air Force was sent a bill for new wheels.

Our subsequent port of call, a small town called Hartley, was next to be favoured with a flyby. It was just bad luck that nineteen windows in a girls' school shattered as we went past, but of course we did not know that at the time. Now the lead Hunter pulled up to an altitude of 25,000 feet where I moved out to a wide battle formation position and where I sat in what felt like motionless wonder at the beauty of the Hunter and the silence of jet flight. After a while my reverie was interrupted by a voice on the aircraft radio. Using non-standard phraseology the voice merely said: "I've got a hard on." I had no idea what he meant, nonetheless I had my suspicions but unfortunately it was too late to turn back for Salisbury to get it fixed so instead we flew on to Gwelo, landed, taxied in, shut down and wandered along to the squadron buildings in order to enjoy post-flight mugs of coffee.

It was not long before the commanding officer entered the crew room, darted a glance in our direction and said: "John, Tony...come here a second." He beckoned us towards his office where he asked: "Have you two been naughty boys?" These were the only recriminatory words he ever used in connection with the incident.

Of course, we owned up at once and the Royal Air Force legal system swiftly swung into action. A wing commander was assigned to take witness statements, including those from the headmistress of the girls' school at Hartley. When she claimed that two jets had flown past at window height, matters did not look good. However, when the school gardener was called for, it turned out that he had been a member of the RAF during the war. The wing commander asked him: "How high up were these jets?" and the gardener hesitated. He glanced around while, in the ensuing pause, John Volkers and I moved the palms of our hands surreptitiously and pleadingly upwards as if contestants in a TV quiz show. The gardener appeared pensive, took his time as befitted a professional witness and eventually declared: "About 1,500 feet."

"1,500?" The wing commander looked surprised.

"Yes," said the gardener.

By now under military arrest, we two miscreants were flown in a Beverley back to Aden where we were grounded. The case for the prosecution was sent to the Air Ministry where a recommendation for court martial was declared. The air officer commanding, though, deemed that it would be too expensive to fly witnesses from Rhodesia so he would deal with the matter himself. Summoned to the air vice-marshal's presence, I was ushered into his office where my mouth went dry as I was subjected to a very one-sided interview. Curiously, I spent the interview struggling to prevent myself from bursting into laughter, an interesting psychological reaction no doubt brought on by nerves. The air vice-marshal at length announced that I would lose six months' seniority. The consequence of this was intriguing, and might even have qualified as record-breaking, for I was now a flying officer with minus four months' seniority. Meanwhile, John Volkers became an even more junior pilot officer by six months and we went back to Khormaksar to join the land of the living as fully restored squadron pilots.

*

At about this time minor political troubles erupted in Arabia which led to occasional military operations. An area west of Ataq had been proscribed because of bad behaviour by local militants and the proscription order seemed to be working: one time, as I flew in the area, I noted that there was not a camel or a goat or a man to be seen. Then, right in front of the Hunter, I caught sight of a lone camel. I turned hard left through 360 degrees, aligned the camel in the Hunter's gunsight and touched the gun button. Immediately after firing, I pulled up and hauled the aircraft round to check what had happened. The camel was nowhere to be seen but suddenly I spotted a large red circle where the animal had been but now wasn't. That big red circle has remained on my conscience ever since and I wished that I had not done it.

From time to time I was sent up country to act as forward air controller. On one occasion our convoy of vehicles suffered a series of setbacks as we made for the Wadi Hadramaut. The Land Rovers got bogged down in sand dunes, our wireless set failed, we drank our normal water supply then the emergency reserve and when, finally, we arrived at the entrance to the legendary wadi, early-years' home of Osama bin Laden, we were very, very thirsty. My lips had become swollen and blackened and all of us needed water badly when, fortuitously, we came across a small irrigation channel. I leapt out of the Land Rover and plunged my face in the small running stream, as did my Arab companions. Eventually, when I had finished, I noticed a camel fifty yards upstream cooling its private parts in the water we had just drunk, however we suffered no ill effects.

Our journey continued through the towns of Shibam, Sayun and Tarim with their fantastic architecture and rich merchants' houses built from wealth generated in the East Indies over the centuries. Heading towards the town of Mukalla we drove through hills up to 7,000 feet when, beyond a tortuous bend, we came across a Land Rover parked by the roadside. Nearby, an Englishman from the Foreign and Commonwealth Service, assisted by two servants, was sitting at a table with a white tablecloth and a silver teapot laid out carefully while he enjoyed teatime as if in the heyday of the Raj. Recollections of this and other Arabian experiences, surprisingly all very favourable, remained imprinted in my memory...the beauty of the edge of the great Empty Quarter of Arabia with its heavy dews at night; the peace of the desert at dawn and the thick mists, a few feet deep, soon to be consumed by the merciless sun; the strange singing of the sand dunes which, in the heat of day, left the ears ringing, yet from no discernible source; the sight of an Arab who emerged from the shimmer of heat haze while he walked to Bir Thamud, a distance of at least 100 miles. Apart from a goatskin water bottle and a large Dhab lizard he had killed, the Arab man carried nothing...amazing, rugged people.

*

It was on our way back to Aden after another visit to Rhodesia that John Volkers, in a philosophical mood, announced that he wanted to live life to the full as he did not expect ever to see his twenty-third birthday. He didn't. After a major emergency in his Hunter he ejected but was caught in the fireball as the aircraft exploded. Years later I called on his parents in Malta where his father had retired from the army as a brigadier. Afterwards, I wished that I hadn't gone as my visit made them sad.

With my two years on 8 Squadron coming to an end, and having eluded the gloomy prediction of the Transport Command adjutant, I did lots of flying. On one of the sorties I achieved sixty-eight per cent on the air-to-ground targets and four yards average error with my rockets. It seemed a pity to have to go home just when my training was finally complete, but go home I did, in a Bristol Britannia, to a wonderfully green and pleasant land called England.

*

It was, in fact, wet, cold and windy when I arrived at RAF Lyneham on 14th April 1961. I almost yearned for the dust and heat of Arabia. My future, though, had to be decided and this involved a visit to a wing commander in the Air Ministry. When I entered the wing commander's office, I sensed something was up even before I'd sat down. In front of him the wing commander had my Form 1369 confidential report which he appeared to study with worrying intensity.

Eventually he looked up, gazed at me, then scowled as if someone had just used frost-fettered fingers to grip his testicles. "This is the worst report I have *ever* seen on *any* officer," he said. I felt the bitter absence of friends, the desolation of the wilderness. "Did you realise that you had four – yes, *four* – starred items?"

Perhaps my face went white; maybe my eyes rolled upwards to the top of my head. Starred items were supposed to be drawn to the attention of the miscreant but no-one had said anything. "I can tell you one thing for certain," went on the wing commander, "and that is that you will never fly another RAF aeroplane while you remain in the service."

"In that case, sir, I must resign my commission." An indignant rage surged within me.

"No you won't and you will go where you are sent." A pause ensued, then: "I'm posting you to air traffic control."

Dear God, I thought, not that. "If there's nothing else," I said, about to deal my trump card, "I'm willing to become a flying instructor."

"You are the last sort of person we want as a flying instructor." It seemed inconceivable but perhaps I blushed. The language of diplomacy appeared to be cowering under the heel of conquest but I had nothing left. Amidst a mounting sense of dismay I wanted to stand up and push this character over a precipice, but perhaps that would have meant yet another starred item.

"I must therefore insist," I said angrily, "on being allowed to resign my commission. If I'm not suitable to serve on a squadron then I'm not suitable in air traffic control or anywhere else."

Reduced, indeed, to the desolation of the wilderness, I was now told to go outside his office and wait in a corridor. I waited and waited. After a while, when a man came down the corridor, the fellow took one glance at me and said: "You look miserable. What's the matter?" I had not realised that I was showing any emotion but there was something about this complete stranger that made me want to pour out my story. He listened with patience and kindness as my tale of woe came flooding out. It turned out to be a lucky break. When, at long last, I was called back to the wing commander's office he said:

"I gather that you have just met Air Commodore Strong, our head of department." My astonished mouth must have dropped open. "He thinks you'll be a good candidate for an *aide-de camp* job – but you won't be able to fly." I would be sent, he continued, to RAF Ouston in Northumberland for an interview with the air officer commanding 11(F) Group.

Two days later, when I was invited to enter the office of the holy of holies, the air vice-marshal smiled and asked me to sit down; he seemed a nice man and almost human. I noticed with a sinking feeling, however, that he held my confidential report in his hand but eventually, when he put it down, he said: "I shouldn't be too concerned about that low flying episode if I were you." He went on to explain that he had suffered a similar fate when he'd been a young flying officer, and his career did not appear to have been greatly harmed. When he asked me if I was qualified to fly the Meteor and I replied in the affirmative, his face lit up and he said: "Excellent! That could save us a good deal of time when we visit remoter stations like Chivenor in Devon and Stornoway in the Hebrides." Things were looking up; it seemed that I would get the job and fly officially. I had to suppress a dangerous desire to telephone that ministry wing commander to tell him my news.

With no idea about the function of an *aide-de-camp* my learning curve was high. My first real test of nerves came within ten days of starting the job. At an important ball attended by all the air ranking officers within Fighter Command I ensured that drink glasses were full and, as I did so, noticed that my boss was talking with the highest of the high, the commander-in-chief himself. When the commander-in-chief, Air Marshal Sir Hector McGregor, put a cigarette in his mouth, he patted his pockets as he searched for a light. As nimble as a thief in an Arab souk, I produced my own lighter and lit the great man's cigarette. "I didn't know that you smoked, Tony," said my boss.

"I don't, sir."

"Very good," he nodded approvingly at which my heart swelled with pride.

My relationship with the air officer commanding was like father and wayward son. On one occasion, by which time the post of air officer commanding had changed hands, the new man declared: "I'm bored, Tony, let's go and fly the Meteor." It was my job to sit in the Meteor T7's rear seat to keep an eye on things while the air vice-marshal did the flying. He flew quite a nice sortie until we turned downwind at Leconfield, by then the new base for Headquarters 11(F) Group. Unfortunately, the Meteor's airbrakes were still out. Always keen to stay alive, I watched the airbrake lever carefully while establishing a two-handed lock on the undercarriage selector. The facts were straightforward: airbrakes in, wheels down, you lived; airbrakes out, wheels down, you didn't. When, to my horror, my hands felt pressure building up on the undercarriage lever even though the airbrakes were still out, I said nothing until a voice cried: "Tony, the undercarriage lever has jammed!" I hastily explained the situation at which a flood of uncomplimentary remarks erupted from the Meteor's front cockpit. After landing, nothing more was said but we both knew that I had saved our lives and that the invective had been a manifestation of shock.

I spent about eighteen months as an *aide-de-camp* and when it was time for me to leave, the air vice-marshal presented me with a pair of gold cufflinks and said that, for my last ten months in the Royal Air Force, I could, within reason, have my own choice of posting. I asked to go to the Hunter operational conversion unit at Chivenor where, posted to the Meteor flight, I knew that I'd get more or less as much flying as I wished.

My non-flying *aide-de-camp* appointment had resulted in an average of twenty flying hours a month, a statistic which, despite a great urge, I did not reveal to the wing commander, that dubious plenipotentiary – a navigator, no doubt – who sat deep within the Air Ministry's tiresome corridors of power.

*

The Meteor Flight at Chivenor was established to tow banners which Hunter students could shoot at to hone air-to-air gunnery skills. In addition to flying the Meteors, members of the flight could help out with Hunter sorties to lead students on various exercises. For the eight months that I spent at Chivenor I averaged just under forty flying hours a month. I relished the flying but I had decided to leave the RAF at my eight-year point on the grounds that, having searched my kitbag for the mythical field marshal's baton that should lie at the bottom, mine seemed to be missing.

One day, when my time in the service was nearly up, the commanding officer called me in to his office and grounded me forthwith. By that stage I had been interviewed, and accepted for, a City job with a merchant bank, a job which was due to start on 1st January 1964.

I started to pack up my belongings and went through the clearing procedure demanded when leaving any RAF station. It was a process that I hated. All was fine apart from a set of Chipmunk Pilots' Notes which I had lost and for which I had to pay half-a-crown (about £2 inflation-adjusted to today's money).

With its strangely inter-muddled population of heroes, workers, leaders, and eccentric characters it was impossible to leave the service without a sense of nostalgia. Perhaps, beneath the surface, I was not entirely convinced that I was doing the right thing. By then, though, it was too late and as I got into my car and drove away from Chivenor, a pair of Hunters on a low-level sortie flew overhead before they disappeared into the distance. It was a symbolic, sentimental farewell and I had a lump in my throat.

Author's Note

With sincere thanks to Old Forge Publishing and Anthony Haig-Thomas whose book *Fall Out Roman Catholics and Jews* formed the basis of this chapter. Copies of that book may be purchased from the Shuttleworth Collection to whom all proceeds are paid.

CHAPTER 15

PROMISE

RICHARD PIKE
AT CHIVENOR

The morning was cool with an opaque fog rising off the Taw estuary. A light breeze from the sea wandered in and out of the station buildings as students and instructors made for the operations set-up at RAF Chivenor where meteorological and other briefings were about to be delivered. The morning fog, not untypical for the Devonshire coast in early summer, would lift before long to herald, we hoped, good flying conditions for the exercises planned on that day in June 1965.

The forecaster confirmed our predictions: "Residual overnight radiation fog, as you know a commonly quotidian phenomenon for this time of year, should disperse quite quickly when ambient temperatures increase," he said. Assembled aces gazed gloomily at swirly charts of isobaric indifference. Apparently anxious to prove algorithmic prowess, the forecaster went on and on to render scientific analysis of this and that; it was as if some of the weathermen liked to make essentially straightforward matters appear complex. Recently, the senior meteorologist at Chivenor had boasted a figure of forty-eight per cent of faultless forecasts over the last twelve months, "a significant improvement on the previous year," he said. His slight air of hubris, however, was somewhat deflated by a presumptuous student who suggested that if all the forecasts had been exactly reversed, the success rate would have improved to a figure of fifty-two per cent.

After the meteorological homily, the range officer stood up to speak followed by the wing commander operations and one or two others after which everyone filed out of the main briefing room as individuals dispersed for separate instructor-student briefings. As a student on No 13 PL (Pre-Lightning) Course I was programmed that day for three flights of air-to-air firing with live ammunition against a towed target. If my aim was good, and if I followed well-rehearsed procedures emphasised by my instructor, the Hunter's powerful 30mm Aden cannon would rip into a long white flag towed by a brave pilot in his Gloster Meteor. On completion of my efforts and those of others, the Meteor pilot would fly back to Chivenor where he would deposit the flag so that each Hunter pilot's individual shots, recognisable from the colour painted onto bullet casings, could be counted up. It was a tense, demanding exercise made all the more so when the score board was updated at the end of flying to reveal the day's 'top gun', as well as, and more poignantly perhaps, the 'bottom gun'.

With briefings over and while we waited for the fog to clear, students congregated in the pilots' crew room where we sipped standard NATO coffee (white with two sugars), swopped yarns, talked about life at Chivenor. As the RAF's Tactical Weapons Unit in the 1960s, RAF Chivenor had an unusual atmosphere; about halfway between a Training Command and a Fighter Command base. It had not always been so. During introductory talks we learned that the airfield, constructed in the early days of World War 2 near the site of a civil airfield, had opened as a Coastal Command training unit with Bristol Beaufighters, Bristol Blenheims and Bristol Beauforts. The latter's unpopular reputation had gained it a popular ditty:

The starting of the Beaufort is a most peculiar art
No matter how you prime it, the bastard will not start
In fact on some occasions when the dew is on the grass
You might as well stick the priming pump right up the engine's arse.

After a couple of years, Chivenor had changed to an operational anti-submarine role and ten years after the war, in mid-1955, the first Hunter operational conversion course commenced with a mix of Vampire and Hunter Mk 1 aircraft. At that stage there were no Hunter two-seaters and we heard that first solos on the early marks of single-seat Hunter often attracted a small audience. Unlike the Meteors and Vampires that pilots had flown in the past, the Hunter had hydraulically-powered flight controls. The consequent instant response to control input evidently had resulted in some remarkable antics when the new-to-type Hunter pilot first launched himself into the air. Onlookers would gaze with amazement at the series of rapid steep banks, first one way then the other, just above the ground as some poor individual struggled to keep the wings level.

When he'd learnt not to over-control, the new pilot would find that the Hunter was a wonderful aircraft to fly. The machine would go much faster and higher than the Vampires and Meteors and, with such improved manoeuvrability, seemed to sense what the pilot wanted to do. When the stick was put hard over the Hunter would roll through 360 degrees in less than a second. A major weak point of the early Hunters, however, was the windscreen's tendency to ice up after about thirty minutes of flight at high altitude. Pilots had to scratch a hole in the ice by hand or by wiping the surface with a sponge, but it was usually impossible to clear the canopy completely. The recommended procedure was to descend to low level for a high-speed run so the heat generated by skin friction could melt the ice, but this required plenty of fuel which was rarely available.

Another weak point was the arrangement of various weapons control, camera, and radio transmit switches and buttons on the tops of the control stick and the engine throttle. We were briefed that a couple of years ago some bright spark at headquarters had decided that these switches should be re-arranged, and a programme was initiated to swop the rocket-firing button and the radio-transmit button. One day, a student pilot on the air-to-ground firing range confused the buttons when he announced: "Tipping-in live" and two rockets consequently sped off in the direction of Cardiff. At once he realised his error and pressed the button again to say: "Oh, I'm terribly sorry," thereby sending two more rockets towards Cardiff. After this, the switches were returned to their original position but the incident was a timely reminder of the non-ergonomic, hotchpotch nature of Hunter cockpits.

Despite cockpit quirks, the Hunter was renowned for its long-term ruggedness. We heard, for example, about a Hunter squadron based in Germany whose successful detachment to the Netherlands was about to succumb to technical difficulties the night before a planned return to RAF Gütersloh. One of the Hunters had developed a faulty hydraulic pump, the ground crew said that they couldn't acquire a spare pump in time so the squadron was resigned to the inconvenience of returning a pilot and a working party later. However, the next morning the squadron's technical warrant officer sidled up to the detachment commander to report all aircraft serviceable and ready to depart.

"Where did you get the hydraulic pump?" asked the amazed detachment commander.

"You don't want to know, sir!" was the reply.

Eventually, word leaked out that, late at night, one of the squadron's chief technicians had crept up to a pensioned-off Hunter acting as a static display 'gate guard' beside the Royal Netherlands Air Force guard room. The chief technician removed the 'gate guard's' old hydraulic pump then sneaked away unnoticed. Back in the hangar, he discovered that the pump, despite years of wind, weather, and lack of attention, was fully serviceable and fit to be used the next day.

Suddenly, I turned round at the unusual sound of an anguished voice. "We have long memories," he cried. He clasped his temples with his hands and spoke with emotion; he appeared to take a deep breath to calm himself. Perhaps, I reckoned, he'd been talking with one of the old hands at Chivenor. Maybe he'd gathered wartime images of bombs and bombers, of doodlebug attacks, of an old house clogged with white dust and cobwebs, of walls reduced to rubble, of a disillusioned old soul who'd planned her dying words but ultimately left them unsaid.

For it was less than twenty years since the end of World War 2, and stories from that conflict were still around, as were some of the pilots involved; a few of 'The Few'. Distinguishable from rows of medal ribbons, these were brave men who were often unwilling to recall dark days, although on rare occasions, if in the right mood, one of them might talk of his experiences. With liberal use of fingers and hands, experiential accounts would describe how, one after the other, Spitfires would peel off in a power dive as a squadron went in to the attack. "I'd pick out one enemy machine and switch my gun-button to 'fire'. At 300 yards I would have it in my sights. At 200 yards I'd open up in a long four-second burst and watch the tracer go into his nose…" After this, the Spitfire pilot would manoeuvre violently to avoid debris. Soon, the sky would fill with a mass of individual dogfights; contrails would paint a dramatic picture of the evidence of battle as, in frenzied eagerness, pilots would hurl their machines about the sky. Then, as if by divine intervention, pilots would find the skies promptly deserted; one moment a bedlam of machines; within seconds, a sudden silence and not an aircraft to be seen.

As budding fighter pilots we were enthralled by such tales and by some of the information we absorbed in general didactic discussions. We learned that the top-scoring fighter pilot of World War 2, indeed of all time, the Luftwaffe's Erich Alfred Hartmann whose boyish, mournful good looks could give him an almost indigent air, claimed 352 victories in 1,404 combat missions during which he crash-landed fourteen times. Remarkably, of the long list of most successful World War 2 fighter pilots, the top 100 or so were all members of the Luftwaffe. In our slightly worried discussions about this, various reasons were put forward, including different assessment standards and dissimilar national policies: the German pilots, for instance, tended to return to the cockpit over and over again until they were killed (although Hartmann himself died of natural causes at the age of seventy-one), whereas successful Allied fighter pilots were routinely rotated to training bases in order to pass on their skills to new pilots. Maybe, as someone suggested, it was to do, also, with national mentality: "The Germans planned well in advance, the Brits planned everything in retrospect, the French planned whilst appearing to have a party, and the Spanish...well, God knows."

The highest-scoring US fighter pilot, Richard Bong, flew the Lockheed P-38 Lightning fighter for all of his forty claimed victories. Grounded one time because he flew a loop over the Golden Gate Bridge, zoomed at low level down San Francisco's Market Street and caused the clothes of an Oakland woman to be blown off her clothes-line, Bong's commanding officer told him: "If you didn't want to fly down Market Street I wouldn't have you in my air force – but you are not to do it any more."

"And by the way," added one of the worthy preceptors, "don't imagine that you could get away with similar mischief here at Chivenor." He went on to discuss the skills of British aces, the likes of Marmaduke Pattle unofficially credited with some fifty victories, Robert Stanford Tuck, Bob Braham and Johnnie Johnson. The latter pilot, credited with thirty-four individual victories as well as seven shared victories, three shared probables, ten damaged, three shared damaged and one destroyed on the ground, flew 700 operational sorties yet engaged enemy aircraft on just fifty-seven occasions. Before the war, Johnson, a qualified civil engineer who worked as a surveyor for a local council, was keen to follow up his interest in aviation so took flying lessons at his own expense. He applied to join the Auxiliary Air Force but met resistance at his interview. The senior officer on the interview panel, knowing that Johnson came from Leicestershire, asked: "With whom do you hunt, Johnson?"

"Hunt, sir?"

"Yes, hunt."

"I don't hunt, sir, I shoot."

"Thank you, Johnson, that will be all."

By the time of the Munich crisis of 1939, attitudes had changed, the Royal Air Force strived to gloss over the niceties of social location and Johnson was called up. In 1965, when I was at Chivenor, he was promoted to the rank of air vice-marshal.

A buzz of information now circulated around the crew room: the fog may be lifting; information from the resident search and rescue unit was about to come through. Equipped with the Westland Whirlwind Mk 10, this unit had access to an Avro Anson ('Faithful Annie') for communication reasons. Recently, when the Whirlwind was under radar control, one of the helicopter pilots jokingly used the 'Annie's' callsign instead of the correct Whirlwind callsign. He wanted to trick the controller into believing that the Anson, not the helicopter, was making an approach to land. The ploy worked: the procedures went routinely until the helicopter pilot, outlandishly gleeful about his ruse, slowed the Whirlwind to a hover then, to the controller's astonishment and dismay, moved the helicopter slowly backwards.

"We've been cleared to start flying!" With this precipitate cry from the duty operations officer, students and staff crowded into the operations room where the

Hunter F6 at RAF Chivenor, 1966.

programme, hastily re-arranged, reflected changed priorities. "The Meteor pilot reckons to be airborne in twenty minutes," the operations officer told me. "Plan to follow him ten minutes later."

"Okay, sir," I said and quickly checked my flying gear: maps, gloves, bone dome, Mae West, range frequencies. An insane amount of stuff was needed, I thought. The telephone had begun to ring insistently; the operations officer looked harassed. I therefore signed the flight authorisation sheet and returned to the coffee bar, glad to leave the hectic atmosphere.

Outside, engineers scurried about while they positioned fuel bowsers, external start equipment, fire extinguishers, oxygen accumulators – all the necessary paraphernalia for aircraft operations. As if by aviation's version of acheiropoieta, more Hunters miraculously appeared when the aircraft were towed to allotted parking places.

Soon, I walked to the engineering line hut, signed the technical log of my assigned aircraft (Hunter F6 XF516) and hastened to the aircraft itself; timing for range slots was critical. At the aircraft I was joined by a member of ground crew who looked hassled and out of breath. He placed a fire extinguisher to one side of the aircraft while I performed the ritual of external checks. The ground crewman now helped me to strap-in before he confirmed that the ejection seat safety pins were removed, then returned to his position by the fire extinguisher.

The engine start procedures did not take long after which, with slick efficiency, air traffic control cleared me to taxi out and take off. When airborne, I turned above Saunton Sands, a vast, veritable carpet of ochre, and spotted a few hand waves from hardy souls below who strolled determinedly along the beach. A popular location for longboard surfers, part of the beach was a designated military training area and occasionally would be cordoned-off to create an airstrip, though not for the use of Hunters. Pilots of suitable aircraft types, the likes of the versatile Lockheed C-130 Hercules (which two years ago, in 1963, had achieved the record for the largest and heaviest aircraft ever to land on an aircraft carrier) could practise short landing and take-off techniques. No such restrictions applied today, however, as I headed initially due north for the range area.

With the camouflaged buildings and runways of Chivenor airfield behind the Hunter, I flew past the village of Croyde with Morte Bay ahead. Inland, as agricultural fields emerged from the fog, I could picture autumnal haymaking as local lads and lasses, invigorated with heady amounts of cider, capered and toiled in the sun. Now, with a scan of the Hunter's cockpit I recorded, like a camera, a dozen or so details at a glance – fuel, oxygen, engine instruments, airspeed, altitude, attitude, compass heading, rate of climb or descent – before looking outside again to concentrate on the visual picture ahead. From force of habit, my head moved ceaselessly from one side to the other in a mechanical, almost clockwork-like routine, while I searched every part of the sky above and below and all around.

My peripheral vision suddenly picked up a movement...yes, there it was, a small black speck set against the backdrop of the sea. I made a radio call, changed frequencies, and checked-in with the Meteor pilot. "You may proceed," said the Meteor pilot whose voice I recognised as that of a master pilot, an old-school type with impeccable manners.

As the black dot gradually materialised into a Dayglo-painted Meteor towing a flag, I manoeuvred to the prescribed 'perch' position above and to one side. A shimmer of reflected light rebounded through the cockpit as the sun, no longer masked by fog, dazzled in the sky. I double-checked the parameters: airspeed, altitude, heading, relative position. These were key. Like someone hanging over the edge of a cliff and searching for a foothold, unless the initial parameters were correct there was no foothold; the bluff would be steep and smooth as if the side of a ship.

But time was at a premium; I needed to act swiftly. Pulse racing, I therefore called: "Tipping-in – dummy run," and the blood momentarily drained away from my head and eyes when I turned vigorously and descended. Rapidly approaching the same height as the flag, I eased the rate of descent, reversed the turn and squinted judiciously through the reflector sight. With the sight's sensitive pipper reacting jerkily to control movements, smooth, accurate flying was of the essence. My overtake speed was high – higher than planned – and the flag began to rush towards me. I pressed the camera button briefly before applying a high angle of bank to avoid collision with the flag.

Now, as I manoeuvred back to the perch position, I knew this was not the moment to relax. There could be no let up in the need for intense concentration. After the practice run was the real thing with live ammunition. I listened to another student call up on the aircraft radio: he would join shortly and the two of us would take turns to 'attack' the flag. The Meteor pilot said that he would hold his current heading for a further run after which he'd turn through 180 degrees. Acknowledging this call, I mentally prepared for the next run by self-analysing errors from the last one. Each run was unique; each had to be assessed for improvements next time.

It did not take long to re-position on the perch after which I faced, as they say, the moment of truth: the first live run. I went through the necessary checks which included the gun switch set to 'live'. I told myself not to tense-up; to be relaxed yet alert, that trying paradox. Then, after a last, anxious, look around the cockpit, I called: "Tipping-in – live," and turned sharply as before.

This time, with the target in my reflector sight, I wanted, as my instructor had said, to "burn a hole in the flag". *"Keep tracking...keep tracking…"* his words echoed in my head as I strived to fly accurately. Having levelled and reversed the turn, and with a measure of control over the pipper's jerky movements, I touched the gun button: the Hunter shuddered and trembled when the Aden cannon sprang into life. Every nerve in my body was quickened. The bullets' terminal velocity was enormous. Ultimately, this would save the homeland from aggressors, just as happened twenty-five years ago in the Battle of Britain. Then it was that, instead of a towed flag, bullets would have torn into an enemy bomber, its crew intent on death and destruction below. Those evil efforts, challenged by gallant Spitfire, Hurricane and other pilots (most of whom lacked current levels of comprehensive training), would have been thwarted; the bombers, ablaze from stem to stern with flames fanned bright by the rush of airflow, would have been forced to peel off as the machines plunged earthwards with plumes of grey-white fuel streaming back from the wings.

Today, though, I had no such confirmation of aim. Not until the end of flying, when all the flags had been checked, would results be known. I flew two more air-to-air sorties that day, in Hunter F6 XF443 followed by Hunter F6 XF516. The sense of exhilaration was high, and after the third flight, when I returned to the aircrew coffee bar to chat with colleagues, we excitedly exchanged ideas and experiences. It seemed that most of the students had flown, like me, three air-to-air firing sorties that day and we waited eagerly for news of the outcome, as if in anticipation of the climax of a well-thumbed adventure book.

When, at last, the duty instructor entered with the required information, he moved silently to the assigned board at one end of the room. He had a robotic, only-half-awake air as he wrote up the day's scores then turned without looking at anyone as he went towards the door again. A small crowd of students now gathered; tension rose with everyone anxious to inspect the board, see who was the ace of spades, who was not. It was my neighbour, my fellow student, who noticed first. "Look!" he said as he nudged me in the ribs with his elbow: "Look who's got the best score!" He glanced at me with brilliant, shining eyes. The effect was electric: I had to check the board twice for I could barely believe that my own name should occupy that coveted position. But it was true; the fact was plain to see.

It wouldn't last, of course, but that did not matter – I would discover soon enough that consistent results were achieved by experience gained from many hours of flying, great persistence, and abundant amounts of honest practice with strict standards applied. Nonetheless, for that one night I reckoned to be able to sleep the sleep of the contented even though I'd wake up feeling a little giddy.

Before long, with the scores inspected and the consequences absorbed, the small crowd of students, still in animated discussion, began to disperse. It was time to go home even though, in truth, I felt no urge to hurry. I preferred to linger, gaze at the board a little longer and dream about future promise.

SELECT BIOGRAPHIES

Alan Pollock

Born on Friday, 13th March 1936, Alan retained clear memories of WW2, and studied classics before a cadetship in 1953 on Chipmunks, Provosts, Balliols and Vampires at Pembrey OCU. 1957-61 saw 2nd TAF years with 26, 4 and 26(AC) Hunter Day Fighter Squadrons and he was ADC to COM2ATAF with many visiting WW2 commanders. Time in Germany allowed for flying the FR10, Swift FR5, Vampires, Meteors T7, F8, NF11 &14, Javelin checkout and nine other aircraft at sixteen airfields, plus Vincent/BMW R69 m/c touring twenty-four countries.

1961-64 brought CFS, a year of Jet Provost flying instruction at Cranwell and Gnat QFI flying, seeing prohibited Gnat formation aerobatics arrive, solo display flying and a splendid 'punishment' Aden 43(F) Sqn Hunter F/GA Mk 9 tour before 1(F) Squadron's excellent NATO mobile role at West Raynham. Civilian highlights included exporting, 1980s Tangmere Museum and Richmond Group launches, plus interesting times campaigning on War Widows, Guildford Four case & HMG's broken pension promises & enjoying the Hunter fraternity.

Nigel Walpole

Nigel passed out from the Royal Air Force College Cranwell in 1954 and joined 26 (Hunter) Day Fighter Squadron in Germany a year later. He then served on 79 (Swift FR5) Squadron in Germany and USAF RF-101 Voodoo units in South Carolina on an exchange posting. On promotion to squadron leader he carried out staff duties in support of the Hunters in Aden before taking command of 234 Hunter DF/GA Squadron at 229 OCU in 1964 and subsequently II (AC) Hunter FR10 Squadron in Germany. He gained a soldier's perspective of air power as the Wing Commander Brigade Air Support Officer with 16 Parachute Brigade before commanding 12 (Buccaneer) Squadron briefly in 1972 and going on to fly Jaguars as OC Strike Wing at RAF Brüggen. Appointed group captain operations, RAF Germany, in 1982, he ended his service career as assistant chief of staff Offensive Operations, Second Allied Tactical Air Force, and retired to become weapons advisor to British Aerospace, Stevenage. He now lives with his wife in Suffolk.

Tim Thorn

After three years Tim graduated from the RAF College and became a first tourist flying instructor. In May 1966, he ejected following a mid-air collision, in which two aircraft crashed on to the outskirts of Nottingham. From there followed a succession of fighter squadron tours beginning January 1968. Four Hawker Hunter tours followed – 8 Squadron (RAF Muharraq), Bahrain (1968-69), 4 Squadron and No II (AC) Squadron (RAF Gütersloh, 1969-71), and 234 (R) Squadron (RAF Chivenor), where he graduated from the Pilot Attack Instructors Course.

In July 1972, he joined the Parachute Brigade where he completed over 100 parachute jumps, during one of which his parachute failed to deploy. On completion of the Indian Staff College, a return to flying duties on the new single-seat Jaguar aircraft followed, first as a deputy OC 41 (F) Squadron (RAF Coltishall) where he was awarded the Queen's Commendation for Valuable Service in the Air (QCVSA). He next took command of No II (AC) Squadron in 1980 flying the Jaguar at RAF Laarbruch, until January 1983. He was awarded the Air Force Cross (AFC). After an MOD staff tour he commanded RAF Cranwell.

In 1990 Tim attended the Royal College of Defence Studies (RCDS) followed by a tour as the SASO HQ RAF Germany and managed to keep flying fighters by qualifying on the Phantom and Tornado aircraft. His final tour, from 1993 to 1995, was as commandant general of the RAF Regiment where he completed his 120th successful parachute jump. He flew a total of 8,000 hours on fast jets. In December 1997, following a total engine failure shortly after take-off in a Bulldog he managed to turn the aircraft back on to the airfield reciprocal runway, and was awarded a 'Green Endorsement' for exceptional flying skill.

Roger Colebrook

A 'Baby Boomer' born in 1946. Roger left school at sixteen, determined to be an RAF pilot and worked on a farm until old enough to join. In 1964 he began an eight-year short service commission and trained on the Jet Provost (3 FTS 1964-5), Folland Gnat (4 FTS 1965-6), Hawker Hunter (229 OCU 1966), then the Lightning (226 OCU 1966-7).

Roger joined 56(F) Squadron, Lightning F3, March 1967, based at RAF Wattisham, Suffolk, then RAF Akrotiri, Cyprus. In July 1969 he was posted to CFS for QFI training, but requested a further air-defence tour of duty, flying the Phantom OCU (700[P] Squadron, RNAS Yeovilton, September 1969) then joined 43(F) Squadron, Phantom FG1, November 1969, based RAF Leuchars, Fife. In 1972 he took his 'eight-year option' to leave.

For the next thirty years Roger worked for a number of charter companies including British Caledonian Airways, Air Europe, Korean Air, Air 2000, and EVA Airways of Taiwan operating, amongst others, Beech 18, Piper Aztec, Britten-Norman

Trislander, the DC10-30, Boeing 757 and Fokker 100. His final appointment was on the Thomas Cook B757 fleet before retiring in 2006.

Jock Heron

Jock Heron was a flight cadet at Cranwell and went on to fly Hunters with 43 Squadron, 54 Squadron and the Central Fighter Establishment's Air Fighting Development Squadron. During his CFE tour he also flew the Lightning and, when detached to AFDS's French counterpart at Mont-de-Marsan, the Mirage 3. After an exchange tour with the USAF flying the F-105 Thunderchief, he was thus qualified on RAF, FAF and USAF Mach 2 fighters. Following a staff tour in the OR branch giving birth to the Tornado he went on to become a Harrier flight commander, Harrier staff officer and, after a tour as OC operations at Gütersloh, his cockpit career came to a close. He was then appointed station commander at West Drayton and Stanley in the Falkland Islands and after retiring he spent twelve years with Rolls-Royce in Bristol.

Harry Anwar

As part of the Pakistan Air Force Harry has performed formation aerobatics with four different air forces across the world, and has also trained others for this specialised task. He went to RAF Leconfield on an exchange posting in 1960. While flying Hunters there, he was selected for the RAF Blue Diamonds sixteen-aircraft aerobatics team. He was the only non-RAF pilot ever to fly in this team.

Tim Webb

Born April 1942 in South Africa, Tim joined the RAF on 5th October 1960 and did his initial officer training at South Cerney with flying training at Tern Hill and Acklington on Piston Provosts. Thus followed advanced training at Oakington and Swinderby – gaining 'wings' on 5th October 1962 on the Meteor. After Hunter conversion at Chivenor he was stationed in the Middle East with 208 Squadron followed by a spell with CFS and at Acklington as QFI on Jet Provosts, Valley as QFI on Hunters, Chivenor as an instructor with 234 Squadron on Hunters – PAI and QFI – then Wittering with 45/58 Squadrons on the Hunter as an instructor.

Next was a posting with the Tactical Weapons Unit at Brawdy as squadron commander on Hunters, Meteors and Jet Provosts, then Hawk Project Pilot, Advanced Staff College, a posting to Ramstein southern Germany as staff officer, Valley on Hawks as wing commander and OC FTS, RAFPMC – as personnel officer for junior officer aircrew.

Tim was then part of the Air Warfare Course prior to a promotion to group captain and became deputy director of Tactical Training in London, then a station commander TWU on Hawks. His final posting was deputy director of personnel air at the RAF Personnel Management Centre. In 1992 he took PVR.

Brian Mercer

Lancastrian born Brian was involved in aviation for fifty years. Starting on open cockpit biplanes at the age of seventeen with the Manchester University Air Squadron he gained his wings at No 4 Flying Training School at Heany, Southern Rhodesia in 1949.

In the course of six fighter squadron tours he was awarded two Air Force Crosses and mentioned in despatches. He was deputy leader of the Black Arrows aerobatic team of 111 Squadron and later commanded 92 Squadron and led the Blue Diamonds aerobatic team. He was also captain of the RAF aerial gunnery team during their most successful year.

As a civilian pilot he rose from junior first officer to become the Boeing 747 fleet manager for Cathay Pacific Airways. Now retired he lives in Perth in Western Australia.

Peter Lewis

Graduating from Cranwell in 1954 Peter was posted to 245 Squadron flying Meteor 8s at Horsham St Faith, and Stradishall. After converting to the Hunter F4 in 1956 there followed a tour as an ADC and then as a QFI/IRE on Aberdeen UAS flying Chipmunks.

In 1962 it was back to Hunters and FR training at Chivenor before joining 8 Squadron at Kormaksar, Aden, flying the FGA9 and FR10. Peter was posted as CO of the newly-formed 1417 FR flight in 1963 to provide low-level photo reconnaissance for the army, Strike Wing and HQ Intel in the Radfan war. He flew 119 operations and was awarded an AFC.

Then followed another ground tour, Staff College, a posting as deputy chief instructor at CFS, and finally HQ RAF Germany to prepare the NATO war plans for the Harrier. Peter left the RAF in 1972 to follow a second career in business.

Anthony Haig-Thomas

Educated at Ludgrove Preparatory School and Eton, he had one ambition which was to fly in the RAF but was rejected four times due to short sight. Never taking no for an answer, and being prepared to bypass official channels, eventually paid off. He joined the RAF in April 1956, training on the Jet Provost and Vampire aircraft, 'wings' were awarded in December 1957 and then he flew the Hunter, Venom and Meteor aircraft in the Middle East. Following a disastrous low-flying incident in Rhodesia, he became a flying officer with minus four months seniority. After returning to England he became ADC to the AOC 11 Group and flew Seahawk, Javelin and Canberra aircraft, eventually leaving the RAF to join a City merchant bank.

Richard Pike

Graduated from the Royal Air Force College, Cranwell in 1964. As part of fighter pilot training, the following year he flew the Hawker Hunter at RAF Chivenor in Devon. The syllabus there included training in air combat manoeuvres, intercept geometry and air-to-air gunnery skills. From Chivenor he was posted to the English Electric Lightning force where, after six months at the operational conversion unit at RAF Coltishall, he was posted to 56(F) Squadron, also at Wattisham, before a posting to 19(F) Squadron at RAF Gütersloh in Germany where he was the squadron instrument rating examiner. Following five years on Lightnings, he was posted to 11 Group at RAF Bentley Priory for a ground tour before converting to the Phantom at RAF Coningsby followed by a tour with 43(F) Squadron at RAF Leuchars. During his time with 43 Squadron he qualified as a Phantom instrument rating examiner. After this, he trained at the Central Flying School at RAF Little Rissington before a tour as a qualified flying instructor on the Folland Gnat at RAF Valley. Following medical re-categorisation which precluded further fast-jet flying, he trained onto helicopters at RAF Shawbury before a posting to 18 Squadron at RAF Gütersloh where he flew the Westland Wessex. On this tour he experienced some of the most diverse and exciting flying of his forty years as a pilot. He retired from the Royal Air Force in 1981 and moved to Aberdeenshire where, as a member of Bristow Helicopters Ltd, he flew the Sikorsky S61 for eighteen years in support of the North Sea oil industry as well as in the search and rescue role.

INDEX

OTHER BOOKS BY RICHARD PIKE

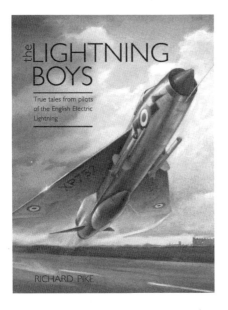

Richard Pike relates the highs and lows, the dramas and the demands of those who operated this iconic aircraft at the sharp end.

Flypast

Richard Pike is to be congratulated on this fascinating compilation of true tales.

Aeroplane

An enlightening canter around the crew room. I recommend it as a good read both to aviators in general and to the Lightning fraternity in particular.

Royal Air Force Historical Society

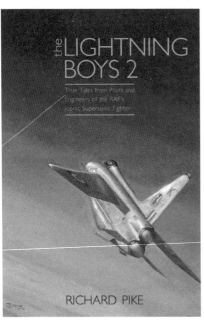

OTHER BOYS' TITLES

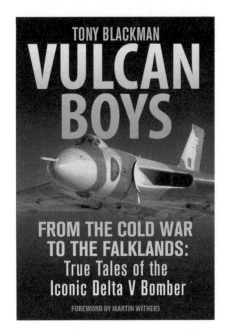

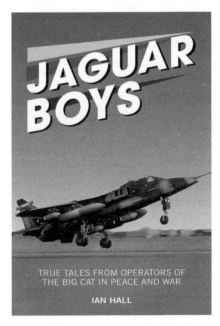

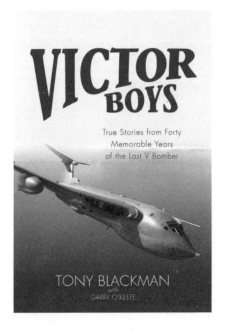